"I know of no other book that so ___ of Old Princeton for today's lay___ accessible, and eloquent work is ___ unacquainted with the giants of Old Princeton."
　—**Matthew Barrett**, Associate Professor of Christian Studies, California Baptist University

"Many have found in Old Princeton Seminary an example of biblical faithfulness, sound theology, and missionary vision. Gary Steward has written an excellent introduction to Old Princeton, telling the story of its major teachers from Alexander to Machen and describing some of their most important writings. Read this book. You will be informed and blessed, and you will want to learn more about Old Princeton."
　—**David Calhoun**, Professor Emeritus of Church History, Covenant Theological Seminary

"Old Princeton justly haunts the conscience of contemporary Reformed and evangelical Christianity. Gary Steward has given us a clear, helpful introduction to its history, figures, and piety. This book will encourage those new to the Princeton tradition to get to know the theology and piety of the Alexanders, the Hodges, Warfield, and Machen."
　—**R. Scott Clark**, Professor of Church History and Historical Theology, Westminster Seminary California

"Gary Steward is to be commended for providing an intelligent and edifying introduction to the theology and leaders of Old Princeton. Part biography and part doctrinal exploration, this volume can be profitably used both by those familiar with the Alexanders and Hodges and by those meeting them for the first time. The tone is warm and balanced, the content rich and accessible, the historical work careful and illuminating. I hope pastors, students, and anyone else interested in good theology and heartfelt piety will 'take a few classes' at Old Princeton. This book is a tremendous resource toward that end."
　—**Kevin DeYoung**, Senior Pastor, University Reformed Church (RCA), East Lansing, Michigan

"I warmly recommend this spiritually edifying book by Gary Steward. This is no dry, historical work about a seminary and its professors in which the author looks back nostalgically on a bygone age of theological giants. On the contrary, here is a book to challenge and encourage every believer—especially ministerial students and their teachers. The book is a pleasure to read: its subject matter is informative and witnesses to Gary's grasp of the issues raised; its style is fresh and readable; and its aim is to show the importance of scholarly, theologically orthodox ministerial training wedded to a piety that is biblical, experiential, practical, and pastorally sensitive."

—**Philip H. Eveson**, Former Principal, London Theological Seminary; Former Director, John Owen Centre for Theological Study, London Theological Seminary

"While publications on the history, theology, and model of ministerial instruction propagated at Old Princeton Seminary continue to flourish, until now readers interested in learning about the spiritual convictions and theological commitments of its leading faculty during its first century of operation have had to rely on specialized studies on these topics. Gary Steward's new work fills the publishing lacunae with an outstanding introductory study on the men and theology that shaped the institutional identity of the school from its founding in 1812 through the early decades of the twentieth century. Marked by the same interest in piety and learning that characterized the faculty of whom Steward has written, his volume is an exceptional combination of biographical, historical, and theological analysis well suited to serve as a gateway text to the rich spiritual history and literary legacy that Old Princeton Seminary has bequeathed to the church today."

—**James M. Garretson**, Ministry Director, Christian Union at Harvard Law School

"Gary Steward's warmhearted and sure-footed guide to the warriors and writings of Old Princeton Seminary is a delight, and the best short introduction to their story for those setting out to discover this often-unappreciated treasure trove. I will certainly be setting it as essential reading for my students. May it help to continue the renaissance of interest in these influential figures of Christian history and the gospel they served."

—**Lee Gatiss**, Adjunct Lecturer in Church History, Wales Evangelical School of Theology

"It is well known that one of the soundest schools of Christian theology in the nineteenth century was what has come to be called Old Princeton; as one author has put it, the school was a veritable 'Gibraltar' of the faith. Regrettably, the opinion has also gained credence, especially among evangelicals, that this was the sum and substance of the Princeton school and that the institution was especially deficient when it came to a robust piety. But nothing could be further from the truth, as this new overview by Gary Steward helpfully demonstrates. I am also thrilled by this book because it delineates a vital strand of the spiritual roots of my school, The Southern Baptist Theological Seminary, for it was at Princeton that James Petigru Boyce and Basil Manly Jr., two of the founders of Southern, learned a Christian faith that was both solid in divinity and red-hot in spirituality."

—**Michael A. G. Haykin**, Professor of Church History and Biblical Spirituality and Director, The Andrew Fuller Center for Baptist Studies, The Southern Baptist Theological Seminary, Louisville, Kentucky

"Gary Steward's *Princeton Seminary (1812–1929): Its Leaders' Lives and Works* contributes significantly to the renaissance of interest in Old Princeton. The sustained combination of scholarship and piety for over a century serves as Steward's leitmotif. What emerges is the Princetonians' breadth of vision that explored not only biblical and theological studies but all of life. Whether probing Archibald Alexander as the quintessential pastor, Charles Hodge's editorship of the *Princeton Review* as 'the true voice of the seminary,' James Alexander's call for a '*Novum Organum* of Christian philanthropy,' or A. A. Hodge's incisive wit and power of illustration, Steward's lucid portrayal will incite readers to explore more of Old Princeton."

—**W. Andrew Hoffecker**, Emeritus Professor of Church History, Reformed Theological Seminary, Jackson, Mississippi

"Whereas David Calhoun's magisterial history of Princeton Seminary awakened this generation to its doctrinal and experiential treasures, and while many recent works on Old Princeton have exhilarated us with their account of its inspiring ministerial and ecclesiastical example, Gary Steward's guided tour of Old Princeton fills the gap for a much-needed compact, yet thorough spiritual guide to this glorious era. May every student and minister begin the study of Old Princeton right here!"

—**Jerry Marcellino**, Pastor, Audubon Drive Bible Church, Laurel, Mississippi; cofounder, FIRE (The Fellowship of Independent Reformed Evangelicals)

"Gary Steward has highlighted elements of the Old Princeton theological tradition that should be of paramount concern to present-day evangelicals in general and Southern Baptists in particular. Seeing that both Basil Manly Jr. and J. P. Boyce studied with this group of theologians, we can detect in our own heritage of theological education, as well as recent efforts to recover this vision, the very values to which Steward gives such clear and forceful exposition. Doctrine, preaching, piety, and defense of the faith once delivered to the saints were central to their understanding of the calling to be ministers of the gospel. This book will put a new resolution into all of us to be faithful to that deposit of truth that is committed to us."

—**Thomas J. Nettles**, Professor of Historical Theology, The Southern Baptist Theological Seminary

"The quality and achievement of Princeton Seminary's leaders for its first hundred years was outstanding, and Steward tells their story well. Reading this book does the heart good."

—**J. I. Packer**, Board of Governors' Professor of Theology, Regent College, Vancouver, British Columbia

"Gary Steward has produced a wonderfully clear and instructive volume on Old Princeton, from its beginnings with William Tennent's Log Cabin through to B. B. Warfield. The thought, aims, achievements, and Christian piety of its leaders—Archibald Alexander, Samuel Miller, Charles Hodge, and their successors—are expounded with sympathy and learning. This book will benefit anyone interested in ministerial training or in the venerable history of Old Princeton."

—**Robert Strivens**, Principal, London Theological Seminary

"Gary Steward is a careful and trustworthy historian. He excels at retrieving wisdom from the past for the edification of God's people today. In this accessible introduction, Steward writes as an unashamed admirer of the Old Princeton theologians, commending the way in which they holistically integrated what so many tend to separate. This is a wise and winsome entry point for study of a neglected but important chapter in church history."

—**Justin Taylor**, Senior Vice President and Publisher for Books, Crossway Books

"This latest addition to the Guided Tour series is a fine study of the men who made Princeton Theological Seminary such a significant force within the world of confessional Presbyterianism and beyond. Setting the stories of the institution and its great early faculty within the larger context of American Presbyterian and Christian history, Gary Steward introduces the reader not only to the great personalities of Princeton but also to key texts from their pens. He opens up not only the history but also the thinking of these men as they sought to articulate a passionate, heartfelt orthodoxy."

—**Carl R. Trueman**, Paul Woolley Professor of Church History, Westminster Theological Seminary

"An entrée to the major figures of Old Princeton. It is an entrée, therefore, into the greatest tradition of Reformed theology in America, one that was deep, true, vital, and rigorous. This study is a gift to the church. It is informative, careful, and engagingly written."

—**David F. Wells**, Distinguished Research Professor, Gordon-Conwell Theological Seminary

"Whether you need an introduction to or a refresher on Old Princeton, this is the book. Steward has provided an evenhanded and informative treatment of the leading names associated with nineteenth-century

Princeton Seminary. Alternating between biographical and topical treatments, Steward has skillfully utilized primary source material to craft a fluid narrative that leaves one wanting to know more of Old Princeton. Timelines, bibliographies, and photographs make this a wonderful addition to Princeton history for the church and beyond. Regardless of your ecclesiastical affiliation, this volume will edify your mind and soul."

—**C. N. Willborn**, Pastor-Teacher, Covenant Presbyterian Church, Oak Ridge, Tennessee; Adjunct Professor of Church History, Greenville Presbyterian Theological Seminary

"Steward provides a most helpful introduction to one of the most significant and interesting institutions in American Christianity. Princeton powerfully shaped American Christianity, bolstering especially its enduring conservatism. This is an excellent resource for students, pastors, and all others who want to understand the course and character of Christianity in America."

—**Gregory A. Wills**, Dean of the School of Theology and Professor of Church History, The Southern Baptist Theological Seminary

"I'm engaged from the start—and it's hard to stop reading. Gary Steward tells the Old Princeton story as if an eyewitness. His thesis is that Old Princeton's dual emphasis on academic erudition and lively spiritual devotion yielded for Christ's church generations of theologically trained and spiritually devout pastors. Each chapter engages with another Old Princeton giant, and Steward amply and convincingly demonstrates the veracity of his thesis. Without delivering it in preachy terms, the inescapable message of the book is that theological seminaries should likewise stand 'like a bulwark for biblical fidelity, revival piety, evangelical activism, and the confessional Calvinism of the Westminster Confession of Faith (1646).' "

—**John Wilson**, Assembly Clerk of the Presbyterian Church of Victoria, Australia; Adjunct Lecturer in Church History and Practical Theology, Presbyterian Theological College, Melbourne, Victoria, Australia

"The giants of Old Princeton, marked by that marvelous combination of learning and piety, have left an impact for the gospel of Christ that only eternity will be able to measure. Their story is one that deserves to be retold, and we are indebted to Gary Steward for capturing its essence and telling it so well. For anyone interested in Old Princeton, this is a must-read."

—**Fred G. Zaspel**, Pastor, Reformed Baptist Church of Franconia, Pennsylvania

PRINCETON SEMINARY

(1812–1929)

The Guided Tour Series

Anne Bradstreet: A Guided Tour of the Life and Thought of a Puritan Poet,
by Heidi L. Nichols

J. Gresham Machen: A Guided Tour of His Life and Thought,
by Stephen J. Nichols

Jonathan Edwards: A Guided Tour of His Life and Thought,
by Stephen J. Nichols

*Katherine Parr: A Guided Tour of the Life
and Thought of a Reformation Queen*,
by Brandon G. Withrow

Martin Luther: A Guided Tour of His Life and Thought,
by Stephen J. Nichols

Pages from Church History: A Guided Tour of Christian Classics,
by Stephen J. Nichols

*Thomas Manton: A Guided Tour of the Life
and Thought of a Puritan Pastor*,
by Derek Cooper

Other Church History Books in the Guided Tour Series

Princeton Seminary (1812–1929): Its Leaders' Lives and Works,
by Gary Steward

Stephen J. Nichols, series editor

PRINCETON SEMINARY

(1812–1929)

Its Leaders' Lives and Works

GARY STEWARD

P&R PUBLISHING

P.O. BOX 817 • PHILLIPSBURG • NEW JERSEY 08865-0817

Page design by Lakeside Design Plus

Printed in the United States of America

ISBN: 978-1-59638-397-5 (pbk)
ISBN: 978-1-62995-139-3 (ePub)
ISBN: 978-1-62995-140-9 (Mobi)

Library of Congress Control Number: 2014945195

To Iain Murray & David Calhoun,
who first introduced me to Old Princeton

CONTENTS

    Hodge's *The Atonement*   263

12. Old Princeton: Past, Present, and Future   283

    Suggestions for Further Reading   301

    Selected Bibliography   305

    About the Illustrations   309

    Index of Persons   315

    Index of Scripture   321

ILLUSTRATIONS

FOREWORD

A number of years ago, I was invited to deliver a lecture at a conference celebrating the two hundredth anniversary of the founding of Princeton Theological Seminary in 1812. As I rose to deliver the remarks I had prepared for that evening, I was overcome with emotion and unable to speak. Those in attendance had just finished singing a hymn that had been sung at my father's funeral a handful of years before, and as I was standing to deliver my address, my mind was flooded with wonderful memories of my father, as well as with gratitude for the theologians at Old Princeton Seminary. While I suspect that some might think it strange that recalling the death of my father would generate gratitude for the Old Princetonians, it makes perfect sense to me, especially in that context. I did not grow up in a household that was committed to the Reformed faith, and neither did my father, yet the Lord in his kind providence used the Old Princetonians and a number of their more faithful interpreters to draw me, and eventually my father and most of the rest of my family, into the broader Reformed camp. I was overcome with emotion that evening because in a very real sense I was both remembering and celebrating the impact that the Old Princetonians had had in my life and in the lives of those I love. The Lord used their works to draw us closer to himself, and for that mercy I remain grateful to this day.

I first encountered the theology and theologians of Old Princeton Seminary when I was working on my doctorate at a Roman Catholic university in the Midwest. I was taking a course in American church history and had the opportunity to read J. Gresham Machen's modern classic, *Christianity and Liberalism*. Machen's work turned my world upside down and introduced me to a theological perspective that was not just revolutionary to me, but instantly compelling. Here was theology that was not only substantive and relevant to the theological issues that I was encountering in my studies, but also faithful to the teaching of Scripture, devotional in the best sense of the word, and beautifully written. The more I read the works of Machen and his colleagues at Old Princeton, the more I came to appreciate their ability to unpack the revelation of God in a way that drove me to worship. They helped me to see the dangers of a kind of dead orthodoxy on the one hand and a kind of unbridled religious enthusiasm on the other, and they persuaded me that because theology is an organic enterprise involving the totality of the whole soul, it is done most faithfully when there is—by God's grace—a symbiotic relationship between the regenerated head and heart. Among other things, they taught me the essential lesson that, as Charles Hodge put it, "the knowledge of Christ . . . is not the apprehension of what he is, simply by the intellect, but also a due apprehension of his glory as a divine person arrayed in our nature, and involves not as its consequence merely, but as one of its elements, the corresponding feeling of adoration, delight, desire and complacency."[*]

As I continue to immerse myself in the literature by and about the Old Princetonians, I am often reminded that relatively few contemporary interpreters share my enthusiasm for both the form and the content of their theology. Many scholars are convinced that the authenticity of the Princetonians' Reformed commitments was compromised by their accommodation of one aspect of the Enlightenment or another, and even more insist that their commitment to the objective nature of religious truth was grounded in a form of naive rationalism rather than in faithfulness to the assumptions of the larger Reformed tradition. Thankfully, something of a renaissance is taking place in the academic study of Old Princeton that is challenging this consensus by returning to the primary sources of the Princetonians themselves. Following the lead of historians such as David Calhoun, W. Andrew Hoffecker, and John Woodbridge, a number of scholars are arguing not only that the Princetonians stood squarely and eloquently in the mainstream of the Reformed tradition, but that their

---

[*] Charles Hodge, "The Excellency of the Knowledge of Christ Jesus Our Lord," in *Conference Papers* (New York: Charles Scribner's Sons, 1879), 214.

works remain particularly relevant in our current context for precisely that reason. The latest addition to this growing body of corrective scholarship is Gary Steward's impressive survey of the theology and theologians of Princeton Seminary from the time of its founding in 1812 to its reorganization in 1929. Steward's survey is judicious and informed by painstaking analysis of the primary and secondary literature. It is sympathetic, yet not fawning; well written and accessible, yet not lacking in substance; and sensitive to those issues that are of enduring interest to scholars, yet always mindful of the pastoral relevance of the Princetonians' labors. Steward has an admirable grasp of the Princeton mind, and for that reason it is an honor for me to commend his analysis to you. May the Lord bless his efforts.

Paul Kjoss Helseth
Professor of Christian Thought, University of Northwestern, St. Paul; Author of *"Right Reason" and the Princeton Mind: An Unorthodox Proposal*

ACKNOWLEDGMENTS

Numerous individuals deserve thanks for helping me write this book. Special gratitude is due to Steve Nichols, who asked me to write it in the first place. Steve has been a wonderful teacher, editor, and friend, and I am thankful for his help in getting this book into print. I am also thankful for the friendship and encouragement of Iain Murray, Andy Hoffecker, Paul Helseth, David Smith, and Jim Garretson, along with many others who have provided wonderful encouragement in things related to Old Princeton. The staff of the Special Collections division at Princeton Theological Seminary, especially Ken Henke, have been most helpful in dealing with their vast archival collections and in providing many of the images that appear in this book. Adam Winters, archivist at the Southern Baptist Theological Seminary, is also to be thanked for providing free access to relevant materials from their collections. Editorial input was graciously provided by John Wind, Derek Butler, Sally Michael, and Amy Steward, for which I am grateful. Personal words of thanks are due to my parents, who nurtured me in the faith and have encouraged me in my studies and writing in countless ways. Without their generous and prayerful support, this book could not have been written. Finally, a special word of thanks is due to my wife, Amy, whose constant help and encouragement freed me to devote so much time to this project. I am deeply thankful to God for bringing her into my life and for making her the joyful mother of our children, Anna, Katie, and Joshua.

PREFACE

When we are in our younger years we need to dig deep, we need to know our position doctrinally so that our reading is focused within that. And if anyone was to ask me as a younger man here today what other authors could be used as benchmarks I would urge the consideration of the Princeton men, you know, Archibald Alexander and Charles Hodge and B. B. Warfield, these are great benchmarks. Three books, you know, Alexander's Religious Experience, *A. A. Hodge's* Outlines of Theology, *Warfield's* Biblical Doctrines, *those three books—if a young man gets hold of those books and they get hold of him, I believe that he's got something, for life. And in case anyone thinks that Princeton is a little too Presbyterian, let me give you another quote from Spurgeon. Spurgeon says: "We have had, of later years, no abler theologians than the Hodges. We fear it will be many a day before we see their like. Finer minds than those of the Princeton tutors have seldom dwelt among the sons of men. No better textbook of theology for colleges and private use is now extant than Hodge's* Outlines. *O for more Princeton theology, for it is the Word of God!"*

—Iain Murray, 1996 Bethlehem Conference
for Pastors (January 29, 1996)

I was in my late teens when I heard a recording of Iain Murray speaking the words above. To my knowledge, I had never heard of "the Princeton men" before. A few years later I came across David Calhoun's masterful two-volume history of Princeton Seminary. Calhoun's soul-stirring history of "Old Princeton" opened up a whole new world of men and books that I have come to deeply appreciate. I have come to admire the Princeton theologians for a number of reasons—for their robust defense of the authority and inerrancy of Scripture, their rich biblical expositions and theological articulation rooted in the very best of Protestant tradition, their emphasis on warmhearted spirituality, their concern for genuine conversion, their love for the church, their zeal for missions, and their social and political concerns for the poor and for the nation. In addition, their vision and priorities in theological education provide a model that is needed for theological education today.

Sadly the theologians of Old Princeton are not as widely appreciated as they once were. While a recent renewal of interest in Jonathan Edwards has occurred, no similar renaissance has yet taken place regarding the Princeton theologians. Things may be changing, however. The year 2012 not only marked the bicentennial of Princeton Seminary's founding, it also brought forth the reprinting of many shorter writings of the Princeton theologians under the editorship of Jim Garretson. The previous year saw the release of two substantial biographies of Charles Hodge—the first produced since the nineteenth century. An Old Princeton Study Group under the auspices of the Evangelical Theological Society Old Princeton Study Group took shape as well in 2011 and has invited evangelical scholars to consider further studies of the Princeton theologians afresh. The year before that saw the publication of Paul Helseth's *"Right Reason" and the Princeton Mind,* which called for a reassessment of the philosophical concerns surrounding Old Princeton. Perhaps a small renaissance is indeed under way. My hope is that this book will contribute to such a renaissance and spark further interest in the Princeton theologians and their writings.

I am all too aware of the many important individuals and books I have had to leave out. Hopefully the readers of this book will not be content with the small sampling provided here and will make deeper explorations on their own. Since I have not sought to engage in an overly critical analysis of the Princeton theologians, some may view this book as a piece of sugar-coated hagiography. I admit that the Princeton theologians had their faults—some of them significant—but I have not attempted to stand above them in a posture of dispassionate critical analysis and point these things out. I love the Princeton theologians, and I have written out of the conviction that we in the church need heroes and models like them from whom we can learn and by whom we can be inspired. Part of the historian's task is to faithfully hold up the true and the good and the beautiful and to proclaim it to be such—to be a moral philosopher in the best sense of the word. That which is truly noble and heroic should be valued and declared as such, even when faults and inconsistencies are acknowledged (see Hebrews 11).

If this is your first introduction to Princeton theologians, I am honored to guide you into their world. Nothing would delight me more than for you to quickly leave this book behind and exchange it for reading the Princeton theologians themselves. A rich feast awaits you if you do.

1

THE FOUNDING OF
PRINCETON SEMINARY

*Few institutions have probably been more useful, in any land or in
any age, than the Theological Seminary at Princeton.*

—Cortlandt Van Rensselaer (c. 1844)

*The agency of the Log College in the establishing of our Presbytery,
and indeed of the Church, has never been properly appreciated.*

—Thomas Murphy (1889)

In the winter of 1742, in the midst of the Great Awakening,
David Brainerd was expelled from Yale. This personal setback
for Brainerd formed part of a chain of events which eventually brought Princeton Seminary into being. While "The Theological Seminary of the Presbyterian Church in the United States
of America at Princeton, New Jersey"—or Princeton Theological
Seminary as it is now known—was not established until 1812, the
events that brought it about were set in motion many years before,
with godly men like Brainerd from both sides of the Atlantic
having a part in its eventual formation. Once established, "Old
Princeton" (the seminary as it existed from its beginning in
1812 to its reorganization in 1929) became a vibrant center for

theological education and spiritual cultivation. It operated within the historic, confessional stream of Protestantism and Reformed orthodoxy, and it supplied thousands of churches in America with theologically trained and spiritually devout pastors. As the religious landscape in America fragmented into differing denominations and sects in the nineteenth century, Old Princeton stood like a bulwark for biblical fidelity, revival piety, evangelical activism, and the confessional Calvinism of the Westminster Confession of Faith (1646).

Being established and run by great men, Old Princeton produced great men. James Petigru Boyce, a Baptist, studied at Princeton Seminary for two years before becoming the founding professor of theology at the Southern Baptist Theological Seminary in 1859, first in Greenville, South Carolina, and later in Louisville, Kentucky. Basil Manly Jr., another prominent Baptist leader, graduated from the seminary in 1847. Charles Colcock Jones, the famous slave evangelist of Georgia, studied at Princeton from 1829 to 1830 before embarking on his tireless work of evangelism among Southern slaves. John Bailey Adger graduated from the seminary in 1833 and went on to become a missionary to Armenia and one of the leading figures in the Southern Presbyterian Church. The prolific pastor-theologian William Swan Plumer attended Princeton, as did biographer extraordinaire William Buel Sprauge. Ashbel Green Simonton graduated from Princeton in 1859 before enjoying great success as a pioneer Protestant missionary in Brazil. Before becoming a chaplain at West Point and a respected Episcopal bishop, Charles P. McIlvaine graduated from Princeton in 1820, as did Samuel Simon Schmucker, later a renowned Lutheran theologian and educator in antebellum America. In addition to these, Cortlandt Van Rensselear noted in 1844 that "some of the most useful ministers of the Dutch Reformed Church received their instructions at Princeton [Seminary]," listing Samuel Blanchard How, Thomas Edward Vermilye, George Washington Bethune, and others as examples. In countless ways such as these, Old Princeton shaped the development of both American and global Christianity far beyond the bounds of its espoused Presbyterianism.

At the seminary's centennial celebration in 1912, E. Y. Mullins noted the widespread impact Princeton Seminary had made on other centers of theological learning in its first one hundred years by stating:

As Mt. Blanc enriches the valleys so Princeton Seminary has stood like Mt. Blanc among the seminaries of this country. In a thousand ways, you have not known, she has sent down her largess of blessing into the valleys, and we rejoice in what she has done. And the reason Mt. Blanc can thus bless the valleys is because she lifts her head to the very skies where, from the inexhaustible heavens themselves, she draws her supply, and so Princeton has drawn her supplies from the eternal sources.

It is hard to overstate the impact of Old Princeton on the development of Christianity in America. While some have continued to draw theological guidance and spiritual encouragement from Old Princeton, the men of Old Princeton and their writings are not as widely known as they should be. How this seminary came to be is a worthy story in and of itself—one which has its roots in the Great Awakening and in the humble beginnings of Presbyterian higher education in colonial America.

William Tennent and the Log College

In the seventeenth and early eighteenth centuries, it was almost universally expected that clergymen would be credentialed by an institution of higher learning. Given this need, the founders of the Massachusetts Bay Colony wasted no time in starting a university for the training of its clergymen. In 1636 they established Harvard University in Cambridge, Massachusetts, just sixteen years after the *Mayflower* landed at Plymouth. This was the first institution of higher learning in America. Harvard very quickly departed from its original Puritan and Calvinistic roots, and in 1701 a more conservative group of Congregationalists started Yale University in New Haven, Connecticut. The Anglicans had started the College of William and Mary in Williamsburg, Virginia, in 1693, but this was not an attractive option for dissenting (non-Anglican) Protestants. For non-Anglicans in colonial America wanting to become clergymen before 1746, there were only three main options for receiving the expected education: Harvard, Yale, or Europe.

Many clergymen came to the colonies from Europe having already received their education. One such individual was William Tennent. Tennent, who was born in 1673, served as a chaplain in northern Ireland before immigrating to the American colonies. He arrived in Pennsylvania with his wife and five children and was admitted into the Presbyterian Church in 1718. At the time of Tennent's arrival, the Presbyterian Church in America had only recently been established. The first presbytery in America, made up almost entirely of Scottish or Irish immigrants, was formed in Philadelphia in 1706— just twelve years before Tennent became a part of it. While formally orthodox in their theology and thoroughly committed to the Westminster Confession of Faith, the Presbyterians of the early 1700s had lapsed into a spiritually cold and lifeless state, not unlike other Protestant groups at that time in the English-speaking world. Spiritual vitality was at a low ebb, and a complaisant coldness had replaced the fervent spirit which had defined the Presbyterians and Congregationalists for much of the seventeenth century.

William Tennent stood out from his contemporaries as a man of great spiritual zeal. Although highly-educated, perfectly fluent in Latin, and well-read in theology, Tennent believed that fervent piety was as important a ministerial qualification as a good education. In 1726, adjacent to his manse in Bucks County, Pennsylvania, not far from the Neshaminy Creek, Tennent built a simple building made of logs to serve as an informal school and seminary for his four boys and others. Located some twenty miles north of Philadelphia, this structure became known derisively as "the College" or "the Log College." While other clergymen looked down upon his school, Tennent labored away at it faithfully all the while engaged in his normal pastoral ministry, giving his students a general and theological education infused with his own emphasis on fervent piety and genuine religious experience.

Tennent's concern for authentic spirituality and genuine conversion united him with others in his day who were zealously proclaiming the need for conversion, especially George Whitefield. Tennent had heard of the young evangelist before Whitefield arrived in Philadelphia in 1739, and he rode close to thirty miles on horseback to meet White-field in person. Almost two weeks after their first meeting, Whitefield accompanied the elder Tennent to his home, where Whitefield preached to a crowd of roughly three thousand people. Whitefield also saw Tennent's humble seminary firsthand, and recorded his impressions of "the College" in his famed *Journal*, stating:

> The place wherein the young men study now is, in contempt, called *the College*. It is a log-house, about twenty feet long, and near as many broad; and to me it seemed to resemble the school of the old prophets, for their habitations were mean. . . . From this despised place, seven or eight worthy ministers of Jesus have lately been sent forth; more are almost ready to be sent, and the foundation is now laying for the instruction of many others. The devil will certainly rage against them; but the work, I am persuaded, is of God, and will not come to nought. Carnal ministers oppose them strongly; and, because people, when awakened by Mr. Tennent, or his brethren, see through them, and therefore leave their ministry, the poor gentlemen are loaded with contempt, and looked upon as persons who turn the world upside-down.

Even though they had just met, Whitefield quickly recognized how out of step Tennent's ministry was with the prevailing religious climate. While the Log College was nothing impressive to look at, Whitefield realized that Tennent shared the same evangelical spirit as those leading the trans-Atlantic awakening. Whitefield noted of Tennent that:

> He is a great friend of Mr. [Ebenezer] Erskine, of Scotland; and as far as I can learn, both he and his sons are secretly despised by the generality of the Synod, as Mr. Erskine and his friends are hated by the judicatories of Edinburgh, and as the Methodist preachers (as they are called) are by their brethren in England.

It was not long before the animosity sensed by Whitefield came out into the open. Within a few short years, the four to five "Log College men" that made up the Presbytery of New Brunswick (New Jersey) came into open conflict with the body of fifty or so clergymen that made up the Presbyterian Synod. The immediate cause of the conflict was the licensure of John Rowland, a student of the Log College, but the central issues that divided the two sides were much deeper. At issue was the adequacy of a "Log College" type of education for ordained ministry, along with the appropriateness of the preaching itinerancies of Log College revival preachers like Gilbert Tennent and Samuel Blair. The success of Whitefield's 1739–40 preaching tour through the Middle Colonies crystallized the differences between the two sides, with the "Old Side" Presbyterians viewing the itinerant preaching of Whitefield as a serious assault on Presbyterian propriety, and the "New Side" Presbyterians welcoming it as a divine blessing. The two sides separated in 1741, with the larger presbyteries of New York and New Castle (Delaware) joining with the Presbytery of New Brunswick in 1745 to form the Synod of New York, a rival to the Old Side Synod of Philadelphia.

Although the spiritual coldness of some Old Side Presbyterians was certainly deplorable, Tennent and his sons were somewhat at fault for unduly provoking the separation between the two sides. In their zeal to promote the new birth and genuine piety among Presbyterian churches, they were guilty of giving undue offense to those who were sincerely evangelical but simply took a more cautious approach to the Awakening. After accompanying Whitefield on his initial tour through the middle colonies, Gilbert Tennent, William Tennent's oldest son, began an itinerant ministry of his own that generated a fair amount of controversy in and of itself. Going far outside the bounds of his New Brunswick Presbytery, Tennent preached a number of sermons denouncing the local Presbyterian clergymen and calling congregants to leave the churches whose clergy did not exhibit the kind of fervent piety that the Log College men felt was essential. The lack of charity in Gilbert Tennent's fiery sermon entitled "The Danger of an Unconverted Ministry" was singled out by Charles Hodge as being "one of the principle causes" of the division between the Old Side and New Side. Archibald Alexander would also fault the New Side for showing "harshness, censoriousness, and bitterness" toward those on the Old Side.

The Old Side Presbyterians eventually reunited with the New Side Presbyterians in 1758, but only after the New Side had significantly outgrown its Old Side counterpart. In the terms of reunion, the New Side's approval of the Great Awakening and revival spirituality was affirmed. This reunion came about, however, only after a new tone of conciliation was adopted by the New Side, and by Gilbert Tennent in particular.

William Tennent died in 1746, but his and the New Side's perspective on the importance of religious experience eventually shaped the course of the whole Presbyterian denomination. While only twenty or so individuals were trained at Tennent's Log College, almost all of these became significant preachers and leaders in the next generation of the Presbyterian Church. According to Archibald Alexander, by these men "a new spirit was infused into the Presbyterian body" and the denomination's "evangelical views" were established.

With its emphasis on spiritual experience and intellectual cultivation, the Log College would serve as a model for ministerial education at Old Princeton. It was kept in hallowed memory by many of the first faculty members of Princeton Seminary. When the logs of the Log College had all but rotted away, a local Presbyterian minister rescued a piece of wood sufficient to make into a walking stick, which he presented to Samuel Miller, Princeton Seminary's second professor. Archibald Alexander, the first professor at Princeton, was an ardent admirer of the men who were trained at the Log College and stated of them:

> One advantage which they possessed who were educated in the Log College was, that the spirit of piety seems to have been nourished in that institution with assiduous care. All those, as far as we can learn, who proceeded from this school were men of sound orthodoxy, evangelical spirit, glowing zeal and in labors very abundant. They had the teaching of the Holy Spirit, and, without the advantages which many others enjoyed, they became burning and shining lights. . . . I cannot express how much the Presbyterian Church in these United States is indebted to the labors of this very corps, who studied successfully the sacred oracles in the Log College, or, more probably, under the beautiful groves which shaded the banks of the Neshaminy. There they studied, and there they prayed, and there they were taught of God.

When the General Assembly was debating in 1811 where the new Presbyterian seminary should be located, there were not a few who argued that it should be built in Bucks County, Pennsylvania, on the very spot of Tennent's Log College.

Jonathan Dickinson and the College of New Jersey

After the aging William Tennent ceased to run his Log College in the early 1740s, New Side Presbyterians were left without an educational institution to rally around. Some of Tennent's students had formed academies modeled after the Log College, including the Fagg's Manor academy in Pennsylvania (founded by Samuel Blair) and the Nottingham academy in Virginia (founded by Samuel Finley). One of Samuel Blair's students, Robert Smith, established another academy in Pequea, Pennsylvania. All of these academies carried forward the dual New Side emphasis on education and piety, but they did not give their students educational credentials that were universally recognized. Many New Side Presbyterians in the New York and New Castle presbyteries continued to view Yale University as a suitable place for ministerial education, but this all changed in 1742, when David Brainerd was expelled from Yale.

As a student at Yale in his early twenties, David Brainerd's life had been touched by a spiritual awakening which spread across the campus in 1740. As the revival lingered, many of those genuinely affected become over-zealous and proud. Even young Brainerd slipped into an episode of indiscretion, one which would have significant consequences. During his third year at college, Brainerd was conversing privately with a handful of friends about spiritual matters. When asked by one of his friends what he thought of a Mr. Whittelsey, one of his tutors, Brainerd replied: "He has not more grace than this chair." As Brainerd uttered this reply, another student happened to pass by outside the room and overheard his remark. Brainerd's words were gossiped around town, and his friends were eventually made to confess of Brainerd's statement. Further gossip ensued, and the authorities at Yale attempted to force Brainerd to give a public apology. Feeling publicly wronged already for an offhand comment made in private, Brainerd refused. For not complying, he was expelled.

Even though disgraced in this manner, Brainerd was soon appointed by a Presbyterian Mission Society as a missionary to Native Americans. Numerous high profile ministers and alumni of Yale—including

Jonathan Edwards and Aaron Burr Sr.—appealed to Yale on Brainerd's behalf, but the rector, Thomas Clap, remained unmoved. Clap was actively trying to suppress the spread of pro-revival fervor, and Brainerd's punishment was allowed to stand no doubt as an example to others. Brainerd would likely have graduated at the top of his class, but instead, he never graduated at all.

FIG. 1.1

Events Leading Up to the Founding of Princeton Seminary

1726	William Tennent established the "Log College" in Neshaminy, Pennsylvania.
1730s–40s	The Great Awakening.
1739–40	George Whitefield first toured New England and the Middle Colonies, welcomed by William Tennent, Gilbert Tennent, Jonathan Dickinson, Jonathan Edwards, and others.
1741	American Presbyterians split into New Side and Old Side factions.
1742	David Brainerd expelled from Yale.
1746	Jonathan Dickinson established the College of New Jersey in Elizabethtown, New Jersey.
1747	The College of New Jersey moved to Newark, New Jersey, and was placed under the leadership of Aaron Burr Sr.
1756	The College of New Jersey (renamed Princeton University in 1896) relocated to Princeton, New Jersey.
1758	Old Side and New Side Presbyterians reunited.
1776–83	The American Revolution.
1810	Presbyterian General Assembly acted to establish a seminary.
1811	Presbyterian General Assembly ratified Ashbel Green's "Plan of a Theological Seminary."
1812	The Theological Seminary of the Presbyterian Church in the United States of America at Princeton, New Jersey (i.e., Princeton Theological Seminary) was established.

Another close friend of Brainerd who interceded on his behalf was Jonathan Dickinson. Dickinson, himself a Yale graduate, had been an intellectual force in the Presbyterian church since 1717. A theological stalwart in colonial America, perhaps second only to Jonathan Edwards, Dickinson was a New Side Presbyterian who supported the Great Awakening with critical discernment and a keen mind. With many of his revival writings predating those of Edwards, Dickinson defended the supernatural origin of the revival while criticizing the fanaticism and divisiveness spawned by its excesses. Dickinson's suitability for such writings grew out of his own personal dealings with individual souls during what would become an almost forty-year pastorate in Elizabethtown, New Jersey.

Brainerd's expulsion from Yale impressed upon Dickinson and other New Side Presbyterians how unsuitable Yale had become for pro-revival candidates for the ministry. Given the state of Yale, Dickinson was encouraged to start a new institution of higher learning in the state of New Jersey, one which would carry forward the New Side emphases on religious experience and revival spirituality. This school, now Princeton University, would be known for many years as the College of New Jersey. The first of its kind between Connecticut and Virginia, it would likely never have been started had Yale looked more favorably on the Great Awakening and less sternly on David Brainerd. Aaron Burr Sr. of Newark, the college's second president, was certainly of this opinion, stating: "If it had not been for the treatment received by Mr. Brainerd at Yale, New Jersey college would never have been erected."

Working independently of a synod or presbytery, Dickinson, Burr, and other New Side clergymen and laymen successfully obtained a charter for the establishment of the College of New Jersey in 1746. This charter was renewed and expanded in 1748 under the evangelical governor of New Jersey, Jonathan Belcher. Belcher was a lover of learning, a friend and patron of Whitefield, and a man of fervent piety. While most of the seven men named on the original charter were New Side Presbyterians who had graduated from Yale, the five additional trustees added shortly thereafter were all men who were closely connected with the Log College: Gilbert Tennent, William Tennent Jr., Samuel Blair, Samuel Finely, and Richard Treat. Given this connection, Archibald Alexander, for one, was of the opinion that the Log College was "the germ from which proceeded the College of New Jersey." Writing in his laudatory *Biographical Sketches of the Founder and Principal Alumni of the Log College*, Alexander stated:

> Besides Dickinson and Burr, who were graduates of Yale College, the active friends and founders of Nassau Hall [i.e., the College of New Jersey] were the Tennents, Blairs, Finley, [Robert] Smith, [John] Rogers, [Samuel] Davies, and others who had received their education in the Log College, or in schools instituted by those who had been instructed there.

Given the numerous Log College men who were involved with the fledgling college from its very beginning, the College of New Jersey was established to carry forward the vision for theological education and piety that had flourished previously at Tennent's Log College.

The trustees of the College of New Jersey appointed Dickinson to be its first president, and the first class of students began their studies in Dickinson's home in Elizabethtown in 1747. Dickinson's tenure as

1.2 Nassau Hall. Built in 1756 as the first building in Princeton for the College of New Jersey.

president was short-lived, as he died only a few months after classes formally began. The students under Dickinson were moved to the home of Aaron Burr, and Burr was appointed the next president of the college as well. Burr had been a friend of Whitefield, Dickinson, and the Tennents, and he tirelessly labored as president to carry forward the original vision for the school, namely that "religion and learning should be unitedly cultivated." In 1756, some nine years later, Burr relocated the new college and its seventy students from Newark to what would become known as Nassau Hall, the first building constructed for the college's permanent location in Princeton, New Jersey.

Aaron Burr died only a few months after the move to Princeton. His death, like Dickinson's, would leave the fledgling college bereft of a president at a crucial time. While Burr's young son, Aaron Burr Jr., would go on to become the third vice president of the United States, he would not carry his father's evangelical ideals and piety into public life. The trustees of the college secured someone who could carry forward Burr and Dickinson's vision for the college when they looked outside their Presbyterian circles to another member of Burr's family: Burr's father-in-law, Jonathan Edwards.

Edwards and the Decade After

While not inclined to leave his writing projects and pastorate in Stockbridge, Massachusetts, Jonathan Edwards bowed to what he felt was his duty and accepted the call of the trustees to be the College of New Jersey's next president. Though a Congregationalist, Edwards had great affinity for the New Side Presbyterians in America and many Presbyterians in Scotland as well. He very quickly found delight in accepting what he had first embraced out of duty. Edwards's time as president was cut off unexpectedly, though, when he died in 1758, less than three months after relocating to Princeton. Edwards would be buried in the college president's plot of the Princeton Cemetery next to Burr, in the same cemetery where the Alexanders, Hodges, Miller, and Warfield would later be buried as well. It is fitting that Edwards the Congregationalist is buried beside the great Presbyterians of Old Princeton, with whom he held so many things in common.

In the same year of Edwards's death, the Old Side and New Side Presbyterians joined together. For the next ten years the presidencies of the College of New Jersey fell to those who had been prominent New Side Presbyterians, many of whom had been personally connected with Tennent's Log College.

Jacob Green was selected to serve as an interim president immediately after Edwards's death. Green was the son-in-law of John Pierson, one of Jonathan Dickinson's closest friends. Both Green and Pierson were original trustees of the College of New Jersey, and both had been close friends of Aaron Burr as well. The revival preaching of Whitefield and Gilbert Tennent had left a deep impact on Green, and he served as acting president of the college while concurrently serving what would be a forty-five year pastorate in Hanover, New Jersey. Green's interim presidency, while short-lived, provided stability and continuity with the past while the trustees searched for a more permanent successor to Edwards.

Samuel Davies was welcomed by the trustees as president in 1759. Davies was a popular and powerful preacher; in fact, Martyn Lloyd-Jones once referred to Davies as "the most eloquent preacher America has ever produced." Davies had been educated at Samuel Blair's academy in Fagg's Manor, Pennsylvania, a school which Blair modeled after his own *alma mater*, the Log College. Through his evangelistic and pastoral work in Virginia, he had also established his reputation as one of the founding fathers of Southern Presbyterianism. Davies had been an enthusiastic supporter of the college since its beginning, and in 1753 had accompanied Gilbert Tennent on a successful fundraising trip to Great Britain and Ireland on behalf of the college. Although Davies's arrival at Princeton looked promising for the school, he too died shortly after moving to Princeton, presiding as president for only eighteen months.

Samuel Finley was elected president next in 1761. A graduate of the Log College and one of the original trustees of the College of New Jersey, Finley was noted by one as being "a very accurate scholar and a very great and good man." While serving as a pastor for seventeen years in Nottingham, Maryland, Finley ran an academy out of his home, and many of Finley's students were some of the best and brightest scholars of their day. In 1763 Finley was awarded a Doctor of Divinity degree from the University of Glasgow, making him one of the first Americans to receive this distinction from abroad. After serving the school as president through five years of expansive growth, Finley died in 1766 and was buried next to his friend Gilbert Tennent in Philadelphia.

For a brief period after Finley's death, John Blair served as acting president of the college. Like his brother Samuel, John was a graduate of Tennent's Log College. Before his appointment at Princeton, he had for ten years advanced the pastoral and educational work of his brother at Fagg's Manor. Blair had also served briefly as a professor of divinity at the college prior to taking over as acting president.

FIG. 1.3

Early Presidents (and Interim Presidents) of the College of New Jersey (Princeton University)

Jonathan Dickinson	1747
Aaron Burr Sr.	1748–57
Jonathan Edwards	1758
(Jacob Green)	1758–59
Samuel Davies	1759–61
Samuel Finley	1761–66
(John Blair)	1767–68
John Witherspoon	1768–94
Samuel Stanhope Smith	1795–1812
Ashbel Green	1812–22
(Philip Lindsley)	1822–23
James Carnahan	1823–54
John Maclean Jr.	1854–68
James McCosh	1868–88
Francis L. Patton	1888–1902
Woodrow Wilson	1902–10

In the decade after Jonathan Edwards's death, all of these men carried forward the New Side Presbyterian emphasis on fervent piety and religious experience. Each one who served as president was intimately connected with the Tennents and the Log College. Heads and hearts were nurtured together at the College of New Jersey in these years, with classical instruction coming from accomplished pastors who were first of all devout men of God.

The Witherspoon Revolution

In 1767, the trustees of the College of New Jersey called upon Samuel Finley's nephew and former student, Benjamin Rush, to help persuade John Witherspoon of Paisley, Scotland, to become the college's next president. Witherspoon's writings and reputation as an evangelical leader in the Church of Scotland made him the chief candidate on their list, and it was hoped that Witherspoon might help unite the newly rejoined branches of the Presbyterian church. Rush, a graduate of the College of New Jersey, was at that time studying medicine in Edinburgh. After many months of personal lobbying from both Rush and Richard Stockton, an alumnus and influential trustee of the college, Witherspoon accepted the offer and relocated to Princeton in 1768.

Without anyone realizing it at the time, Witherspoon's immigration to New Jersey would prove significant beyond the affairs of the church and college. Witherspoon, Rush, and Stockton would all go on to become signers of the Declaration of Independence, as would Joseph Hewes, another graduate of the college. Although Jacob Green had been an early and earnest proponent of American independence, it was John Witherspoon who most significantly connected the College of New Jersey to American political life and the cause of American independence. Witherspoon's impact on the emerging nation was immense. James Madison, the fourth president of the United States and "Father of the Constitution," studied under Witherspoon at the College of New Jersey from 1769 to 1771. Many other American statesmen were similarly influenced by Witherspoon. While Elias Boudinot, an influential trustee of the college from 1772 to 1821, questioned whether or not a minister such as Witherspoon should be so involved in political matters, Boudinot himself would follow suit, serving briefly as president of the Continental Congress and signing the Treaty of Paris, which brought the Revolutionary War to an end.

Immediately upon his arrival at Princeton, Witherspoon started a revolution of his very own right at the college, raising its academic standards and greatly expanding the scope of the college's curriculum. According to Samuel Miller,

> He produced an important revolution in the system of education. . . . He extended the study of mathematical science, and introduced into the course of instruction on natural philosophy, many improvements. . . . He placed the plan of instruction in moral philosophy on a new and improved basis, and was, it is believed, the first man who taught in America the substance of those doctrines of the philosophy of the human mind. . . . Under his presidency more attention began to be paid than before to the principles of taste and composition, and to the study of elegant literature.

Witherspoon was the first president of the college who was not personally connected with the New Side Presbyterianism, and with Witherspoon the college moved away from the original priorities of the New Side. His new emphasis on political, moral, and natural philosophy left a deep mark on the college. Witherspoon was to serve a full twenty-six years as president of the college—longer than all of the previous presidents combined, and his impact upon the school was immense. In the words of Mark Noll, "Witherspoon altered the course of the college and defined its direction for at least the next century."

This new educational trajectory set by Witherspoon, with its emphasis on the sciences and secular branches of learning, was carried forward by his son-in-law, Samuel Stanhope Smith. Smith, an accomplished scholar in his own right, had graduated from Princeton in 1769. In 1775 he became the founder and first president of the Hampden-Sydney College in Prince Edward County, Virginia. After a successful four years in Virginia, Smith was called back to Princeton to assist Witherspoon, who was deeply involved in the political affairs of the emerging nation. Smith was named vice president of the college in 1786 and became president upon Witherspoon's death in 1794.

Smith, even more than Witherspoon, emphasized the emerging sciences and was privately more enthralled with philosophical pursuits than with his inherited tradition of evangelical orthodoxy.

Samuel Stanhope Smith's presidency at the College of New Jersey was a tumultuous one. Although Smith communicated an air of gentility and propriety, the moral climate of the school declined rapidly under his leadership, with persistent student uprisings beginning around the turn of the century. An apparent act of arson devastated and gutted Nassau Hall in 1802. In 1807 the student uprisings culminated in a full-blown student revolt. Gradually, the trustees began to grow more and more nervous about Smith's theology and ability to lead the school in the right direction. With the trustees stepping in to take more direct oversight over the college, Smith resigned in 1812. The curricular revolution started by Witherspoon and carried out by Smith had left the college far afield from its original purpose of training ministers and cultivating piety alongside of a traditional education.

Almost immediately after Smith's resignation, Ashbel Green was unanimously elected as president of the College of New Jersey. Green had been an active trustee of the college since 1790. He had also studied at Princeton under John Witherspoon, and had been the valedictorian of the class of 1783. From 1787 to 1812, Green was the foremost preacher in Philadelphia. He also served in Philadelphia as chaplain to Congress from 1792 to 1800, and in this role frequently dined with President Washington. The son of Jacob Green, Ashbel Green was known for his fervent and earnest piety. Even though he was a highly educated member of the American Philosophical Society and the recipient of an honorary doctorate from the University of Pennsylvania, Green believed that a renewed emphasis on piety and religious devotion was what was needed to rescue education at Princeton from what it had become under Smith. He would write, "It is not the understanding, but the heart, which needs to be addressed. . . . It is not argument, but piety which is requisite to exterminate [errant views]."

While Smith had sought to carry forward Witherspoon's appreciation for philosophy and the sciences, Green sought more to carry forward Witherspoon's Calvinistic orthodoxy and evangelical piety.

EARLY PRESIDENTS OF

1.4 Jonathan Dickinson (1688–1747).

1.5 Aaron Burr (1716–57).

1.6 Jonathan Edwards (1703–58).

1.7 Samuel Davies (1723–61).

THE COLLEGE OF NEW JERSEY

1.8 Samuel Finley (1715–66).

1.9 John Witherspoon (1723–94).

1.10 Samuel Stanhope Smith (1751–1819).

1.11 Ashbel Green (1762–1848).

Whereas Smith looked optimistically to new developments in philosophy and science, Green stressed traditional evangelical thought and conservative religious orthodoxy. In the person of Ashbel Green, the College of New Jersey, at least temporarily, found someone who could bring the college closer to its original ideals.

The Founding of Princeton Seminary

A few years into Samuel Stanhope Smith's presidency, it became increasingly clear to many trustees of the College of New Jersey, especially Ashbel Green, that the college was failing to carry out its original vision—a vision that "religion and learning should be unitedly cultivated." From its earliest days, a central purpose of the college had been to provide competent ministers for the churches, as Jonathan Dickinson stated in 1747: "Our aim in the undertaking [of establishing a college] is to promote the interests of the Redeemer's kingdom; and to raise up qualified persons for the sacred service to supply . . . qualified candidates for the ministry." Around half of the college's graduates in its first twenty years did in fact become ministers, but in the years just after the American Revolution (1784 to 1812), fewer than 15 percent of those who graduated from the college entered the ministry. This meager output contributed to what became a severe shortage of ministers. In 1810 the Presbyterian General Assembly would report "near four hundred vacant congregations within our bounds."

For trustees like Green, a reformation of the college, albeit desirable, was not the most promising way to meet the needs of the Presbyterian churches. While continuing to work at changing the direction Smith had set for the college, Ashbel Green came to view the intellectual and spiritual climate of the school as too injurious to train pious and orthodox men for the ministry. In the early 1800s, he began contemplating the creation of a separate Presbyterian seminary, all the while serving as a trustee of the college. Green was encouraged along these lines by Samuel Miller, a fellow trustee who shared his concern. Miller implored Green with these words in an offhand letter written in 1805:

> We have, if I do not mistake, a melancholy prospect, indeed, with respect to a supply of ministers to our churches. Cannot the General Assembly,

at their next sessions, commence some plan of operation for supplying this deficiency? . . . It appears to me, that we ought, forthwith, either to establish a new theological school, in some central part of our bounds; or direct more of our attention to extend the plan and increase the energy of the Princeton establishment. On the latter part of the alternative many doubts occur to me; and, with respect to the former, I know difficulties of the most formidable kind will arise. I can think of no person in the United States, who has so good information of the state of the Presbyterian Church as yourself, or who is so capable of devising and putting in motion the plan best adapted to our situation. I hope, therefore, you will devote your leisure time . . . to the consideration of the subject, and the preparation of some plan to be acted upon by them.

Green responded to Miller and in 1805 formally urged the Presbyterian General Assembly to focus its attention on the urgent need to train up more ministers. In the following years, Green continued to correspond with Miller, Edward Dorr Griffin, and others about potential plans for a Presbyterian seminary.

In 1808, the idea of a seminary received fresh impetus from a rousing speech made by Archibald Alexander at the General Assembly. In this speech Alexander stated:

The deficiency of preachers is great. Our vacancies are numerous, and often continue for years unsupplied. . . . This state of affairs calls loudly for your attention. . . . In my opinion, we shall not have a regular and sufficient supply of well-qualified ministers of the Gospel, until every Presbytery, or at least every Synod, shall have under its direction a seminary established for the single purpose of educating youth for the ministry, in which the course of education from its commencement shall be directed to this object; for it is much to be doubted whether the system of education pursued in our colleges and universities is the best adapted to prepare a young man for the work of the ministry. The great extension of the physical sciences, and the taste and fashion of the age, have given such a shape and direction to the academical course, that I confess, it appears to me to be little adapted to introduce a youth to the study of the sacred Scriptures.

Encouraged by Alexander's remarks, Ashbel Green led the Presbytery of Philadelphia to formally propose the establishment of a seminary at the 1809 General Assembly. Some debate ensued as to whether or not there should be one seminary, a separate seminary for each of the Northern and Southern regions, or a seminary for each of the four Synods, but Samuel Miller was able to convince the 1810 General Assembly that the option of establishing a single, unifying seminary was the best option and the one that the majority preferred. The 1810 General Assembly also made its hopes for the new seminary clear by adopting this statement:

> That, as filling the Church with a learned and able ministry without a corresponding portion of real piety, would be a curse to the world and an offence to God and his people, so the General Assembly think it their duty to state, that in establishing a seminary for training

Fig. 1.12

From Ashbel Green's *Plan of the Theological Seminary* (1811)

It ought to be considered as an object of primary importance by every student in the Seminary, to be careful and vigilant not to lose that inward sense of the power of godliness which he may have attained; but, on the contrary, to grow continually in a spirit of enlightened devotion and fervent piety; deeply impressed with the recollection that without this, all his other acquisitions will be comparatively of little worth, either to himself, or to the Church of which he is to be a minister....

It is expected that every student in the Theological Seminary will spend a portion of time every morning and evening in devout meditation, and self-recollection and examination; in reading the holy Scriptures, solely with a view to a personal and practical application of the passage read, to his own heart, character, and circumstances; and in humble fervent prayer and praise to God in secret.

The whole of every Lord's Day is to be devoted to devotional exercises, either of a social or secret kind. Intellectual pursuits, not immediately connected with devotion or the religion of the heart, are on that day to be forborne. The books to be read are to be of a practical nature. The conversations had with each other are to be chiefly on religious subjects. Associations for prayer and praise, and for religious conference, calculated to promote a growth in grace, are also proper for this day; subject to such regulations as the professors and directors may see proper to preup ministers, it is their earnest desire to guard as far as possible against so great an evil. And they do hereby solemnly pledge themselves to the churches under their care, that in forming and carrying into execution the plan of the proposed seminary, it will be their endeavour to make it, under the blessing of God, a nursery of vital piety as well as of sound theological learning, and to train up persons for the ministry who shall be lovers as well as defenders of the truth as it is in Jesus, friends of revivals of religion, and a blessing to the Church of God.

In addition to approving the establishment of a seminary to be "a nursery of vital piety as well as of sound theological learning," the 1810 General Assembly selected a committee to draft the plan for this new seminary, with Ashbel Green, Samuel Miller, Archibald Alexander,

scribe. It is wished and recommended, that each student should ordinarily set apart one day in a month for special prayer and self-examination in secret, and also that he should, on suitable occasions, attend to the duty of fasting....

If any student shall exhibit, in his general deportment, a levity or indifference in regard to practical religion, though it do not amount to any overt act of irreligion or immorality, it shall be the duty of the professor who may observe it, to admonish him tenderly and faithfully in private, and endeavour to engage him to a more holy temper, and a more exemplary deportment.... If a student, after due admonition, persist in a system of conduct not exemplary in regard to religion, he shall be dismissed from the Seminary....

The professors are particularly charged, by all the proper means in their power, to encourage, cherish, and promote devotion and personal piety among their pupils, by warning and guarding them, on the one hand, against formality and indifference, and on the other, against ostentation and enthusiasm; by inculcating practical religion in their lectures and recitations; by taking suitable occasions to converse with their pupils privately on this interesting subject; and by all other means incapable of being minutely specified, by which they may foster true experimental religion, and unreserved devotedness to God.

and a few others chosen for this task. Green, who chaired this committee, drafted the plan for the seminary on his own. It was eventually adopted in 1811 with no substantial changes made by other committee members or by the General Assembly, and the plan to establish a Presbyterian seminary was settled.

Whereas the College of New Jersey had been chartered as an independent institution, Princeton Seminary was placed under the control of the Presbyterian General Assembly acting through a board of its choosing. It was decided in 1812 to place the seminary in Princeton, next to the college. Even though the two institutions were formally independent of each other, they would enjoy a close partnership in the seminary's early years, given the number of individuals who were involved with both. This harmonious relationship was established when Green was elected to succeed Smith as the college's president in 1812, the same year he was made the president of the new seminary's board of directors. While only serving ten years as president of the College of New Jersey, Green would serve in his official capacity with the seminary board until his death in 1848.

According to Green's plan for the seminary, students were to become accomplished scholars of the Bible, "well skilled in the original languages of the Holy Scriptures." They were to be trained as theologians in accordance with the Westminster Confession of Faith and Catechisms, able to apply their theology practically to ethical questions, as well as to defend their theology directly from Scripture. They were also to have "a considerable acquaintance with general history and chronology, and a particular acquaintance with the history of the Christian Church." In a special way, they were to be prepared to meet objections raised against the Christian faith by "the deistical controversy." The students were also to be schooled in the Presbyterian form of church government, as well as in sermon composition and delivery and pastoral care. In keeping with Green's concern for religious experience, students "must have read a considerable number of the best practical writers on the subject of religion," and a whole section of Green's *Plan of the Theological Seminary* was devoted to the cultivation of "devotion" and the "improvement of practical piety."

The 1812 General Assembly chose Archibald Alexander to serve as the seminary's first and, for the first year, only professor. Their choice could not have been better suited to carry out Green's vision for the seminary. A pastor as well as a scholar, Alexander was as concerned with promoting true spirituality in the heart as with developing orthodox thinking in the mind. On August 12, 1812, the vision for theological education shared by Tennent, Dickinson, and Green came to fruition when Princeton Seminary formally opened, and it would go on to flourish there for more than a hundred years.

Conclusion

When the College of New Jersey failed to fulfill the hopes of its founders, Princeton Seminary emerged to educate and train spiritually minded ministers of the gospel. Ashbel Green's vision for Princeton Seminary, embraced by the Presbyterian General Assembly of 1811, was in many ways a renewal of the vision embodied previously in William Tennent's Log College—a vision which stressed both learning and piety. The cultivation of true religious experience, as well as education in orthodoxy, was central to Princeton Seminary's original purpose. Through the work of Ashbel Green, Samuel Miller, and Archibald Alexander, the emphasis on spiritual experience that flourished during the Great Awakening found a renewed expression at Princeton, where it was fused to evangelical orthodoxy for over a century.

2

ARCHIBALD ALEXANDER

Archibald Alexander of Virginia gave to Princeton Theological Seminary distinctive characteristics which it retained for more than a century. As the seminary's first professor and as a man of strong convictions, he was the principal formative influence on the institution.

—Lefferts A. Loetscher

Using the word "Pope" in its best sense, as a spiritual father, I may say that if the Presbyterian Church ever had a Pope it was Archibald Alexander.

—William M. Paxton

His piety . . . was earnest, simple-hearted, equable, transparent, commanding in influence, constantly cultivated, predominating through life and sustaining to its end. His peculiar piety was the basis of all his excellence.

—Cortlandt Van Rensselaer

While Samuel Miller and Ashbel Green were more directly involved in the founding of Princeton Seminary, it was Archibald Alexander who personally gave it its distinctive character. The fledgling seminary was nurtured by Alexander from the very day it began with just three students in 1812, and he was a "spiritual father" to the young men who prepared for ministry in Princeton for almost forty years. In some ways, he was larger than life. Mark Noll calls Alexander "a forceful and engaging personality of nearly heroic proportions," noting that it was Alexander who "constructed the framework which shaped the theology at the seminary for over a century." Personally loved and admired as a man of profound spirituality, pastoral sensitivity, and wide-ranging scholarship, Alexander brought into reality Ashbel Green's vision for a seminary that would be just as devoted to spiritual nurture as it was to theological education.

A great deal of what we know about Alexander's life comes from the large biography written by his oldest son, James Waddel Alexander. This biography was originally published in 1854 and is entitled *The Life of Archibald Alexander, D.D.* It contains extended quotations from Alexander's autobiographical reminiscences, which he compiled in the latter half of his life but never published. Unattributed quotations in this chapter are Archibald Alexander's own words or the words of his son as recorded in this biography.

Early Beginnings

Archibald Alexander was born in a log house on April 17, 1772, at the foot of the Blue Ridge Mountains, not far from Lexington, Virginia. Born to parents of Scots-Irish descent, he was named after his paternal grandfather, who had immigrated to Pennsylvania from Northern Ireland in 1736. His grandfather had been converted during the Great Awakening, and he moved his family to the Shenandoah Valley of Virginia in 1747, where Alexander was born and spent his earliest years. He was the third of nine children, and he grew up in the home of a frontiersman. Before attending school, he was taught to read from the Bible and learned the Westminster Shorter Catechism. In 1776 Alexander's father "purchased several convict servants" who had been brought from Britain as "redemptioners" (i.e., bondservants) to work off their punishment. These unlikely teachers were Alexander's introduction to formal education. At the age of ten, however, Alexander was enrolled at the newly established Liberty Hall Academy not far from his home. This classical academy, which

FIG. 2.1

Timeline of Archibald Alexander's Life

April 17, 1772	Born near Lexington, Virginia.
1782	Began studies under William Graham.
1788–89	Served as tutor near Fredericksburg, Virginia.
1789	"The Great Revival" in Virginia.
1791	Licensed for the Ministry.
1792	Missionary in Virginia and North Carolina.
1794	Ordained by the Hanover Presbytery.
1794–98	Pastor near Charlotte Court House, Virginia.
1797–1806	President of Hampden Sydney College.
1801	Received an honorary master of arts degree from the College of New Jersey.
1802	Married Janetta Waddel.
1807	Became pastor of Pine Street Church, Philadelphia.
1808	Preached before the General Assembly as outgoing moderator, calling for a Presbyterian seminary.
1810	Received an honorary doctor of divinity degree from the College of New Jersey.
1812	The opening of Princeton Seminary.
1812–51	Professor at Princeton Theological Seminary.
1825	First major work, *A Brief Outline of the Evidences of the Christian Religion*, published.
1838	Old School/New School Presbyterian Split.
1841	Published *Thoughts on Religious Experience*.
1845	Published *The Log College*.
October 22, 1851	Died at Princeton, New Jersey.

would later become Washington and Lee University, was run by William Graham, a graduate of the College of New Jersey and a former student of John Witherspoon. Graham also served as young Alexander's pastor and had a deep impact on the mind and character of his bashful young student, teaching him theology, philosophy, Greek and Latin classics, and the natural sciences.

Alexander's studies with Graham were broken off suddenly by an arrangement his father made for Alexander to serve as a private tutor for the family of General John Posey, who had been a commander of riflemen in the Revolutionary War. The Poseys lived more than a hundred miles to the southwest in Wilderness, Virginia, just beyond Fredericksburg. While initially disappointed by his father's decision, the year spent at the Poseys would be one of the most important years in Archibald's life. Providentially, an elderly Baptist woman named Mrs. Tyler was also residing in the Poseys' home. Mrs. Tyler soon befriended the young Alexander and began to guide him in his reading. This devout woman also shared with Alexander an account of her conversion experience and took him to hear local Baptist preaching. Since Mrs. Tyler's eyesight was poor, she often asked Alexander to read her favorite author, John Flavel, to her. At first Alexander complied out of courtesy, but gradually he grew more and more interested in what he was reading. One Sunday evening as he was reading one of Flavel's sermons to the Posey household, he was powerfully and emotionally gripped by Flavel's description of Christ's patience and kindness toward sinners. His emotions caused his voice to falter in his reading, and he immediately retreated to a secluded place for prayer, where he was "overwhelmed with a flood of joy." He was furthered along spiritually by reading Soame Jenyns's *Internal Evidences of the Christian Religion* and a book on justification by Benjamin Jenks entitled *Submission to the Righteousness of God.* Clear views of the gospel and of Christ were gradually coming to him through his reading of these books and through his conversations with Mrs. Tyler. Regarding this period of his life, Alexander would later write:

> I now began to read Flavel for my own instruction. . . . The two great
> doctrines of Justification and Regeneration I began to understand, at

least in theory. A good sermon was now a feast to me. . . . This year, 1788–89, was in many respects the most important of my life. If I had not the beginnings of a work of grace, my mind was enlightened in the knowledge of truths, of which I had lived in total ignorance. I began to love the truth, and to seek after it, as for hid treasure. To John Flavel I certainly owe more than to any uninspired author. During the year I paid one visit to my friends in Lexington, and heard Mr. Graham preach a sermon on the text, "For our righteousnesses are as filthy rags.". . . It was the first intelligent discourse to which I had listened since my new understanding of the doctrines in question, and it gave me great satisfaction; but when I looked around upon the people, I had the impression that they were generally in the same state of darkness and legality in which I had lived so long.

Light began to shine upon Alexander's heart and mind, and it set him apart from what he had previously known.

Even with his newfound understanding of the gospel, it would take a bit more time for Alexander to have assurance that he had truly been born again. In 1789 Alexander returned home to Lexington where the news of "an extraordinary religious awakening" across the other side of the Blue Ridge Mountains soon greeted him. Alexander traveled with Graham on horseback to see and participate in this wonder firsthand. The journey had a significant effect on Alexander, bringing him into contact with revival preaching from great preachers of his day like John Blair Smith. Over the course of this journey, Alexander heard of many who had experienced dramatic conversions by first being "deeply convulsed with severe conviction" of sin. Rather than being encouraged by these revival incidents, Alexander stated: "I concluded that the hopes which I entertained [of being born again] must be fallacious." After failing to be deeply moved by John Blair Smith's preaching as others had been, Alexander became more deeply discouraged about the state of his soul. He spoke with Smith about this, and Smith concluded "in his decided and peremptory way" that Alexander must yet be lacking in genuine spiritual grace. Smith's assessment left him devastated. In his own words: "From this time I abandoned all persuasion that I had experienced regenerating grace. My desire now was to be brought under such alarming convictions of sin, as

I had heard of in the case of others." While yet on his journey with Graham, Alexander conversed with a wise minister named James Mitchell, who encouraged him by explaining that no degree of conviction was required for a true conversion and that the only purpose of conviction was to show us our need of Christ. These words of counsel shone a ray of hope into Alexander's troubled heart: "This mere probability of salvation, after having given up all hope, was like the dawn of morning upon a dark night; it was like life from the dead."

Alexander continued to struggle with doubts and fears about the state of his soul after he returned from his revival tour with Graham. He gave himself wholly to Bible reading, prayer, and religious conversation with other zealous "seekers." He also spent much time in meditative solitude in the wilderness around him. Back in Lexington, he also witnessed the occasional individual who was struck down with sudden conviction and "convulsions," and this caused Alexander to continue doubting whether he had received real saving grace. Many distresses about the state of his soul continued to plague him, both before and after he became a communicant member of his church in the fall of 1789.

Alexander would eventually come to believe that he was genuinely converted while residing with the Poseys in 1788. The many months of spiritual anguish which followed gave him a pastoral sensitivity for those weighed down by doubts and fears about their spiritual condition. As Alexander watched those who were touched by the revival of 1789 (sometimes called "the Great Revival"), he carefully documented a number of revival instances in his journal, taking "copious notes" on particular cases. Seeing some who had made a profession of faith later fall away altogether, Alexander began to think deeply about such subjects as conversion, genuine versus spurious religious experience, the nature of saving faith, and the place of "legal conviction" prior to conversion. Although only a young Christian, Alexander was in the process of becoming a spiritual diagnostician through these early encounters with revival.

Throughout the rest of his life, Alexander continued to be a strong advocate of religious awakenings and revival preaching. He truly believed that what he had witnessed in the Great Revival of 1789 was a special outpouring of the Holy Spirit where many had been truly converted. Yet, like Dickinson and Edwards before him, he also saw the need to distinguish between the genuine working of God's Spirit and the more superficial and temporary workings in the heart that often accompany these genuine outpourings.

Early Steps in Ministry

Archibald Alexander had all but made up his mind to go to Princeton in 1790 to further his education under John Witherspoon when, at the last minute, his mentor William Graham persuaded him to remain in Virginia to continue his studies with him. Under the guidance of Graham, Alexander soon began studying for the ministry. Meeting in Graham's study, a half-dozen students gathered weekly to debate and discuss theological topics which "entirely absorbed" Alexander's thoughts. All this happened while he was still only in his midteens. Graham led Alexander into a careful reading of books by Jonathan Edwards, William Bates, John Owen, and Thomas Boston, but his persistent counsel to Alexander was: "If you mean ever to be a theologian, you must come at it not by reading but by thinking."

Alexander was deeply influenced by Graham's "strictly Calvinistic" views, but he came to differ with Graham on certain points, especially regarding regeneration and the nature of faith. Alexander later wrote about the differences he had with Graham on these things:

> He [Graham] maintained that as conversion is the change of a rational agent, it must be a matter of conviction and choice; and that it was absurd to suppose any physical operation on the soul itself to be necessary or even conceivable. The opposite, supposed to be that of many called Hopkinsians, was that no change takes place in the views of the understanding, but such as arises from a change in the feelings of the heart. But some of us were not satisfied with either of these explanations. We supposed that a soul dead in sin was incapable of spiritual views and feelings, until made partaker of spiritual life; that this principle of life was imparted in regeneration; so that the natural order of exercises was, that the quickened soul entertained new views, which were accompanied by new feelings in accordance with the truths presented to the mind.

According to Alexander, Graham "considered faith to be simply a belief of the truth, under a spiritual apprehension of its nature" and would not "agree that any affection or emotion which flowed from such belief properly belonged to its nature, as distinguished from other graces." Graham also gave special prominence to human rationality in his understanding of regeneration, arguing that "regeneration is produced by [the] light [of truth]," apart from any distinctly spiritual operation on the unregenerate heart and mind. Alexander rejected these and other "peculiar" idiosyncrasies of Graham's thinking that grew out of Graham's special affection for metaphysical and epistemological speculation.

When Alexander's abilities were put to the test by the Presbytery of Lexington, he was surprised to find that he had a gift for extemporaneous speaking, and he was made a traveling "exhorter" by the local presbytery that same year at the age of eighteen. In this capacity, he traveled with Graham on many of his itinerant preaching tours. Also that year, Alexander was licensed to preach the gospel as a "probationer" by his presbytery. He accepted this position reluctantly, feeling too young and inexperienced for this responsibility. Alexander continued to itinerate throughout Virginia, now speaking as a *bona fide* preacher instead of as a mere "exhorter." While delivering one of his first sermons as a newly-licensed preacher, Alexander was embarrassed by a gust of wind that carried his sermon outline away, completely halting his preaching. This incident left him "determined to take no more paper into the pulpit," and for the next twenty years he did not use notes of any kind for his preaching. Instead, it became his usual practice to preach extemporaneously from a memorized and well-rehearsed sequence of thoughts. Being thus freed from notes, Alexander was able to proclaim the Word with a directness that quickly gained him the reputation of a powerful preacher.

Pastoral vacancies abounded in the Presbyterian churches in the 1790s, and many rural areas in the South did not have established evangelical churches. Alexander was appointed as a missionary by the Synod of Virginia in 1792 to build up groups of believers who were without the means of regular Christian instruction. His missionary labors took him through southern Virginia and North Carolina on horseback, and in this itinerant work he spent most of his mental energies on sermon preparation. According to Alexander: "I had no books with me but my small pocket Bible, and found very little to read in the houses where I stopped. I was therefore thrown back entirely on my own thoughts. I studied every sermon on horseback, and in bed before I went to sleep, and some of the best sermons that I ever prepared were digested in this way and at this time." By meditatively rehearsing his sermons on horseback, the young itinerant learned a discipline which he continued throughout his life. By extended meditation on a specific sequence of thoughts, Alexander learned an approach to sermon preparation which both fed his soul and prepared him for fruitful extemporaneous preaching without notes.

Hampden-Sydney and Philadelphia

Archibald Alexander left his itinerant ministry in 1794 to become the pastor of two small congregations near the town of Charlotte Court House in southern Virginia. In this rural setting, Alexander labored to make up for what he felt were deficiencies in his education. He devoted himself to disciplined study, paying close attention to the challenges posed to the Christian faith by Thomas Paine's popular *The Age of Reason*. The fruit of these studies would eventually spill over into some of the earliest books written by Alexander, which defended the rationality of the Christian faith.

Alexander's pastoral charge in southern Virginia was a part of the Hanover Presbytery, which had oversight of the nearby Hampden-Sydney College, a school modeled after the College of New Jersey. Hampden-Sydney opened in 1775, with Samuel Stanhope Smith serving as its first president. When Smith went to Princeton to assist John Witherspoon in 1779, his brother John Blair Smith became president, serving in this position for ten years. When John Blair Smith was called to a church in Philadelphia in 1789, the college carried on without a president for eight years, and it was during this time that Alexander, just a few years into his ministry, began teaching at the college as well. Along with his pastoral duties, Alexander labored to keep the school going alongside of some who would become his lifelong friends: Drury Lacy, John Holt Rice, and Conrad Speece. Driven by the necessities of teaching, Alexander explored numerous philosophical and theological issues in depth, thus developing his own character as a scholar. His son James described the effect of these early years at Hampden-Sydney:

> At no time in his life did he feel more keenly the stimulus to application, and he declared in later years that whatever accuracy he possessed in classical and scientific knowledge was acquired during this period, under the spur of necessity. . . . These years, spent amidst many anxieties, were, nevertheless profitable in no common degree, in the corroboration of principles, and the molding of character.

As Alexander wrestled through theological issues, he began at this time to entertain serious doubts about the doctrine of infant baptism. He communicated his uncertainties with his church and presbytery, and he requested that he might cease baptizing infants while continuing to explore the matter. This request was granted, and in the course of almost three years Alexander arrived at a settled conviction in favor of his initial paedobaptist views. Years later, he concluded that the origin of his doubts "was in too rigid of a notion as to the purity of the church, with a belief that receiving infants had a corrupting tendency."

The trustees of Hampden-Sydney had originally tried to obtain William Graham as their next president, but they quickly noted the giftedness of Graham's former student, and they invited Alexander to become Hampden-Sydney's third president in 1797. Alexander accepted this position and eventually resigned his two pastoral charges. As president of Hampden-Sydney, he spent himself building up the school. He labored tirelessly in study, teaching, preaching, and college administration for the next several years, to the point of experiencing many bouts of sickness in the midst of his work. In the spring of 1801 Alexander temporarily resigned his position at Hampden-Sydney with the hope of regaining his health. He decided to journey to New England, but just a few days into his journey, he contracted a severe fever and was forced to turn aside from his trip to recover. He found himself in the home of James Waddel, the celebrated blind preacher of Virginia. Waddel was known for his learning and eloquence, and he labored in fruitful service for many years as a preacher, even after completely losing his eyesight. Alexander stayed in Waddel's home for several days and was immediately impressed by Waddel's daughter, Janetta. In devoted service to her father, Janetta had read numerous volumes of theology to him, some of which were in Latin. Before leaving the Waddel home for New England, Alexander received permission to seek Janetta's hand in marriage. The two were married the following year, after which Alexander resumed his presidency at Hampden-Sydney.

Alexander's tour through New England brought him into contact with many notable leaders in the American church. During his travels he attended the General Assembly in Philadelphia, where he made the acquaintance of Samuel Miller of New York. His travels also took him to Princeton for the first time, where he renewed a previous friendship with Samuel Stanhope Smith. While in New England, Alexander took part in a joint "General Association" gathering of Presbyterians and Congregationalists, where he met many leading Congregationalists. He was also introduced to several of the leading "Hopkinsian" theologians and clergymen of New England—theologians in the tradition of Jonathan Edwards who had made several significant modifications to Edwards's more traditional Calvinism. Alexander was introduced to Samuel Hopkins himself and even preached in Hopkins's pulpit during his visit. He spent quite a few days with Nathanael Emmons as well. Although Alexander considered himself as "quite a follower of Edwards" and "open to receive light from any quarter," his encounter with Hopkins and Emmons left him convinced that the New England theologians had fallen into serious error, particularly in their governmental understanding of the atonement, their belief in the mediate imputation of Adam's sin, and their understanding of human ability.

As a result of his 1801 tour, Alexander received a number of calls to serve in other locations. In testimony to both his learning and dynamism in the pulpit, the congregation of the First Presbyterian Church in Baltimore called him to be their pastor, and Dartmouth College invited him to be a professor of theology. Both of these calls were declined, however, and Alexander returned to his previous employment as the president of Hampden-Sydney in 1802. For four more years, Alexander labored there, teaching a wide variety of subjects, preaching in local churches, and overseeing students who were not always easily managed. A period of "much turbulence and insubordination" among the students in 1806 encouraged him to reconsider the repeated calls from a church in Philadelphia he had previously declined. Alexander eventually accepted the call to the Third Presbyterian Church on Pine Street, arriving in Philadelphia in the fall of 1807 with his wife and two young sons.

As the former seat of the national government, Philadelphia was a leading American city in 1807. It was also the unofficial capital of American Presbyterianism. For many years the Presbyterians held their General Assembly there, and the four Presbyterian churches in Philadelphia boasted clergymen of distinction, including James Wilson, Ashbel Green, and Jacob Janeway. Upon arriving in Phila-

2.2 Archibald Alexander (1772–1851).

delphia, Alexander took advantage of all the educational benefits the city had to offer. He began applying himself with "assiduous application" to "every thing [sic] connected with the criticism and interpretation of the sacred text." He quickly acquired a personal library of theological books, and "his shelves began . . . to fill themselves with those folios and quartos, bound in vellum, of Latin theology, which always continued to be characteristic of his library." He also immersed himself in the works of sixteenth- and seventeenth-century theologians, reading Reformed, Roman Catholic, and Lutheran works of this period. As he now preached regularly to large assemblies in Philadelphia, his reputation grew as a preacher and also as a theologian.

In the urban setting of Philadelphia, Alexander excelled as a pastor. He was moved with compassion by the spiritual state of the poor on the outskirts of the city. With great zeal, Alexander worked to reach the poor with biblical truth. Anticipating the later work of the Sunday school and City Mission movements, Alexander started an organization in 1808 called "the Evangelical Society." While it originally started with a handful of men from his church, Alexander's Evangelical Society grew to include numerous evangelical clergy and laymen throughout the city, including Ashbel Green and Jacob Janeway. According to Alexander's plan, this group met together on Sunday evenings and separated into groups of two "to gather the children of the poor in some convenient place, to talk with their parents, and read the Scriptures and other good books." Sunday evening church services were not then common, but these Evangelical Society meetings became very popular among the poor. He also labored to construct a "free" church in Philadelphia, a church which had no pew rental or reserved seating. His idea of a religious newspaper to spread gospel truth to the masses resulted in *The Christian Remembrancer*, one of the first newspapers of its kind. Through all these efforts, Alexander successfully brought the gospel to the poor, and his work eventually resulted in many new churches in the Philadelphia area.

A Professor at Princeton

At the age of forty, the midpoint of his life, Alexander was chosen to be the founding professor for the Presbyterians' new theological seminary. Through his service at Hampden-Sydney and his preaching in Philadelphia, Alexander attained the reputation of a wise and experienced churchman and was elected moderator of the Presbyterian General Assembly in 1807. His intellectual abilities were noted by many within Presbyterian circles as well, and in 1801 he was awarded an honorary master of arts degree from the College of New Jersey, and in 1810 an honorary doctor of divinity from the same. In 1810 Alexander was elected as president of the University of Georgia, but he quietly declined this call away from his church. Other calls came to him from other institutions of higher learning, but when the General Assembly almost unanimously elected him to serve as the first professor of its new theological seminary, it was an offer he felt duty-bound to accept. Speaking to his Philadelphia congregation about his decision to go to Princeton, Alexander stated:

> I did expect to live and die with you, unless ill health (of which I have been threatened of late) should have made a removal expedient. But we know nothing of the designs of Providence with regard to us. God's dispensations are unsearchable. In the whole of this business, thus far, I have been entirely passive. I never expected or sought this appointment. . . . To train up young men for the ministry, has always been considered of higher importance to the Church of Christ than to preach the Gospel to a particular flock already gathered into the fold; and it has always been considered as a sufficient reason for dissolving the pastoral relation between minister and people. . . . In addition to this it ought to be considered that this call comes to me in a very peculiar way. It is not the call of a College, or University, or any such institution, but it is the call of the whole Church by their representatives. . . . I do believe that the majority of this congregation are convinced in their judgment, whatever their feelings may dictate, that I should be out of my duty to refuse.

Alexander was inaugurated as the Presbyterian seminary's first professor on August 12, 1812, and shortly thereafter began teaching its first class of students.

As a professor of theology, Alexander began to teach what had become the study of his life. While residing in Philadelphia he had continued to expand his theological library and immerse himself in theological writings. By purchasing the library of a minister from Holland, he had greatly added to his stock of material on Dutch Reformed theology. It was to these Dutch masters that he gave his highest praise, and he came to view the theology written during the Synod of Dort (1618–19) as a high point in the history of Reformed theology. By the time he became a professor he was also well acquainted with the whole history of Christian thought, especially of Protestant theology. He was well versed in the writings of the early church fathers, Renaissance philosophers, Lutherans, Arminians, Socinians, and the English Puritans. His travels through New England had made him familiar with the New Divinity of the Hopkinsians as well.

Though widely read in the area of theology, Alexander had grown to heartily embrace the theological positions expressed in the Westminster Confession of Faith. According to his son James:

> As it respects his own conclusion, he has left on record the statement, that on his return from New England, and during his residence in Philadelphia, his views, which had been somewhat modified by eastern [i.e., New England] suggestions, began to fix themselves more definitely in the direction of the common Westminster theology.

As a theology textbook for his classes, Alexander chose the Latin text of Francis Turretin's *Institutes of Elenctic Theology*. Even though it was "ponderous, scholastic and in a dead language," according to James Alexander, "he believed in the process of grappling with difficulties" and "he had felt the influence of this athletic sinewy reasoner on his own mind, and had observed that those who mastered his arguments were apt to be strong and logical divines." His own original lectures supplemented his students' reading and discussion of Turretin. Charles Hodge, one of Alexander's brightest students, described Alexander's practice as a teacher of theology as follows:

> In teaching theology he adopted all the methods of a text book, lectures, catechetical examinations, and written exercises. His students were for many years accustomed to read Turretin, on which they were examined. Lectures were delivered on prominent topics. Questions were handed out, to which the students were expected to write answers; and themes were proposed for extended dissertations. On Thursday

evening, the two lower classes assembled for public speaking, Dr. Alexander presiding and criticizing the performances. On Friday evening there was a meeting of the theological society for the discussion of points of doctrine and ethics. The professors attended these exercises, and concluded the debate with whatever remarks they saw proper to make. It was here that Dr. Alexander appeared in his element. His talent for extemporaneous remark found its fit occasion. His older pupils will remember while they live, the knowledge and mental excitement derived from these exercises.

In his early days as a professor, Alexander also taught Greek and Hebrew exegesis, even though his grasp of Hebrew was not perfect in the beginning. In his interpretation and instruction of the Old Testament, his son James states:

> No man looked more reverently on the typical Christology of the levitical law; and none of his pupils can forget the awe with which he approached the recesses of the expiatory system. . . . Though far from the extreme of Cocceius, and though falling short of Witsius in his interpretation of Mosaic symbols, he nevertheless differed still more from that rationalizing school of American divines, then becoming loud and influential, who were disposed to reduce the contents of the levitical typology to a minimum.

His grasp of Hebrew would eventually match his grasp of Latin and Greek, and singing from the Hebrew Psalter would become a regular part of his devotional practice. Alexander continued his instruction in biblical studies until 1820, when he was relieved by his student Hodge.

In addition to teaching biblical and theological studies, Alexander devoted himself to his students' personal and spiritual development. In the early days of the seminary, the students met mostly in Alexander's home and frequently joined in with the Alexanders' meals and family worship. In the first year of the school, there were only three students, but by the fifth year there were forty-seven. Even when the school grew to more than a hundred students, Alexander did not refuse visitors and made himself readily accessible to all who wanted pastoral counsel. According to his son James, "They [the seminary students] had constant access to his fireside and his study; and were aided by him in their pursuits, and encouraged to propound difficulties and scruples for his resolution." Alexander was also involved in assisting students with financial needs, bringing him into the personal lives of his students.

As a new professor, Alexander almost immediately began to preach to the students and other invited guests on Sunday evenings. When this gathering outgrew his modest-sized home, he was invited by the college faculty to preach in a large room in one of the college buildings. The tradition of gathering the students together for practical instruction on Sundays was later continued on the seminary campus through the long-standing Sunday afternoon "Conference" held by Alexander and other members of the seminary faculty. These gatherings invited students to share on a topic related to "experimental or practical religion," after which the professors would close with a sermon or discourse on the same topic, addressing the points that were raised by the students. Topics regularly covered by Alexander in this setting included: the work of the Spirit in the heart, spiritual pride, the dangers of seminary life, walking with God, the symptoms and cure of backsliding, saving faith, and fasting. His concern for the spiritual development of his students was demonstrated in his introductory lectures he gave at the outset of each academic year— lectures on subjects such as "The Importance of Vital Piety and Holy Living," "Defects of Character among Ministers of the Gospel," "Raising the Standard of Piety in This Seminary," and "The Use and Abuse of Books." When a revival broke out at the college next door in 1815, Alexander assisted Dr. Green in giving personal consultation on spiritual matters, furthering his reputation as a trustworthy spiritual advisor. James Alexander stated that this "quiet department of Christian service," in which Alexander frequently engaged until the end of his life, was perhaps Alexander's area of "chief influence" in the lives of others:

> It was undoubtedly by this very means, noiseless and unobtrusive as it was, rather than by formal teaching, by sermons, or by authorship, that he built up that character and attained that influence, which were so universally recognized in the church. He lives now, in the memory of great numbers, especially of the clergy, as eminently a wise counselor and a spiritual guide.

In all these varied areas, Alexander's concern for cultivating "vital piety" stands out.

Even while fully engaged as a teacher and spiritual counselor, Archibald Alexander continued throughout his life to progress as

2.3 This lecture by Archibald Alexander on the moral qualifications for ministry highlights one of Alexander's main charges to his students.

a scholar, especially during his early years as a professor. According to his son James:

> This was the time of his arduous labour and rapid accumulation. With a restless activity he pushed his inquiries far beyond the field of his prescribed course. . . . From this time forward he lost no opportunity of procuring every accessible volume of Latin theology, belonging to the German, French, Dutch, and Helvetic schools. . . . Nor did he confine himself to dogmatic or polemic works, but read largely in the departments of Criticism and Hermeneutics. . . . The reigning controversies of the day awakened his lively attention, and he repeatedly dipped into the Greek and Roman classics, and even into works on mathematical and physical science. It was characteristic of his habits to seek mental relaxation in a change of grave studies, rather than in what is denominated light reading, and for many years nothing was more common than to find his evening hours spent over some ponderous tome of the seventeenth century.

Alexander's intellectual breadth and productivity are evidenced by the more than seventy-five articles he produced for the *Princeton Review*, a quarterly journal begun in 1825 by Charles Hodge. Some of Alexander's articles include: "Early History of Pelagianism" (1830), "German Works on Interpretation" (1833), "Indian Affairs" (1838), "Instruction of the Negro Slaves" (1843), "Independent Nestorians" (1842), and "Chalmers's Mental and Moral Philosophy" (1848). This sampling illustrates the breadth of Alexander's intellectual and theological interests.

While serving at Princeton, Alexander continued to receive calls to serve in his native Virginia. In 1820 he was again elected as the president of Hampden-Sidney College when his friend and successor Moses Hoge passed away. He declined this position, along with many others from Virginia he would receive. Regarding his lifelong attachment to Virginia, his son James said in 1854:

> Until his last breath, he was intensely a Virginian; and nothing more kindled his restless eye, or animated his nervously mobile frame, or called out his colloquial fires, than any occasion for vindicating the honour of the "old colony and dominion" . . . as it regards his judgments, feelings, and policy, he was uniformly reckoned, in every good

sense, a Southern rather than a Northern man. More especially in his abhorrence of extreme and fanatical abolitionism, he never bated a jot; having constantly and firmly predicted its degradation into infidelity, which has now become patent to the world.

Though a loyal Southerner in an age of increasing sectionalism, Alexander was not a political partisan. He remained interested in political matters and read widely on current political affairs, but he kept his political opinions to himself, never preached political sermons, and seldom voted in elections.

When divisions and strife developed in the Presbyterian church in the 1830s, Alexander exhibited his characteristic moderation. Even though strict in his own theology, he was moderate in his tone and temper regarding the idiosyncrasies and deviations of various individuals in his denomination. When the Presbyterian church was dividing over Finney's "New Measures" and the "New Divinity" of Lyman Beecher, Albert Barnes, and others, Alexander wrote in 1835 in a letter to one of his earliest students: "We go on here upon our old moderate plan, teaching the old doctrines of Calvinism, but not disposed to consider every man a heretic who differs in some few points from us." Alexander and the Princeton faculty were clearly on the side of the "Old School," but they were not ones (like Ashbel Green) to lead the charge in excising the New School men from the Presbyterian denomination.

Through the ups and downs of his denomination, Alexander carried out at Princeton almost forty years of tireless work of studying, writing, teaching, counseling, preaching, and corresponding with former students. Old age did nothing to diminish his output; in fact, his last ten years of life were some of his most productive. Although stooped with age in the end, Alexander's mind and voice remained strong, and he continued to serve as the venerated "father" of Old Princeton up to his eightieth year—even lecturing until the month preceding his death. Princeton Seminary flourished under his guidance, and as Alexander's life drew to a close, his heart was filled with peace and contentment in the will of God. As death drew near, Alexander called Charles Hodge to his side for one final farewell. After giving Hodge some instructions about his funeral, he symbolically turned over the charge of the seminary to his former student and friend. In Hodge's own words: "He then, with a smile, handed me a white bone walking-stick, carved and presented to him by one of the chiefs of the Sandwich Islands, and said, 'You must leave this to your successor in office, that it may be handed down as a kind of symbol of orthodoxy.'" In this way, Alexander passed on the mantle to Hodge, who would in fact carry forward the warmhearted orthodoxy that Alexander had exemplified during his long and fruitful years at Princeton.

FIG. 2.4

Selected Works of Archibald Alexander

A Brief Outline of the Evidences of the Christian Religion, 1825

The Canon of the Old and New Testament Ascertained; or the Bible Complete without the Apocrypha and Unwritten Traditions, 1826

Suggestions in Vindication of Sunday Schools, 1829

A Selection of Hymns, 1831

The Lives of the Patriarchs, 1835

Thoughts on Religious Experience, 1841

Biographical Sketches of the Founder and Principal Alumni of the Log College, 1845

A Brief Compend of Bible Truth, 1846

A History of Colonization on the Western Coast of Africa, 1846

Practical Sermons, 1850

A History of the Israelitish Nation, 1852, posthumously

Outlines of Moral Science, 1852, posthumously

Conclusion

When Archibald Alexander passed away in the fall of 1851, the loss was felt in many parts of the church in America. The New School Synod of New York and New Jersey, in session at the time, passed the following resolution in honor of this venerated Old School Presbyterian leader:

> That the rare constellation of excellencies which met and blended in the life and character of this eminent servant of God; his child-like simplicity, warm-hearted piety, rich religious experience, fervid Christian eloquence, together with a sound practical judgment, fine natural endowments, accomplished scholarship, and fidelity and perseverance in the discharge of every duty, conspire to make him one of the highest ornaments which have adorned the Church of Christ in our country. The cause of Theological Education, to which his ripest years were devoted, found in him one of its most active and successful promoters; and the Christian Ministry, especially of the Presbyterian Church, is under an inestimable and lasting obligation to his truly apostolic service and example.

The genuine earnestness and warmhearted piety that won him the respect of even his theological opponents also brought him the universal love and respect of his closest acquaintances. When James Alexander asked his friend John Hall of Trenton to reflect upon his father's life, Hall made the following observation:

> Christians, and especially clergymen, of strong intellect, of studious habits, of scholastic attainments, often find their professional pursuits so absorbing to their taste, as to become their great temptation. They bury themselves in books—exhaust their minds in researches, which though they may be theological in their relations, are purely intellectual in their process. But I think that no one who intimately knew Dr. Alexander, can think otherwise, than that profoundly as he studied the range of theological and philosophical science, his heart was in the Bible, and in experimental religion; that *his* musings were not on the speculative theories of his own, or other men's minds, but on the revelations of the Divine Spirit, and the actual workings of the human heart, in its relations to God and inspired truth.

Alexander's dual concern for both learning and spiritual experience made him the ideal "founding father" of Princeton Seminary. He did not approach theological study as merely an intellectual or speculative exercise, thus establishing the pattern for those who would follow in his footsteps at Old Princeton. His concern for spiritual experience and piety as a teacher and theologian exemplified the combination of learning and piety that had marked Tennent's Log College and had been envisioned by Ashbel Green's *Plan of the Theological Seminary*.

3

OLD PRINCETON AND SPIRITUAL EXPERIENCE: ARCHIBALD ALEXANDER'S *THOUGHTS ON RELIGIOUS EXPERIENCE*

[Archibald Alexander] lives also in his writings. . . . In that book on "Religious Experience," Dr. Alexander lives. The book itself is a breath of life. A frontispiece gives us his picture, but the book is himself. The one shows us his face, the other makes us feel the pulsations of his heart. There was only one man who could have written The Pilgrim's Progress, *so there was but one who could have written this book on religious experience.*

—William M. Paxton

His volume entitled Thoughts on Religious Experience . . . *contains the results of his matured thinking upon the inward work of grace, and has been extensively useful. No one of his writings more fully reveals his own opinions and feelings upon the rise and progress of godliness in the soul.*

—James W. Alexander

Archibald Alexander's *Thoughts on Religious Experience* contains his extensive and insightful analysis of spiritual and religious experience, based on his own biblical, theological, and personal reflections. The book appeared in 1840 to help believers evaluate their own religious experience and the experiences of others. Early nineteenth-century revivalism had produced a climate of confusion surrounding the nature of genuine religion, causing him to state in the book's introduction: "In our day there is nothing more necessary than to distinguish carefully between true and false experiences in religion."

For Alexander, genuine religious experience occurs when the truths of Scripture are impressed upon the soul by the efficacy of the Holy Spirit. A knowledge of the truth, then, is absolutely necessary for genuine piety and religious experience. In this spiritual experience of the truth, the heart is not left in a cold and detached state but is moved to have a variety of feelings or "affections." Alexander understood that one could have a kind of "theoretical knowledge" without having a genuine spiritual knowledge. True knowledge of Christ always leaves an impression on the heart. Since false religious experiences can easily be mistaken for genuine ones, Alexander believed that individuals must be cautious and careful in evaluating the religious experiences of themselves and others. In his words, "We know very little, however, of what is passing in the minds of thousands around us. . . . Those impressions which manifest themselves by a flow of tears are not the deepest, but often very superficial; while the most awful distresses of the soul are entirely concealed by a kind of hypocrisy which men early learn to practice, to hide their feelings of a religious kind from their fellow creature."

According to Alexander even the act of discerning between true and false experiences in one's own heart is made difficult for a variety of reasons. Above all, the human heart is "a fallible guide" and prone to self-deception and delusion. Also, the truth of God may be impressed upon the heart with different levels of force and different degrees of theological accuracy. The true work of the Spirit can often coexist alongside of "much darkness and confusion . . . and much that is of a nature directly opposite to the effects of the engrafted word," making it difficult to ascertain the extent to which one has grasped the truth. A wide variety of temperaments and differences among individual personalities make the issue of spiritual examination difficult as well. After years of observation, then, Alexander issued his *Thoughts on Religious Experience* to help believers understand the various ways and workings of God in the souls of men.

Conversion and the Various Ways of God

The first nine chapters of *Thoughts on Religious Experience* address various issues related to conversion, regeneration, and saving faith. Alexander began his discussion of this topic by addressing the issue of childhood conversions. Children may indeed be the recipients of regenerative grace, but all indications of regeneration in children

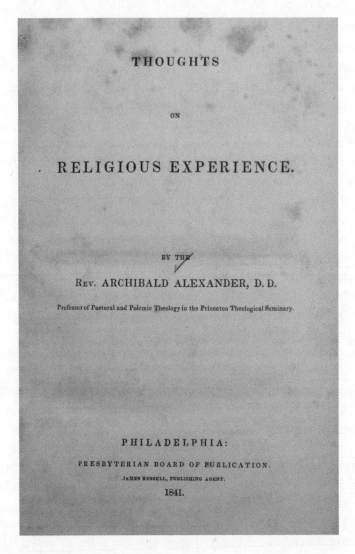

THOUGHTS

ON

RELIGIOUS EXPERIENCE.

BY THE

Rev. ARCHIBALD ALEXANDER, D. D.

Professor of Pastoral and Polemic Theology in the Princeton Theological Seminary.

PHILADELPHIA:

PRESBYTERIAN BOARD OF PUBLICATION.

JAMES RUSSELL, PUBLISHING AGENT.

1841.

3.1 Title Page of *Religious Experience.*

should not be necessarily received as such. Children raised within the sphere of Christian influence frequently experience a variety of striking religious impressions and experiences, and yet these are often "transient impressions" that should be "ascribed to the common operations of the Spirit of God." While many childhood experiences are often a genuine work of God and may be linked to the child's future conversion, in and of themselves they are generally insufficient indications of true conversion.

Alexander did believe it was possible for children to be converted at an age so early that they might not be able to remember the "first exercises" of saving grace in their hearts. These cases of early conversion, however, are difficult to discern with certainty, though genuine piety and love for Christ in a child are good indications that regeneration has occurred. Alexander even believed that a child might be regenerated before he is able to hear and understand the gospel, but he believed that these instances are rare and that "very few are renewed before the exercise of reason commences." In such cases, however, Alexander believed that a child will embrace Christ and demonstrate genuine piety as soon as he is made aware of Christ and the gospel.

Parents should make their children the focus of special spiritual instruction, even though they may not be able to accurately ascertain the progress of God's grace in their children's souls. Alexander believed that children who have received "sound religious instruction" and have "commit[ted] the catechism to memory" have an "unspeakable advantage" over children who have not. Such instruction often remains dormant and hidden away in the heart of a child until the Lord "awakens" him to spiritual concerns. Once awakened, such a child has a storehouse of spiritual instruction within him to guide and encourage the healthy growth of grace in his life. Alexander believed that parents should give religious training and instruction to their children and proceed on the assumption that their children (whether baptized or not) are in "an unregenerate state until evidences of piety clearly appear."

Adults, like children, frequently experience a variety of spiritual experiences that precede actual regeneration and conversion. While the passing from death to life in regeneration is instantaneous,

Alexander believed that there often is "a gradual preparation, by common grace, for regeneration." The supernatural regeneration of the soul is instantaneous and often imperceptible, but it may be preceded by a preparatory "law-work." Alexander did not believe that such a preparatory work was absolutely necessary, and he disagreed on this point with former New Side Presbyterian leaders such as the Tennents and the Blairs. He did believe, however, that such a work of conviction *often* precedes God's work of regenerative grace and stated that "it does appear to be a common thing for awakened persons to be at first under a mere legal conviction." "Legal conviction does in fact take place in most instances, prior to regeneration." Even so, he could conceive of repentance and conviction of sin immediately *following* upon regeneration in the hearts of some. According to Alexander:

> All who ever became pious must have begun with serious consideration, whatever means were employed to produce this state of mind. But all who, for a season, become serious, are not certainly converted. There may be solemn impressions and deep awakenings which never terminate in a saving change, but end in some delusion, or the person returns again to his old condition, or rather to one much worse. . . . In general, those impressions which come gradually, without any unusual means, are more permanent than those which are produced by circumstances of a striking and alarming nature. But even here there is no general rule. The nature of the permanent effects is the only sure criterion.

All in all, Alexander believed that "there is no general rule" on how God prepares an individual for his regenerative work, though a preparatory work of conviction and humiliation is not uncommon.

The actual event of regeneration, or what Alexander calls "the implantation of spiritual life in a soul dead in sin," reveals itself in a variety of ways in different individuals. While "the agent is the same, the deadness of the subject the same, the instrument the same, and the nature of the effect the same in every case," there are still "great diversities in the appearances of the motions and actings of spiritual life in its incipient stages." The clarity with which one grasps key biblical and theological truths at regeneration greatly affects how regeneration displays itself in the life of a new believer. While some who are born again may immediately exhibit high degrees of spiritual vigor, joy, and assurance, others who are born again remain clouded with doubts and struggles, as was the case with John Newton and Richard Cecil. The early religious experience of Henry Martyn, Philip Henry, and Matthew Henry were likewise by "no means strongly marked, but seem to have been rather obscure and feeble." According to Alexander, "genuine faith may consist with much ignorance and error," as well as with doubts and fears.

Alexander believed that a major reason why the spiritual experience of individuals differs so widely is the difference in individual temperaments. In chapter 4 of *Religious Experience*, Alexander explained how varying human temperaments have a significant impact upon an individual's religious experience and religious expression. Some temperaments are more "cold" and "phlegmatic," while others possess a more "sanguine" temperament. A due appreciation of the variety of temperaments should "shake the vain confidence of those who imagine they can decide with certainty whether another individual is a truly converted person, merely from hearing a narrative of his religious experience."

Alexander believed that failing to appreciate the diverse ways in which regeneration shows itself can lead to significant spiritual problems. He recognized that "the experimental exercises of religion . . . take their complexion from the theory of doctrine entertained, or which is inculcated at the time," and that a kind of "sectarian peculiarity in the experimental religion of all the members of a religious denomination" can emerge. New believers may be expected to conform and understand their conversion experience according to what is normal for their religious community, even though their actual experience might have followed any number of patterns that have been common throughout the history of the church. If their experience of regeneration falls outside the norm, they may be filled with great doubts as to the legitimacy of their experience. Great care should be taken, then, in counseling new believers about their experience. Above all, Alexander believed that new believers should not be made to give their "testimony" in a public setting until they have matured enough to understand more accurately what has happened to them.

Alexander believed that it was important to have a clear theological understanding of what regeneration and conversion entail. In chapter 6 of *Religious Experience*, Alexander explained his own doctrine of conversion in detail, contrasting it with other views. He faulted the views of those who emphasized the role of gospel truth in conversion and yet downplayed the need for a supernatural "operation on the mind itself" to bring about conversion. In order to be converted, man needs the light of the gospel but also a divine renovation of the spiritual faculties (a "new heart") in order to perceive this light correctly. This "supernatural" and "spiritual" operation on the soul produces "illumination" as "the first effect of regeneration." As such, the regenerate soul experiences "new views of divine truth," whereby it "discerns in the truth of God a beauty and excellence of which it had no conception until now." This "spiritual knowledge" is tantamount to the gift of saving faith, which not only "contemplates the truth" of God's Word but also "the beauty, excellence, and goodness" of what is revealed in it. Faith is the "first act of the regenerated soul" and it "draws all holy emotions and affections in its train."

In his discussion of regeneration and conversion, Alexander revealed his indebtedness and substantial agreement with Jonathan Edwards. According to Alexander,

> Few men ever attained, as we think, higher degrees of holiness, or made more accurate observations on the [spiritual] exercises of others [than Edwards]. . . . Perhaps no man who has lived in modern times has had a better opportunity to form an accurate judgment of facts of this kind than Jonathan Edwards; and few men who ever lived were better qualified to discriminate between true and false religion.

One can hear similarities with Edwards in Alexander's description of saving faith:

> The difference between a saving faith and a historical or merely speculative faith consists not in the truths believed, for in both they are the same; nor in the degree of assent given to the proposition, but in the evidence on which they are respectively founded. A saving faith is produced by the manifestation of the truth in its true nature to the mind, which now apprehends it, according to the degree of faith, in

its spiritual qualities, its beauty, and glory, and sweetness; whereas a historical or speculative faith may rest on the prejudices of education, or the deductions of reason; but in its exercise there is no conception of the true qualities of divine things.

In chapter 6 of *Religious Experience*, Alexander quoted at length from Edwards's *Faithful Narrative* of the conversions witnessed in the 1734 revival in Northampton, a narrative he found helpful and instructive. And yet Alexander's appreciation for Edwards was not without critique. He believed that Edwards's own conversion narrative had too little of a reference to Christ and that his writings on the subject of "experimental religion . . . seem to represent renewed persons as at the first occupied with the contemplation of the attributes of God with delight, without ever thinking of a Mediator." While he also believed that Edwards's *Religious Affections* was "an excellent work," he nevertheless believed it was "too abstract and tedious for common readers," and that "his fourteen signs of truly gracious Affections might with great advantage be reduced to half the number, on his own plan." Mostly likely referring to some of Edwards's nineteenth-century followers, Alexander stated:

> In our own country, faith and love have not been kept distinct. . . . When love is confounded with a justifying faith, it is very easy to slide into the opinion that as love is the substance of evangelical obedience, when we are said to be justified by faith, the meaning is, that we are justified by our own obedience. And accordingly, in a certain system of divinity valued by many, the matter is thus stated: faith is considered a comprehensive term for all evangelical obedience. The next step is—and it has already been taken by some—that our obedience is meritorious, and when its defects are purged by atoning blood it is sufficient to procure for us a title to eternal life. Thus have some, boasting of the name of Protestants, worked around, until they have fallen upon one of the most offensive tenets of Popery. . . . But while it is of importance to distinguish faith from every other grace, yet it is necessary to insist on the fact that that faith which does not produce love and other holy affections is not a genuine faith.

Even with the minor criticisms aimed at Edwards and the more significant criticisms aimed at Edwards's followers, Alexander regarded

Edwards highly as a "great and good man" and a "master in Israel" and held his writings on conversion in high regard.

Alexander's writings on regeneration and conversion are a rich production of biblical, theological, and pastoral reflection. He covers a wide range of topics, including an extended discussion of the nature of saving faith and its relationship to love in the Christian life. While Alexander understood that the Bible is to be our guide in understanding the nature of regeneration and conversion, he also understood that much insight could be gained from considering the historical accounts of conversion and the varied experiences of others. For this reason, Alexander also included in his *Religious Experience* the extended conversion narratives of Thomas Halyburton, Richard Hill, and others. The combination of historical, theological, and practical reflections makes Alexander's account of conversion especially edifying and instructive.

Melancholy, Sympathy, and Revelation through Dreams

As a supplement to his discussion of regeneration and conversion, Alexander explored the issues of melancholy, human "sympathy," and revelation through dreams. The better part of a chapter in *Thoughts on Religious Experience* is devoted to a discussion of melancholy, which is today called *depression*. Alexander recognized that true believers may struggle with depression, and often this struggle takes on a religious dimension. For Alexander, melancholy (or "a morbid temperament") is a "frightful malady," and when "religious melancholy" becomes "a fixed disease" it is one of "the heaviest calamities to which our suffering nature is subject." He believed it was important to distinguish between "religious melancholy" and "spiritual desertion," which he held was a less severe state of spiritual dryness, darkness, and temptation.

Alexander's discussion of melancholy and its causes and cures is helpful and insightful. Certain temperaments and physical conditions make some individuals more prone to melancholy, and Alexander believed that for many it may be a "bodily disease." He also recognized that it may have "moral causes" as well as physical ones. It may also be triggered by certain events in one's life, such as a severe blow to one's hopes. Alexander also believed that those who fall into religious "enthusiasm" or fanaticism are more prone to melancholy as well, especially when their delusions leave them disappointed and defeated.

In Alexander's view, pastors are often not as familiar with cases of melancholy as they should be. He stated that "many of our young preachers, when they go forth on their important errand, are poorly qualified to direct the doubting conscience or to administer safe consolation to those troubled in spirit." Those who seek to bring the comfort of gospel truth to others must understand how to handle delicately the hearts of those so afflicted and should draw upon older resources, since in his opinion, "in modern preaching there is little account made of the various distressing cases of deep affliction under which many serious persons are suffering. If we want counsel on subjects of this kind, we must go back to the old writers." Alexander quoted extensively from Timothy Rogers (1658–1728), a pastor in London who himself fell into a time of "deep melancholy" and later recovered after an extended period. Alexander cites thirteen points of instruction from Rogers's *A Discourse on Trouble of Mind and the Disease of Melancholy* on how to minister to those who are afflicted with "religious melancholy." Some of Rogers's directives include: "Treat those who are under this disease with tender compassion," "Encourage them to hope for speedy deliverance," "Put [them] in mind, continually, of the sovereign grace of God in Jesus Christ," and "Teach them . . . to look unto God, by the great Mediator, for grace and strength, and not too more to pore over their own souls."

Just as individual temperament affects one's religious experience, so also do one's social condition and religious environment. Alexander understood that man is "a social being" and that there is "a mysterious bond" whereby individuals often involuntarily take on the mental and emotional state—as well as the actions—of those around them. Alexander called this invisible social link "sympathy" and stated that it can be seen in group tendencies to yawn, cry, cough, and (under certain conditions) engage in mob violence together.

Alexander believed that by the human principle of sympathy, religious agitations and excitements are often spread naturally from one individual to another in religious assemblies. Those who are brought to experience such natural feelings and experiences may easily confuse them for a genuine work of grace. According to Alexander, "We have known instances of persons professing conversion at a camp meeting, and filling the camp with their rejoicing, who relapsed into their old habits of sin before reaching their own dwellings. In these strong excitements of the animal sensibilities there is a great danger of deception." When God is genuinely working among a group of people in a powerful way, it is often difficult, Alexander believed, to distinguish between the experiences of those who are truly experiencing a work of grace and those who are being carried along with it merely on the grounds of sympathy.

Alexander criticized Charles Finney's and other preachers' use of "new measures" in evangelism, such as calling people forward to kneel at an "altar" or sit on an "anxious bench." He believed these means used the principle of sympathy illegitimately to produce results that were often more natural than supernatural. Calls for a physical reaction to the gospel, Alexander feared, were influencing many into making a premature "response" that inadvertently turned them from the genuine path of grace that they were on. God's way of grace often brings about conversion slowly and gradually. According to Alexander,

> If they [truly] have the seed of grace, though it may come forth slowly, yet this principle will find its way to the light and air, and the very slowness of its coming forward may give it opportunity to strike its roots deep in the earth. . . . The language of experience is that it is unsafe and unwise to bring persons who are under religious impressions too much into public view. The seed of the Word, like the natural seed, does not vegetate well in the sun. Be not too impatient to force into maturity the plant of grace. Water it, cultivate it, but handle it not with a rough hand.

Individuals should not be psychologically pressured or manipulated in a group setting into performing actions and making responses that they might not be spiritually ready to make.

Just as individuals may be carried away into a kind of religious experience by the natural workings of human "sympathy," so too might they be carried away by delusions of enthusiasm or various impressions that they feel are from God. Alexander recounted a time of "general excitement" in Virginia during the beginning of the American Revolution when some were "impressed with the idea that they possessed precisely the same gifts and powers which had been bestowed upon the apostles." The idea was also promoted that some had received "an extraordinary call from God to preach, such that they needed neither learning nor study [nor pulpit preparation] to enable them to preach the gospel." After the promoters of these ideas "failed, in some private attempts, to work miracles," these beliefs ceased to spread. But when the idea of "immediate inspiration" was common, some individuals were also led to believe that extraordinary events and occurrences—hearing a voice, receiving a prophetic dream, seeing a vision—were normally connected with the converting and regenerating work of God.

Alexander stated that "whether God ever now communicates any thing by dreams is much disputed" and that "certainly people ought not to be encouraged to look for revelations in dreams." Alexander recognized that in the Bible God "frequently made His communications to His servants by dreams," but he believed that in his day there were many who deluded themselves "by fancying that their dreams are supernatural." And yet at the same time, Alexander admitted that

> there is nothing inconsistent with reason or Scripture in supposing that, on some occasions, certain communications, intended for the warning or safety of the individual himself, or of others, may be made in dreams. To doubt of this is to run counter to a vast body of testimony in every age. And if ideas received in dreams produce a salutary effect, in rendering the careless serious, or the sorrowful comfortable, in the view of divine truth, very well; such dreams may be considered *providential*, if not divine.

As an example of this, Alexander quoted at length from the testimony of John Newton and also from John Fletcher of Madeley, whose dream of the judgment day left a deep and lasting impression upon him and was ultimately used by God in the course of time to bring about his conversion. God may use dreams in his providence to bring about the conversion of the lost, but Alexander's position was that "most dreams are undoubtedly the effect of the previous state of mind, and of the peculiar circumstances and state of the body at that time."

Alexander believed that the counselor of souls must be aware of the varied nature of human frailty and the kinds of influences to which humans are susceptible if he is to give good spiritual counsel regarding conversion. Individual variations in temperament, and the unique cases of religious melancholy in particular, require patient and careful applications of gospel truth. The natural reality of human "sympathy" and its implication for group dynamics should shape how one thinks about leading in corporate worship, preaching, and evangelism. To ignore the fundamentals of group dynamics might cause one to misinterpret what is spiritual and what is merely natural. Finally, the tendency toward delusion and "enthusiasm" in some must be recognized for what it is, and the desire for direct revelation may wrongly turn people away from carefully studing and reflecting on the Bible.

Even while acknowledging counterfeit forms of religious experience, Alexander was no enemy of genuine spirituality. He recognized that a Christian profession of faith without real spiritual experience in the heart is no true profession at all. All the same, certain experiences are to be handled with great care, and spiritual counselors need an extra measure of wisdom in handling the more unusual cases.

Christian Growth and Struggles

Alexander went on in chapters ten through fifteen of *Religious Experience* to discuss the struggles that accompany the growth of grace in the life of a believer. According to Alexander, once God implants the principle of spiritual life in the believer, he leaves his work of renewal incomplete and "imperfect," such that this imperfection continues throughout the believer's entire life. Indwelling sin continues to have a "seat" in the soul of the believer, and the existence of these two contradictory principles causes much struggle and requires much diligence on the part of the Christian for his entire life. According to Alexander, "Where two opposite principles exist in the same soul, there must be a perpetual conflict between them, until 'the weaker dies.' But as the 'old man,' though crucified, never becomes extinct in this life, this warfare between the flesh and the spirit never ceases until death." "As the one gains strength the other must be proportionately weakened," and therefore, "the most effectual way to subdue the power of sin is to cherish and exercise the principle of holiness." Sin may "deceitfully hide itself" and often appears to be dead in the face of a new believer's "lively feelings" of love for God, but once these feelings have abated it often pounces and seeks to overcome once it has lulled them into "the sleep of carnal security." The Christian life, for Alexander, is understood as a life of conflict and struggle against the remains of the sinful nature.

Alexander elaborated next on the variety of challenges a believer faces in living out the Christian life. Following Christian tradition, he believed that "the world, the flesh, and the devil . . . resist the Christian soldier by their combined powers." While acknowledging that we are "often led astray by the enticements of sin within us, without the aid of Satan," Alexander also warned against the tendency among some to deny the reality of spiritual warfare and to "make a mock of Satan's temptations, as though they were the dreams of superstitious souls." The subtlety of temptation reveals itself in the fact that "lawful pursuits are more frequently a snare than those which are manifestly sinful." Alexander believed that Christians are especially prone to falling away from God because of love for the world: "Worldly prosperity has ever been found an unfavourable soil for the growth of piety. It blinds the mind to spiritual and eternal things, dries up the spirit of prayer, fosters pride and ambition, furnishes the appropriate food to covetousness, and leads to sinful conformity to the spirit, maxims, and fashions of the world."

Alexander recognized that many new believers are often naïve about the nature of the spiritual temptations they will face as their relationship with Christ matures:

> The young convert may well be likened to a raw recruit just enlisted. He feels joyous and strong, full of hope and full of courage. When the veteran Christian warns him of coming dangers and formidable enemies, and endeavors to impress on his mind a sense of his weakness and helplessness without divine aid, he does not understand what he says. . . . he is ready to think that the aged disciples with whom he converses have been deficient in courage and skill, or have met with

obstacles which are now removed out of the way. He views the contests of which they speak as the young soldier does the field of battle at a distance, while he is enjoying his bounty-money, and marches about with a conscious exultation on account of his military *insignia*, and animated with martial music.

It was Alexander's view that God often treats the young Christian with "peculiar tenderness" and protects him from temptations:

He is like a babe dandled on the knee, and exposed to no hardships. His frames are lively and often joyous, and he lives too much upon them. His love to the Saviour and to the saints is fresh and fervent, and his religious zeal, though now well regulated with knowledge, is ardent. He often puts older disciples to the blush by the warmth of his affections . . . he delights in social exercises, especially in communion with those of his own age.

After a while, however, "the glow of fervent affections subsides" and "worldly pursuits . . . steal away the heart," along with "various perplexing entanglements." Young Christians should learn from this to be vigilant over their souls, no matter how strong their feelings of love for God are:

Young Christians . . . are often greatly deceived by the appearance of the death of sin, when it only sleeps or deceitfully hides itself, waiting for a more favourable opportunity to exert itself anew. When such an one experiences, in some favoured moment, the love of God shed abroad in his heart, sin appears to be dead, and those lusts which warred against the soul, to be extinguished; but when these lively feelings have passed away, and carnal objects begin again to entice, the latent principle of iniquity shows itself; and often that Christian who had fondly hoped that the enemy was slain and the victory won, and in consequence ceased to watch and pray, is suddenly assailed and overcome by the deceitfulness of sin. Christians are more injured in this warfare by the insidious and secret influence of their enemies lulling them into the sleep of carnal security, than by all their open and violent assaults. No duty is more necessary, in maintaining this conflict, than watchfulness. Unceasing vigilance is indispensable. 'Watch and pray, that ye enter not into temptation.'

Alexander further detailed in chapter ten the slow progression of decline into which a once zealous believer can easily fall. Once a new believer's zeal lessens and he "enters into more intercourse with the world," he "imbibes insensibly some portion of its spirit," which "has a deadening effect on his religious feelings." Once this occurs, his daily "devotions" and "daily duties of the closet," which Alexander referred to as "precious seasons of grace," become less fervent, regular, and meaningful.

Alexander believed that the battleground for the soul is often lost when one loses the battle against "vain, wandering thoughts." He describes the battle against a distracted mind in this way:

> Swarms of vain thoughts may be reckoned among the first and most constant enemies of the servant of God. . . . No human mind in this world is free from the incursion of vain thoughts. . . . If the current of these thoughts is so continuous that they leave no room for spiritual meditations, they become sinful by their excess. . . . If the mind [during set times for prayer and other devotional exercises] wanders off from the contemplation of those objects which should occupy it, such forgetfulness of God's presence, and vain wandering of the thoughts, are evidently sinful. And here is an arena on which many a severe conflict has been undergone, and where, alas! many overthrows have been experienced by the sincere worshipper of God.

Alexander argued that wandering thoughts must be battled, and often battled at the level of one's affections. We are often distracted, he believed, out of "a secret aversion to spiritual things" which is the result of our fallen nature. He quoted extensively from Bernard and Chrysostom, noting that the struggle with "vain and wandering thoughts" is "common to all Christians," even the most devout.

Alexander further believed that "backsliding" was also an all too common occurrence among professing Christians, given the remains of the sinful nature and the spiritual battles that believers face. He distinguished between "perpetual backsliding" (what others have called "apostasy"), whereby a "partially awakened" individual falls away from a superficial and temporary profession of faith, and "temporary backsliding," whereby a real Christian departs from

God in his heart. Alexander described the backsliding of believers as follows:

> [Backsliding] occurs when the Christian is gradually led off from close walking with God, loses the lively sense of divine things, becomes too much attached to the world and too much occupied with secular concerns; until at length the keeping of the heart is neglected, closet duties [prayer and seeking of the Lord in private] are omitted or slightly performed, zeal for the advancement of religion is quenched, and many things once rejected by a sensitive conscience are now indulged and defended. . . . The forms of religion may still be kept up, and open sin avoided. But more commonly backsliders fall into some evil habits; they are evidently too much conformed to the world, and often go too far in participating in the pleasures and amusements of the world; and too often there is an indulgence in known sin into which they are gradually led.

Alexander believed it was the duty of believers to give "Christian reproof" or for the churches to exercise formal discipline in order to bring a backslidden Christian to repentance. God, in his mercy, will often "smite the offender with His rod" of affliction to turn a backsliding believer back to himself. It was also Alexander's view that God frequently "employs" afflictions in order to prevent his children from backsliding in the first place.

Alexander believed that "growth in grace" is the best means for avoiding the pitiful state of the backslidden. Real spiritual growth is essential for real Christian experience, for "when there is no growth there is no life." At the root of all Christian growth is growth in one's spiritual knowledge of Jesus Christ: "Just so far as any soul increases in spiritual knowledge [of Christ], in the same degree it grows in grace." An increased knowledge of Christ comes through the Word of God, and therefore those "who are most diligent in attending upon the Word in public and private, will be most likely to make progress in piety." When one is truly growing in grace, he grows in "clear and deeper insight . . . into the evils of his own heart." This can make him mistakenly conclude that he is growing worse instead of better!

True growth in grace is also shown clearly "by a more habitual vigilance against besetting sins and temptations, and by greater self-denial in regard to personal indulgence." Other indications of real Christian growth include: a "growing conscientiousness" to "minor duties," "increasing spiritual mindedness," "continued aspirations [brief prayers] to God," "victory over besetting sins," "increasing solicitude for the salvation of men," increased "meekness" and longsuffering, "diligence in the duties of our calling," "increasing love to the brethren," "a healthy state of piety," as well as increased trust and contentment in God. He went on to say, "there is no surer standard of spiritual growth than a habit of aiming at the glory of God in everything."

Alexander believed that gradual growth in grace requires believers to exert themselves toward greater godliness and that "we should aim to do something in this work every day." He laid out a number of practical directives for making "progress in piety," including: "Pray constantly and fervently for the influences of the Holy Spirit," "Take more time for praying 'to the Father which is in secret' and for looking into the state of your soul," "Be much in the perusal of the Holy Scriptures, and strive to obtain clear and consistent views of the plan of redemption," and "Practice self-denial every day." Alexander laid great emphasis on the devotional reading of Scripture for spiritual growth:

> Learn to contemplate the truth [of Scripture] in its true nature, simply, devoutly, and long at a time, that you may receive on your soul the impression which it is calculated to make. Avoid curious and abstruse speculations respecting things unrevealed, and do not indulge a spirit of controversy. Many lose the benefit of the good impression which the truth is calculated to make, because they do not view it simply in its own nature, but as related to some dispute, or as bearing on some other point. . . . It is not the critic, the speculative or polemic theologian, who is most likely to receive the right impression, but the humble, simple-hearted, contemplative Christian. It is necessary to study the Scriptures critically, and to defend the truth against opposers; but the most learned critic and the most profound theologian must learn to sit at the feet of Jesus in the spirit of a child, or they are not likely to be edified by their studies.

He also emphasized "religious conversation" as a means of spiritual growth:

> Religious conversation, in which Christians freely tell of the dealings of God with their own souls, has been often a powerful means

of quickening the sluggish soul, and communicating comfort. It is in many cases of a great consolation to the desponding believer to know that his case is not entirely singular; and if a traveller can meet with one who has been over the difficult parts of the road before him, he may surely derive from his experience some salutary counsel and warning. . . . There is, no doubt, an abuse of this means of grace, as of others; but this is no argument against its legitimate use, but only teaches that prudence should govern such religious intercourse.

In order to truly grow in godliness, "[Progress in piety] must be considered more important than all other pursuits, and be pursued in preference to everything else which claims your attention." Alexander also elaborated on a variety of hindrances to spiritual growth that need to be overcome, including deficient views on the absolute necessity and freeness of God's grace, a religious life separated from everyday life, the failure to establish specific practices of devotion, and the failure to deal with specific sins. In all these things, spiritual growth is achieved through an increased spiritual knowledge of Jesus Christ in the heart.

The Death-Bed Experiences of Believers

Alexander handled in great detail the varied experiences of believers as they encounter death and depart from this world into the next. Chapters sixteen through twenty-two of *Religious Experience* are devoted to this topic. It is natural for even Christians to recoil from the thought of death, for death is "a formidable evil, and can be desirable to none." It is a thing "abhorrent to the constitution of man," and yet Jesus has come to remove the sting of death and liberate those who are held in "bondage through fear of death." Because of what Jesus has accomplished at his resurrection, those "who are united to Christ meet death as a conquered and disarmed enemy." Even so, "[death] wears a threatening aspect, and although he cannot kill, he can frown and threaten, and this often frightens the timid sheep" who "often do not know that they are delivered from his tyranny, and that he can do nothing but falsely accuse them, and roar like a hungry lion disappointed of his prey."

We cannot truly know what it is like to experience the transition from this world to the next, and yet the experience of believers as they approach death is instructive. According to Alexander, "No arguments have ever so powerfully operated on my mind to convince me of the reality and power of experimental religion, as witnessing the last exercises of some of God's children." He recounted how he witnessed on separate occasions the supernatural power of God in preserving his dying saints from fear and filling them with a special kind of "spiritual beauty" and a "heavenly serenity of countenance." Alexander went on to describe at length the extended death-bed experiences of such notables as Andrew Rivet, Thomas Halyburton, John Janeway, Edward Payson, Samuel Finley, Richard Baxter, Thomas Scott, and many others. These examples together illustrate "the power of divine grace to support and comfort the true believer, even in the pangs of dissolution." They also demonstrate how the "blessed communications of the joy of the Holy Ghost [on the death-bed] are conveyed to the soul through the promises of God; and that all that is necessary to fill it with these divine consolations is a firm and lively faith."

Alexander admitted that not all true believers die in a state of joy and triumph and many "die under a cloud, and go out of the world in distressing doubt respecting their eternal destiny." This led Alexander to "exhort all professors of religion . . . to begin in time to make preparation for death . . . [and to show diligence] in making our calling and election sure. . . . especially let us see to it that we have on . . . the perfect and spotless robe of Christ's imputed righteousness." He also believed that a variation in death-bed experiences of believers can be attributed to a number of causes, including different degrees of grace and consolation which God sovereignly distributes, different temperaments, different biological causes of death, and different treatments and medicines administered as death approaches: "[A]s the hopes and comforts of the children of God in life are very various, so . . . a like variety is found in their views and exercises at the time of their departure out of the world."

Alexander believed that upon death the soul of a believer will continue to exist in a new mode and in the presence of God. According to Alexander, "Although we cannot now understand how the soul will act in the future world, when divested of the body of clay, we cannot doubt that its consciousness of its identity will go with it. The memory of the past, instead of being obliterated, will in all probability be much more perfect than while the person lived upon the earth." Believers will enjoy "perfect purification of the soul from sin" and great joy in the presence of Christ in the "intermediate state between death and judgment," after which time the body will be resurrected and the full salvation of the Lord realized.

Alexander concluded his lengthy section on death-bed experiences with an extended prayer that might be used devotionally by "one who feels that he is approaching the borders of another world." In 1840 Alexander himself felt that death might not be far off from him personally, and he wrote:

> The writer confesses also that, in dwelling so long on this subject, he had some regard to his own edification and preparation for death. As he knows from infallible evidence that he will soon be required to put off this tabernacle, and to emigrate from this lower world, he was solicitous to acquire as much information as he was able from those who have gone before, what were the difficulties, sufferings, and encouragements of pilgrims in this last stage of their journey.

The contemplations of death-bed scenes gave Alexander "instruction and encouragement," and he addressed this topic as a counselor of souls, hoping that others might profit from it as well.

Pastoral Letters

Alexander concluded his *Thoughts on Religious Experience* with a series of "pastoral letters" directed to specific groups of individuals. He addressed the first five of these letters to older believers, or "the aged." As an older man himself, Alexander penned these letters with pastoral sensitivity and encouraged the elderly "not to give way to despondency, and unprofitable repining at the course of past events." The elderly are encouraged to "live by faith" and to hope in God's mercy and faithfulness. Alexander exhorted older believers to remember that "Your work is never ended while you are in the body." He went on to state,

It is a sad mistake for aged persons to relinquish their usual pursuits, and resign every thing into the hands of their children. Many have dated their distressing melancholy from such a false step. The mind long accustomed to activity is miserable in a state of stagnation; or rather, having lost its usual nutriment, it turns and preys upon itself. Lighten your burdens, but do not give up business or study, or whatever you have been accustomed to pursue. Imbecility and dotage are also prevented or postponed, or mitigated, by constant exercise of the mind.

With this and many other counsels, Alexander gave warmhearted and sympathetic encouragements and exhortations to elderly saints to direct their spiritual life, their reading, and their labors in profitable paths for their own souls and for the souls of others to whom they might minister.

Alexander's next letter is written to the young and contains twenty extended sections of specific counsel on a wide variety of topics. In this letter, Alexander addressed himself to "the rising generation" as "an affectionate friend." His warm counsel commends such things as learning, good habits, carefully chosen friends, frugality, integrity, self-restraint, and diligence. Alexander also gave spiritual counsels and commended the cultivation of genuine piety and "incessant fervent prayer," saying: "You need grace to help you every day. Your own wisdom is folly, your own strength weakness, and your own righteousness altogether insufficient." He concluded his address by encouraging readers to consider the brevity and uncertainty of life and to "make immediate preparation for death." All of his counsels to the young are affectionate, direct, and oriented toward Christ.

Alexander also included a short, practical, and powerful letter of counsel to Christian mothers. He began by underscoring a mother's need for genuine Christian piety, saying "no woman destitute of religion is fit to become a wife and mother." While "consistent piety" is commended, "fanaticism" and "extravagant expressions of religious feeling" are to be avoided, since these often have "a contrary tendency." Alexander's aim in this letter was to "arouse [mothers] to the consideration of the importance of the station which they occupy, and to persuade them to exert that influence which they possess."

He believed that mothers bear a great responsibility in nurturing the faith of the next generation, and that the health of the nation and of all civil and religious institutions depends upon godly mothers faithfully laboring to cultivate faith and godliness in their children. According to Alexander,

> No eloquence equals that of a sensible and pious mother, because no impressions made by human speech are so deep and indelible. These lessons, whether she knows it or not, she is engraving on fleshy tablets, from which the inscription can never wholly be obliterated. Impression after impression may be made on the same, but these have the advantage of being first and deepest; and when all the others are gone, these will be left.

Alexander warned mothers of showing "injudicious indulgence" on the one hand and "discipline too rigorous" on the other. He also warned them from trying to completely preserve their children from temptation "by external restraints and confinements." This "general principle is good, but may be pushed too far. A gradual exposure to such temptations as must be encountered in the world is safer than for a son to be suddenly subjected to the whole influence of the world at once." Alexander's letter is filled with other wise and practical directives on raising children, disciplining children, and leading children to faith and genuine godliness.

Alexander closed his book with two short letters of comfort and encouragement—one to a bereaved widow and another to a bereaved widower. In both these letters, as with his others, Alexander expressed much wisdom and sensitivity. These model letters of tenderness in dealing with the bereaved are instructive, encouraging, and illustrative of Alexander's pastoral tenderness and compassion.

Conclusion

Archibald Alexander's *Thoughts on Religious Experience* is a unique book full of pastoral wisdom and insight into the various experiences a Christian may encounter. It illustrates the Princeton theologians' spiritual discernment and devotion to cultivating genuine religious experience in the lives of others. As a pastor and counselor,

Alexander's spiritual counsels demonstrate his vast experience in shepherding souls. His godly wisdom, balance, and good sense are evident throughout. For those desiring pastoral counsel about their own experiences, or for those seeking to speak into the religious experiences of others, *Thoughts on Religious Experience* is a helpful distillation of the kind of spiritual wisdom that benefitted those who came to Old Princeton for pastoral training.

4

SAMUEL MILLER

No man in the Church had been more zealous and active in founding this institution [Princeton Seminary] than Dr. Miller. He and Dr. Green may more properly be considered its founders than any other persons. Others aided by their counsels and occasional exertions, but these two devoted themselves with untiring zeal to the prosecution of the object, and had the pleasure of seeing their exertions crowned with success.

—Archibald Alexander

For half a century, Dr. Miller occupied a prominent and distinguished place in the Presbyterian Church in the United States of America; so that his biography, in his public relations, would be the history of that Church for fifty years.

—James Carnahan

Resolved, that I will endeavor, by the grace of God, to set such an example before the candidates for the ministry committed to my care, as shall convince them, that, though I esteem theological knowledge and all its auxiliary branches of science very highly, I esteem genuine and deep piety as a still more vital and important qualification.

—Samuel Miller, December 3, 1813

Old Princeton's dual emphasis on learning and "vital piety" was further secured when Samuel Miller joined Archibald Alexander as a faculty member just a year after the seminary began. An accomplished scholar and experienced pastor, Miller left his pastoral charge in New York for Princeton in 1813, and he remained there until his death in 1850. Miller became distinguished in Princeton as a defender of Presbyterian ecclesiology, an active churchman, and a model Christian gentleman. His sober humility and gracious sociability endeared him to his students and colleagues alike. Sharing a common theological outlook and a deep bond of affection between them, Miller and Alexander provided the fledgling seminary with a unified faculty that exhibited maturity, godliness, and pastoral sensitivity to a whole generation of students.

Early Beginnings

Samuel Miller was born in 1769 in a rural area outside of Dover, Delaware. His grandfather had emigrated from Scotland in 1710 and had married into a New England family which extended back to the earliest of the area's Pilgrim families. Miller's father, John, grew up in Boston and was converted under the preaching of Joseph Sewell, pastor of the Old South Church. Although he was raised as a Congregationalist, Miller's father became the pastor of a Presbyterian church in Dover in 1749, and this is where Samuel and eight other children were raised. Even though Miller's father received inadequate support from his church for such a large family, he acquired a large personal library and was diligent to give his children a classical education at home. From age twelve to eighteen, young Samuel was instructed in the Latin and Greek classics under the direction of his father and two older brothers. Since he aspired in these early years to be a businessman, he endured his classical studies with little interest. At the age of eighteen, however, Miller experienced a work of God's grace that set him on a different path. His experience of grace led him to make "a profession of religion" before his church in Dover and also produced a dramatic change in his feelings toward education. In Miller's words, God was pleased "to excite in me a desire for the acquisition of knowledge, though without any settled purpose as to a future profession." Shortly thereafter Miller's father cobbled together the funds to send him to the University of Pennsylvania, the first school outside of home he ever attended. His father strongly believed in the value of education, and he sent young Samuel there with the desire that he might be prepared for some "important use-fulness in the world." Miller's father wrote to Samuel's older sister and brother-in-law who lived near the university in Philadelphia, stating his hopes in sending young "Sammy" to school:

> You well know what my desire is respecting him; viz., that he may be a well-informed, sincere, prudent and humble follower of Christ. Unless his education is sanctified, by divine grace, for this purpose, I think he had better be without it. Were he, from right principles, disposed and prepared for the gospel ministry, it would be inexpressibly pleasing to me.

In other letters John Miller would express his concern that his son "may be serious, and with deep solicitude pursue an early and experimental acquaintance with vital religion, without which every other accomplishment will avail him nothing."

FIG. 4.1

Timeline of Samuel Miller's Life

October 31, 1769	Born in Dover, Delaware.
1789	Graduated from the University of Pennsylvania.
1791	Licensed for pastoral ministry by the Presbytery of Lewes.
1791–92	Studied theology under Rev. Charles Nisbet.
1793–1808	Associate pastor, First Presbyterian Church, New York City.
1801	Married Sarah Sergeant.
1809–13	Pastor, Wall Street Church, New York.
1803	Published *A Brief Retrospect of the Eighteenth Century*.
1804	Awarded a doctor of divinity degree by the University of Pennsylvania.
1813–49	Professor of ecclesiastical history and church government at Princeton Theological Seminary.
1838	Old School/New School Presbyterian Split.
January 7, 1850	Died at Princeton, New Jersey.

Miller made good use of the opportunity provided to him by his father and graduated with a "first honor" in 1789 after only one year of study. Upon his return to Dover that summer, Miller felt uncertain as to what profession he should pursue. He set apart a special day for seeking God's guidance, and before the day was done he had come to a decision. According to Miller,

> [I] set apart a day of fasting and prayer for the divine direction in my choice of a profession. Before the day was closed, after much serious deliberation, and, I hope, some humble looking for divine guidance, I felt so strongly inclined to devote myself to the work of the ministry, that I resolved, in the Lord's name, on this choice.

Upon making this choice, Miller recorded this prayer in his journal:

> O my Father's and my Mother's God, I yield myself to thee! Yet, what an office for a poor, polluted, weak creature, who is helpless in himself, to aspire unto! Lord, help me to realize my own weakness and unworthiness; to lie in the dust of abasement, and habitually to look for strength to him who can "make me strong in the power of his might." Lord, I, this day, devote myself to thy most worthy service. I am thine by creation and preservation; I ought to be thine by a holy regeneration and a gracious adoption; and I would humbly devote myself to the promotion of thy glory to my latest breath.

With this new direction in life, Miller immediately began to study theology under the direction of his father. He also sought counsel regarding his studies from Ashbel Green, whose pastoral encouragement he had received while in Philadelphia. After beginning his studies in Dover, Miller's mother died, leaving him to care for his aging and ever-weakening father by himself. In a state of near poverty and with frequent interruptions, Miller continued to study theology under his father's guidance for almost two years until he presented himself to the Presbytery of Lewes as a candidate for ministry in the spring of 1791. In the midst of his final round of examinations, Miller's father died as well, leaving him without his much-beloved guide and mentor. To obtain a license from his presbytery, Miller was examined on his "experimental acquaintance with religion," his "views in seeking the holy ministry," his facility with Greek and Latin, his attainments in rhetoric and logic, and his abilities in scriptural exegesis and preaching. All of these concluded with "a long and strict examination on college studies and especially on Theology." Miller passed all these exams successfully and was licensed in the fall of 1791, just shy of his twenty-second birthday.

Having obtained a license to minister, Miller relocated to Carlisle, Pennsylvania, where he put himself under the instruction of Charles Nisbet, principal of Dickinson College. The college had been founded in 1783 by Benjamin Rush, and Nisbet had left his ministry in Scotland in 1785 to become its first president. A close friend of John Witherspoon, Nisbet shared Witherspoon's zeal for Presbyterian orthodoxy in Scotland from the time he first entered the ministry in 1764. Like Witherspoon, Nisbet was a strong supporter of American independence during the Revolution. By age 31 Nisbet was considered a "walking library" due to his diligent acquisition of knowledge and a memory that "bordered on the prodigious." Nisbet became Miller's mentor after the death of Miller's father in 1791. He received Miller into his home "with all the condescension and kindness of a parent." Miller immediately felt at ease around his new-found mentor, and he came to quickly admire and appreciate his counsel and instruction. According to Miller,

> His practice, in ordinary cases, was regularly, every evening, to sit with him in his domestic circle two or three hours. And on whatever subject he might desire information, whether in Theology or Literature, ancient or modern, he had but to propose the topic, and suggest queries, to draw forth everything that he wished. . . . [This] presented a constant flow of rich amusement and information, and yet so entirely free from ostentation, dogmatism, or pedantry, that every listener was at once instructed, entertained, and gratified. Probably no man on this side of the Atlantic ever brought into the social circle such diversified and ample stores of erudition; such an extraordinary knowledge of men, and books, and opinions; such an amazing fund of rare and racy anecdotes; and all poured out with so much unstudied simplicity, with such constant flashes of wit and humor, and with such a peculiar mixture of satire and good nature, as kept every company, whether

young or old, hanging on his lips, and doing constant homage to his wonderful acquirements.

His hours spent with Nisbet caused Miller to recognize "the immense advantage to be derived from coming into contact daily with an acute, active and richly furnished mind, from which as much might be learned in one hour . . . as from the private study of a week." Miller would go on to pen an appreciative *Memoir of the Rev. Charles Nisbet, D.D.*, in 1840, in which he stated:

> The compiler of this volume has never seen a man so well adapted to benefit those around him, in these respects, as Dr. Nisbet. The rapidity and force of his mind in conversation; the preeminent richness of his mental furniture; his vivacity; his wit; his inexhaustible store of striking anecdotes and of happy classical allusions, rendered him at all times a most instructive and entertaining companion; and served more indelibly to impress upon the mind what came from his lips than from those of almost any other man.

Miller would spend less than a year with Nisbet, but the time he spent with him was invaluable.

After leaving Carlisle in the spring of 1792, Miller made his first visit to New York City, where he visited his father's friend and former Delaware pastor, John Rodgers. Rodgers was the much respected pastor of the First Presbyterian Church in New York City from 1765 to 1809. Converted under George Whitefield at a young age and trained under Samuel Blair and Gilbert Tennent, Rodgers was a decidedly New Side Presbyterian. While neither an intellectual nor a particularly powerful preacher, Rodgers won universal respect for his zealous piety, his "affectionate earnestness," and his deep spirituality. In 1813, Miller would pen a lengthy biography of him, entitled *Memoirs of the Rev. John Rodgers, D.D.*, in which he would write:

> The American church has not often seen his like; and will not, it is probable, speedily or often "look upon his like again." . . . In that happy assemblage of practical qualities, both of the head and the heart, which go to form the respectable man; the correct and polished gentleman; the firm friend; the benevolent citizen; the spotless and exem-

plary Christian; the pious, dignified, and venerable ambassador of Christ; the faithful pastor; the active zealous, persevering, unwearied laborer in the vineyard of his Lord; it is no disparagement to eminent worth to say, that he was scarcely equaled, and certainly never exceeded, by any of his contemporaries.

Miller spent a few weeks with Rodgers in the spring of 1792 and had the opportunity to preach in Rodgers's New York City church. Although the church of his upbringing in Dover sought to secure him as pastor, Miller instead accepted a pastoral position at Rodgers's First Presbyterian Church in 1793. Although Miller was only twenty-three at the time, and although this Presbyterian church was one of the most prestigious and wealthy churches in the nation, the church members were deeply impressed with what they saw of Miller's pulpit eloquence, his literary and social refinement, and his pastoral sensitivity. He was ordained later that year after successfully passing another battery of exams in "Latin, Greek, Geography, Logic, Rhetoric, Natural Philosophy, Astronomy, Moral Philosophy, Divinity, Ecclesiastical History, and Church Government."

As the "boy preacher" (as some called him) passed his ordination trials and entered the ministry, he had the immense privilege of having been mentored by Green, Nisbet, and others. But most significantly it was the influence of his parents, his father in particular, who gave him the bulk of his education and made the duties of the pastoral office almost second nature to him. Miller's son and biographer, Samuel Miller Jr., states that "it was in that retired, rural, Delaware home, that [Miller] laid the foundation of every accomplishment, which particularly characterized his subsequent life; and, if so, the fact is but one proof among many of the power of early home influences." John Miller died in virtual poverty and had sacrificed most of his worldly possessions for the education and advancement of his children. He would undoubtedly have been pleased to see his young "Sammy" successfully ordained and settled as a pastor in New York City.

A Young Pastor in a Big City

Samuel Miller had never aspired to any position other than "an ordinary country charge," and he was quite surprised to be thrust from rural anonymity into such a public and demanding ministry. When he began his work in New York City in 1793, the First Presbyterian Church was composed of two congregations united as one church. Both the Wall Street congregation and the congregation meeting in "the Brick Church" would become independent churches in 1809, but in 1793 the two congregations were supplied by pastors John Rodgers and John McKnight. When McKnight's health kept him from preaching the usual three sermons that were expected every Sunday from both men, Miller was called to assist with preaching and other pastoral responsibilities. Even with two colleagues, Miller found his pastoral duties in New York incredibly demanding. It was Miller's practice to write out his sermons in full, and then to commit them to memory, preaching from only a scrap of paper with the first few words of every paragraph written down as an aid to his memory. The effort Miller put into sermon preparation was duly noted and appreciated, and many of his sermons were secured for publication, including two preached on the anniversary of American Independence (in 1793 and 1795), a sermon against slavery (1797), two sermons related to the yellow fever plague of 1798 (1798, 1799), a sermon eulogizing George Washington (1799), and a sermon in support of the New York Missionary Society (1802). Miller produced these and many others in the midst of numerous pastoral demands, as well as during the waves of yellow fever which ravaged the city in these years and claimed thousands of lives. The demands of ministry took a toll on Miller's health, and he himself struggled with various ailments during his first years in New York.

Miller's relocation to New York also brought with it a host of temptations that led him down certain paths he would later renounce. Even in the midst of pressing responsibilities, the young Miller was soon drawn into a variety of social and literary societies which the city had to offer. Miller's brother Edward practiced medicine in the city, and the two bachelors lived together and joined a number of societies which further stimulated Miller's interest in broader literary and intellectual concerns. One such society was called "the Friendly Club," which Miller may have helped form. It met every Tuesday evening for social interaction and the discussion of a passage of literature. Miller also joined the Masonic Lodge and ascended to the degree of a Royal Arch Mason. With an increasing interest in secular affairs, he began gathering historical materials with the intention of writing a history of New York. He also labored in these early years to produce what would become a monumental two-volume intellectual survey of the eighteenth century entitled *A Brief Retrospect of the Eighteenth Century* (1803). This was Miller's first substantial publication. The wide-sweeping survey it provided of eighteenth-century science, art, and literature established Miller's reputation as a scholar. Miller had planned additional volumes on politics, theology, and ethics, but these never materialized. While his *Retrospect* won him widespread acclaim, it also illustrates the degree to which Miller was involved in these years with secular intellectual concerns.

As Miller grew more interested in such studies, he also became increasingly involved in partisan politics. While a student in Philadelphia in 1787, Miller had excitedly gone to the State House to observe men like Washington, Hamilton, and Franklin as they gathered to draft the Constitution, and these experiences likely gave him an early interest in public affairs. While in New York, Miller became a strong partisan for the Democratic-Republican party of Thomas Jefferson, over against the Federalist party of Hamilton and Adams. Even though he knew that Jefferson was "suspected of Deism," his own adherence to democratic ideology caused him to write in 1800 that "I had much rather have Mr. Jefferson President of the United States, than an aristocratic Christian." Miller was also, in his own words, "among the thousands of his countrymen who regarded the French Revolution, in its early stages, with a favorable eye, as the triumph of the spirit of liberty over misrule and oppression." Along with others in the party of Jefferson, he tenaciously clung to these hopes "long after every truly favorable aspect had vanished."

A Pastor and a Scholar

It was as a pastor in New York City that Samuel Miller became established in his family and professional life. He met and married his life's companion, Sarah Sergeant, in 1801. Sarah was the daughter of Jonathan Dickinson Sergeant, a noted Revolutionary patriot, and a granddaughter of Jonathan Dickinson, the first president of the

College of New Jersey. She also was a descendant of the noted Sergeant family of New Haven, Connecticut. Sarah proved to be a wonderful companion to Miller, even though she hadn't made a public profession of faith and wasn't a communicant member of a church until after their marriage. Miller noted on their first anniversary that "her natural and moral qualities are such as have more and more endeared her to me, and impressed me every day with a deeper conviction of the wisdom and happiness of my choice." Sarah would become a communicant member later that year, though she struggled with spiritual doubts and fears for several years after. The two would have ten children together, and Sarah would remain at Samuel's side throughout his life, outliving him by more than ten years.

In response to the appearance of his *Brief Retrospect of the Eighteenth Century* in 1803, Miller was awarded doctor of divinity degrees from Union College and the University of Pennsylvania. He was only thirty-four years old at the time. According to William Sprague, "it was uncommon, if not unprecedented, for a person so young to receive that honour." Miller's work was quickly republished in England, though at least one of his British editors felt it needed significant editing and criticized it for its "dogmatism." This comment was likely due to the fact that Miller's work forthrightly opposed the "theories, falsely called philosophy, which pervert reason, contradict Revelation, and blaspheme its divine Author."

Miller's reputation as a Christian thinker was also established by the theological controversies in which he engaged as a pastor. He was not a strident controversialist, and it was with great moderation that he met many of the issues of his day. Miller did not believe, for example, that the deviations of Samuel Hopkins posed a significant threat to the Presbyterian church. And even though Miller was thoroughly committed to traditional Calvinism, he did not stand in the way of ordaining Presbyterian candidates for ministry (like Gardiner Spring) who held to moderate Hopkinsian positions. According to his son, Miller "certainly did not regard with as much alarm as some others, the introduction of this so called moderate Hopkinsianism into the Presbyterian Church, and constantly by voice and vote contended for its toleration." He did, however, view the Hopkinsianism of Nathaneal Emmons and others to be in more significant error and withheld his support of those who held to Emmons' more extreme positions on moral ability, original sin, imputation, and atonement. Because of his moderation, Miller himself fell temporarily under the suspicion of being a Hopkinsian himself. Regarding Unitarianism and other forms of heterodoxy, though, Miller took a much sharper stand. Miller supported Rev. John Codman in 1810 when Codman refused to join in with the long-held practice of the Boston area clergy of regularly exchanging pulpits with Unitarians. In his published support of Codman, Miller wrote: "Is not deliberately sending a man into our pulpits, whom we suspect and more than suspect of heresy, fundamental heresy, something very like being accessory to the propagation of that heresy?" Miller's opposition to Unitarianism would find its fullest expression in his 1821 *Letters on Unitarianism*.

Even with his natural bent toward moderation, Miller also took a strong stance against the encroachment of "high church" Episcopalianism, which he believed sought to "gain a mastery over every other denomination in the state, and particularly in the city." Drawing on their "immense wealth," Miller noted in 1805, the New York Episcopalians were promoting their "high-toned doctrines of Laud and his successors" through a deluge of "sermons, tracts, and much larger works." The leading proponent of these views was John Henry Hobart, the episcopal bishop of New York. Writing to Ashbel Green, Miller stated that Hobart and his associates "are printing, and distributing through the United States, very large editions of books, both polemic and practical, replete with high church doctrines. . . . [They are attempting] both in public and private, to impress upon the minds of the people a belief of the invalidity of all ministrations, excepting those of men who are episcopally ordained." According to Miller, the Episcopalians were aggressively promoting the belief that

> the power of ordination to the Christian ministry is, by divine appointment, vested exclusively in Diocesan Bishops; that where these Bishops are wanting, there is no authorized ministry, no true Church, no valid ordinances; that, of course, the Presbyterian and all other non-Episcopal churches and ministers are, not only unauthorized and perfectly destitute of validity, but are to be viewed as institutions founded in rebellion and schism.

Writing to his friend Edward Dorr Griffin in 1805, Miller stated that the Episcopalians "are taking unwearied pains, upon a large scale, to disseminate their high church doctrines much beyond the bounds of this city and state. Every minister of the Presbyterian Church ought to be apprized of their designs, and to be particularly armed on the subject of Church Government, and the history of Presbyterian and Episcopal ordination." Miller and his Presbyterian clerical associates in New York believed the threat posed was so significant that they formed a magazine, *The Christian's Magazine*, to counter this form of aggressive Episcopalianism.

Miller's controversy with Episcopalianism would have significant consequences, both for his own career and for the founding of Princeton Seminary. According to his son, the episcopal controversy "more or less marked the whole of his subsequent life." Miller's first major publication after his *Retrospect*, entitled *Letters on the Constitution and Order of the Christian Ministry*, would appear in 1807 to address the issue. *A Continuation of Letters Concerning the Constitution and Order of the Christian Ministry* would appear the following year. These books contradicted the notion of an Episcopalian hierarchy by arguing that the words "elder" and "bishop" are used interchangeably in Scripture. Miller also argued that a distinction should be made between a "ruling elder" and a "teaching elder" (or minister) based on 1 Timothy 5:17, even though the different types of elders shared an essential equality. Throughout the course of his life, Miller would publish many works on church polity and history, including his *Essay on the Warrant, Nature, and Duties of the Office of the Ruling Elder in the Presbyterian Church* (1831) and *The Primitive and Apostolical Order of the Church of Christ Vindicated* (1843).

Miller's first correspondence to Ashbel Green in 1805 regarding the establishment of a Presbyterian seminary was triggered by the threat he felt the Presbyterians were facing from high church Episcopalianism. To keep the Presbyterians from being reduced to a fringe minority, Miller felt it was necessary for the Presbyterian assembly to adopt a new measure to train up additional ministers to supply the numerous vacancies in Presbyterian churches. Green would make an overture to the assembly that year, starting the discussion which would lead to the eventual establishment of Old Princeton.

FIG. 4.2

Selected Works of Samuel Miller

A Brief Retrospect of the Eighteenth Century, 1803

Letters on the Constitution and Order of the Christian Ministry, 1807

A Continuation of Letters concerning the Constitution and Order of the Christian Ministry, 1809

Memoirs of the Rev. John Rodgers, D.D., 1813

Letters on Unitarianism, 1821

Letters on Clerical Manners and Habits, 1827

An Essay on the Warrant, Nature, and Duties of the Office of the Ruling Elder in the Presbyterian Church, 1831

Letters to Presbyterians on the Present Crisis in the Presbyterian Church in the United States, 1833

Memoir of the Rev. Charles Nisbet, D.D., 1840

The Primitive and Apostolical Order of the Church of Christ Vindicated, 1840

Letters from a Father to his Sons in College, 1843

Thoughts on Public Prayer, 1848

From Pastor to Professor

As the Presbyterian work in New York continued to flourish, in 1798 a third congregation on Rutgers Street was added to the two united congregations, along with a fourth minister, Philip Milledolar. Even before this addition of a third congregation, Miller had come to view the one-church, multisite "union of congregations" as "a great evil." While pulpit preparation was lessened through the preachers' repetition of sermons at each of the congregations, the pastoral cares were greatly multiplied by the number of congregants who expected to receive pastoral care and visitations from each of the pastors. Pastoral rivalries and factions were also fostered by the arrangement, even with Rodgers occupying a senior position. By the end of 1808, Miller felt that the congregations had to be separated or he would be forced to seek another position. At his instigation, the congregations separated and formed independent churches in 1809, with McKnight becoming the pastor of the Brick Church, Milledolar the pastor of Rutgers Street, Miller the pastor of Wall Street, and Rodgers maintaining a connection to each of them. The dividing up of the churches caused significant tension and misunderstanding, especially between Miller and McKnight. Their misunderstanding was resolved, but only after much effort. Miller would come to view his push for separation as one of the best things he did for the Presbyterian work in New York, and yet the experience also sensitized him to the need of diligently pursuing and maintaining collegial relationships with fellow ministers.

With the dissolution of the united congregations behind him, Miller gave himself to the duties of pastoring the Wall Street Church for the next four and a half years. With Rodgers's health failing, Miller was virtually the only pastor of the congregation, which numbered around two hundred members. Though the Wall Street church did not have a Sunday school, Miller conducted the weekly catechism class for the children of the church every Wednesday afternoon. His direct involvement in the catechism classes was common for the time, and yet Miller seemed to have taken a special interest in his work with children. In an 1805 letter, he wrote: "I wish to do as much good as possible; and doing good to the young has always appeared to me as, humanly speaking, doing it on the largest scale." On another occasion he would write to another minister: "Take care of the children of your charge. They are the hope of the Church." Miller would make this a regular plea in his advice to younger ministers.

Miller continued to give special attention to his pulpit preparations, and his preaching style was suited to the highly educated and wealthy congregation which made up his church. According to William Sprague,

> Miller early took rank with the best preachers of his day. . . . His utterance was deliberate, possibly too much so to suit the mass of hearers;

but it was marked by an evident sincerity and solemnity which were well fitted to make an impression. He would occasionally deliver a sentence with an air of majesty, and a degree of unction that would make it quite irresistible. . . . Still he could not be considered an impassioned preacher; and his manner was characterized rather by quiet dignity, and occasionally by genuine pathos, than by any remarkable versatility or vigour. But his discourses were decidedly superior to his manner of delivering them. He never shot at random: he always had a distinct object in view, and he went deliberately and skillfully to work to accomplish it. There was the same symmetry about his sermons that there was about his character—everything was in its right place. . . . You expected that everything in the service would be fitting and reverent, and every way up to the dignity of the pulpit; and you were never disappointed. . . . If there were others who had a wider popularity and more control of the passions of the multitude, there were few whose pulpit productions had in them so much of weighty and well digested material, or would so well abide the test of an intelligent criticism.

Those who attended to Miller's public ministry were especially blessed by his public prayers, a means of grace which he valued highly and cultivated carefully. He put his views on public prayer in print with his last publication, *Thoughts on Public Prayer* (1848).

As Miller's reputation continued to grow, he began to be sought after by institutions of higher learning. In 1808 he declined a call to be the principle of Dickinson College in Carlisle, Pennsylvania. In 1811 he was awarded a third doctor of divinity degree, this one from the University of North Carolina, which pursued him to be its president the following year. That same year he also declined an appointment to become president of Hamilton College in Clinton, New York. In 1807 he became trustee of the College of New Jersey, a position he would hold until his death forty-three years later. According to James Carnahan, Miller "took a deep interest" in the concerns of the college and "was rarely if ever absent from the meetings of the Board, and was always an active and influential member." In 1812 the board of trustees pursued him to replace Samuel Stanhope Smith as the president of the college. He declined this invitation and helped secure Ashbel Green for the position instead. While concerned with the well-being of the college, Miller gave increasing attention to the formation of what would become Princeton Seminary. Miller helped steer the General Assembly to establish a single, unifying seminary when it was considering a variety of proposals. He also served with Ashbel Green and Archibald Alexander on the committee that drew up the official "plan" of the seminary. Further, he was elected to serve on the first board of directors, and once Princeton Seminary was launched he labored to raise funds for its establishment.

Miller was surprised when the 1813 General Assembly appointed him to assist Archibald Alexander in Princeton as the professor of ecclesiastical history and church government at the new seminary. The interest he took in the seminary, along with his reputation as a scholar and pastor made him a fitting choice for the seminary faculty. After a few weeks' deliberation, Miller concluded that it was the will of God for him to yield to the Assembly and accept their call to Princeton, but it was not without sadness that he left his congregation in New York. Writing to Ashbel Green, Miller confessed that "I did not know, until now, how much I loved my people nor had I the least idea that they would be so unwilling to part with me." As Miller prepared to take up the task of preparing men for the ministry, he was overwhelmed with the weight of responsibility he felt being placed upon him. Writing in his diary on September 22, 1813, Miller stated:

I must, in candor, say, that when I think of the intellectual, literary and spiritual attainments and qualifications, which the office to which I am appointed demands, my heart sinks within me. I am constrained here to record my honest conviction, that I have not the appropriate qualifications for it, and that if I, in any tolerable degree, succeed, it will be rather owing to the charitable indulgence of the directors and pupils of the institution, and, above all, to the shielding and sustaining power of my covenant God, than to my own preparation for the work. I have not the talents; I have not the varied furniture; especially, I have not the mature spiritual wisdom and experience which appear to me indispensable. The choice to this office, I am well aware, would never have fallen on me, if there had not been a lamentable scarcity, in our Church, of ministers who have in any measure turned their particular attention to the studies appropriate to this office. May the Lord sustain me, and prevent my utterly sinking under the burden laid upon me!

Miller's move to Princeton was almost cut short by two severe bouts of illness, the second of which being "a violent inflammatory fever" which confined him to his home for six weeks. At one point this sickness appeared to be terminal, but God spared his life and sustained him for the important work prepared for him in Princeton.

Professor at Princeton

Before Samuel Miller began his term as a professor at the seminary, he wrote down a series of resolutions to help him meet his new responsibilities. These included the resolve to live completely for Christ in all things, the resolve to avoid giving offense or taking offense from others, and the resolve to put aside the "indulgence in levity and

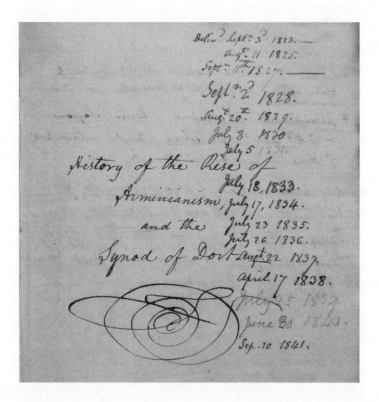

4.3 Samuel Miller's lecture notes on the "History of the Rise of Arminianism and the Synod of Dort" show that he gave this lecture almost once a year from 1823 to 1841. It was eventually published as an "Introductory Essay" to a reprint of the Articles of the Synod of Dort by the Presbyterian Board of Publication in 1841.

jesting," which he called one of his "besetting sins." He also resolved to continue preaching "as often as my Master gives me opportunity," stating: "I am persuaded that no minister of the Gospel, to whatever office he may be called, ought to give up preaching. He owes it to his ordination vows, to his office, to his Master, to the Church of God, to his own character, to the benefit of his own soul, to go on preaching to his last hour." Miller carried out this resolve up until the close of his life, preaching frequently in pulpits in and around Princeton.

When Miller went to Princeton he also renounced many of the former social and political entanglements that had weighed him down in New York. He also focused more narrowly on theological and ecclesiastical concerns than he had done previously. By the time he arrived at Princeton he had already renounced all connections with the Masonic Lodge, and he would later give emphatic instruction to his sons not to join it. He also came to renounce his attachment to Thomas Jefferson. Writing in 1830 he stated that

> There was a time . . . when I was a warm partisan in favor of Mr. Jefferson's politics and administration as President. Before his death, I lost all confidence in him as a genuine patriot, or even as an honest man. And after the publication of his posthumous writings, in 1829, my respect for him was exchanged for contempt and abhorrence. I now believe Mr. Jefferson to have been one of the meanest and basest of men.

As Miller moved away from his Jeffersonian views to more Federalist (or "old line Whig") positions, he also came to view his former involvement in partisan politics in a negative light altogether:

> I look back on that whole part of my early history with entire disapprobation and deep regret. . . . I was wrong in suffering myself to be so warmly and actively engaged in Politics as I was during that period. For though ministers have the rights and duties of citizens, and, probably, in most cases, ought to exercise the right of voting at elections; yet when party politics run high, and when their appearing at the polls cannot take place without exciting strong feelings on the part of many against them; and when their ministry among all such persons will

be therefore much less likely to be useful, I cannot think that their giving their votes can have an importance equivalent to the injury it is likely to do. I think I was wrong in talking, and acting, and rendering myself so conspicuous as a politician, as I did. I fear I did an amount of injury to my ministry, which could by no means have been counterbalanced by my usefulness as a politician.

Turning his back on partisan politics, Miller embraced a new course which he felt was in accord with the "soundest evangelical wisdom" for a pastor and a seminary professor. Specifically, Miller says that he

determined to do and say as little on the subject [of politics] as could be deemed consistent with the character of a good citizen: to attend no political meetings; to write no political paragraphs; to avoid talking on the subject much either in public or private; to do little more than to go quietly and silently to the polls, deposit my vote, and withdraw; and, in the pulpit, never to allow myself, either in prayer or preaching, to utter a syllable from which it might be conjectured on which side of the party politics of the day I stood.

Miller had come to the conclusion that the greatest good he could do his nation was to advance the interests of Christ and in so doing promote the most important concerns of the country.

In addition to politics, the influence of intellectual societies and worldly acquaintances had been too powerful for him to resist while he had been a young pastor in New York. Miller's son would write that

In later years Mr. Miller seemed to look back at his life in New York, as having been, in more than one respect a life of sore temptation; and no one can recur to its remaining records, imperfect as they are, without concluding that he could not have escaped entirely unharmed, from influences far too worldly, by which he was surrounded. The choice of a history of New York as the first great task for his pen, though a task never completed; and his subsequent actual preparation of two volumes of a general "Retrospect of the Eighteenth Century," clearly prove, that he had not yet learned to give himself wholly and rigorously—an absolute condition of great spiritual success—to his bare gospel work.

Miller's son called his father's dalliance with secular intellectualism and Jeffersonian democracy in particular a "temporary hallucination." However much the young New York pastor became co-opted by eighteenth-century political and intellectual culture, it was a fall from which he recovered. Even though, according to his son, Miller's "growth in grace and experimental knowledge" may have been "seriously retarded" while serving in New York, "his spiritual progress was much more decided, constant, and vigorous after his removal to Princeton."

Once settled in Princeton, Miller devoted himself to instructing his students, and he put off large publication projects for a number of years. Like his colleague Alexander, Miller took an affectionate and fatherly interest in his students, listening to their questions and concerns with great tenderness and compassion. According to one of his earliest students, "[Miller] met us with a father's counsels, and brought out to us the ample treasures of his own Christian experience." Another of Miller's students, S. Irenaeus Prime, recounts how Miller graciously offered him the use of his personal library, stating that "while you are in the Seminary it is entirely at your service; take books to your room and use them as long as you please." According to Prime, Miller was a "father and friend of the students, each one of whom he regarded as a son." Miller provided his students with lectures in ecclesiastical history, church government, and sermon composition and delivery. These lectures reflected his essentially conservative and Presbyterian convictions. According to one student:

> A large part of the instruction which Dr. Miller communicated to us was, of course, by lectures. And here I always considered him admirable. I cannot say, that he had any great vivacity of manner, or that he was given to saying brilliant and startling things, which would be remembered and talked about afterwards; but his lectures were remarkable for exhibiting a full, clear and perfectly logical view of his subject. He had none of that miserable affectation of originality, which prefers a doubtful path to a beaten one, and which is never satisfied unless it is following some *ignis fatuus*, or gazing at a sky rocket. There was such perfect continuity of thought in his lectures, whether he read them or delivered them extemporaneously, and withal, his utterance

was so distinct and deliberate, that it required nothing more than an ordinary memory, especially if assisted by brief notes, to retain a large part of what it would take him an hour to deliver.

Miller's course on ecclesiastical history began with the original "dispensation of mercy" in the garden of Eden and embraced the whole scope of biblical history and geography. As a textbook for his historical courses, Miller began, then, with the Bible. He also made enthusiastic use of John Lawrence von Mosheim's eighteenth-century *Institutes of Ecclesiastical History*. Alongside his lecturing in the seminary, Miller produced a number of items for publication. Some of his published sermons and addresses include "The Utility and Importance of Creeds and Confessions" (1824), "The Importance of the Gospel Ministry" (1827), "The Importance of Mature Preparatory Study for the Ministry" (1829), and "The Importance of Gospel Truth" (1832). Miller also contributed some twenty-five articles to the *Princeton Review* as a professor, including: "Thoughts on Evangelizing the World" (1836), "Decline of Religion" (1837), "Attention to Children" (1838), and "The Intermediate State" (1839).

Even as a professor, Miller continued to play an active role in church affairs. As the "New School" adherents grew in numbers and influence in the General Assembly, he began to see them as a serious threat to the Presbyterian church and to the seminary. In the assessment of Miller, "the adherents of Mr. Finney," "the friends of New Haven theology," and "the old Hopkinsians" had converged in the late 1820s and had become "firmly united in policy and purpose to put down [confessional] Presbyterianism." After the 1831 General Assembly, Miller wrote:

> I have no doubt that the apprehensions of danger, felt by our friends of the Old School, are well founded! There is, in my opinion, a crisis at hand. We have much to fear. There is danger, great danger, that our church will be overrun with error, and that the direction and instruction of Princeton, and, I may add, of every other place and institution, will fall into the hands of another set of theologians.

In 1833 Miller published his *Letters to Presbyterians on the Present Crisis within the Presbyterian Church* in the hopes of unifying the fragmenting

Presbyterian church under traditional Old School Presbyterian views. In 1837 he stated,

> I am opposed to a division still [in the Presbyterian Church]. By prudence, fidelity and patience, I am confident it may be avoided. But I have no hesitation in expressing the opinion . . . that if we are to go on, in future, as we have done for the last few years, in a course of continual conflict and strife; and above all, if division can be avoided only by yielding to the inroads of Arminian and Pelagian errors; I do not see how the great ends of Christian fellowship can be attained; and am persuaded it would be better to separate, and that as speedily and quietly as possible.

4.4 Samuel Miller (1769–1850).

Even though Miller and the Princeton theologians did not share Ashbel Green's zeal for removing the New School party, Miller was supportive of the separation once it took place in 1837.

A Unified and Blessed Faculty

The mutual respect and affection between Samuel Miller and Archibald Alexander, the first two members of the faculty, laid a foundation for the harmony that its faculty would enjoy for many years. This unity was not the result of shared personalities, for Miller and Alexander had very different temperaments and upbringings. According to James W. Alexander, Miller "came from the training of city life, and from an eminently polished and literary circle." His "courtly manners" caused him to "set a high value on all that makes society dignified and attractive." He was "preeminently a man of system and method" who governed his life "by exact rule," even in "the minutest particulars." By contrast, Alexander says that his father "was not a man of rules" and was "free from all constraint and plan." Freedom and spontaneity, for him, were "almost his passion," and "eminent natural simplicity was his characteristic." The degree of harmony that existed between the founding faculty can be attributed in at least some degree to Miller's humility. Writing in 1834, Miller reflected on the discord he had experienced in New York and stated:

> Knowing the discomfort, as well as the other mischiefs of the want of entire harmony and cordiality among colleagues in the same institution, one of the "Resolutions" I formed in coming to Princeton was that nothing should tempt me to quarrel with my colleagues: that, however they might treat me, I would merge my own feelings and honour in my Master's glory. By the favour of God, I think no three men [Hodge, Alexander, and himself] were ever more united, in affection and confidence, than we are.

Writing in the last year of his life, Miller paid tribute to Alexander and to the unity and affection that they had enjoyed:

> The sentiment which most strongly and prominently occupies my mind [regarding the seminary] is that of thankfulness that the Lord

has been pleased to unite me with colleagues so wise, so faithful, so much superior to myself, and so eminently adapted to be a blessing to the Church. I consider it as one of the greatest blessings of my life to be united with such men, and pre-eminently with my senior colleague, whose wisdom, prudence, learning, and peculiar piety have served as an aid and guide to myself, as well as to others. . . . I desire especially to feel thankful that I ever saw the face of my venerated senior colleague. He has been for thirty-six years to me a counselor, a guide, a prop, and a stay, under God, to a degree which it would not be easy for me to estimate or acknowledge.

Miller's humility and affectionate respect for his "senior" colleague (who was actually younger than he by two years) cemented a unique partnership and unity of heart. This union, Miller himself attributed to "the perfect agreement on the part of all of us in an honest subscription to our doctrinal formularies," but undoubtedly his humble, respectful, and gentlemanly demeanor contributed to the harmony the faculty members of Old Princeton enjoyed.

Miller continued to experience many bouts with illness during his years at Princeton. As Miller aged, these bouts increased, and the board of trustees began dividing up Miller's duties and lessoning the expectations that were put on him as an instructor. In 1848 Joseph Addison Alexander took over Miller's courses on church history. In 1849 James Waddel Alexander was chosen to replace him altogether. Miller had taught at the seminary for more than thirty-six years, and he spent the last few months of his life in severe frailty and in anticipation of his heavenly reward. William Sprague recounted that in his last encounter with Miller,

His whole appearance was a compound of the deep solemnity that becomes the dying man, and the joyful tranquility that becomes the dying Christian. He had no breath to waste on mere worldly matters, but began immediately to talk of the goodness of the Master whom he had served; of the great imperfection of the service he had rendered; and of the glorious eternal home, which, through grace, he was about to enter . . . I came away convinced that I had been listening to a dying man; and yet such an impression had he left upon me, that I could not think of him, in connection with the grave, but only with the glorious world beyond it.

On January 7, 1850, Miller passed away at the age of 81. It fell to his aged partner and friend, Archibald Alexander, to give his funeral address. In this address Alexander honored the character of the man whom God had raised up to serve at his side in laying the foundation for Princeton Seminary. He summarized the character of Miller in his address as follows:

> In all the private and domestic relations of his life he was exemplary. As a neighbor he was kind and courteous to all, and exactly just in his dealings. As a minister he was faithful and evangelical, and was accustomed to present the truths of the Gospel in a manner so distinct and methodical, that his discourses could not only be understood with ease, but readily remembered by the attentive hearer. As a member of the church judicatories, he was an able advocate for [truth], a warm friend to experimental and practical piety, and of course a friend of revivals. No member of the Church has done more to explain and defend her doctrines than our deceased brother. With his colleagues he was uniformly cordial; and I have never known a man more entirely free from vainglory, envy, and jealousy.

Miller's consistent piety won him the respect of his students and colleagues alike, especially the respect of Archibald Alexander, with whom he shared the honor of being a "founding father" of Old Princeton.

Conclusion

Samuel Miller left to the students of Old Princeton a legacy of piety, grace, and love for God and for the Presbyterian church. He was highly regarded as a warmhearted gentleman full of orthodox convictions, edifying anecdotes, and good humor. He provided an important model for students at Princeton of pastoral demeanor and propriety, as well as of humility and graciousness. In the words of James W. Alexander,

> It is impossible to remember Dr. Miller, without thinking of him as a Christian gentleman. Without an approach to stiffness, he was urbane and elegant in all the forms of the best society, with which indeed he

had always mingled. He was cheerful and cordial in his greetings, lively in conversation, and fond of social intercourse. It was to this that the founding and continuance of a clerical association was due, in which he and his ministerial friends met at one another's houses during many years. He was the charm of mixed companies; being rich in topics of discourse, and happy beyond most men in apposite anecdote and historical reminiscence. Indeed we have never known any one who could give such magical effect to little ebullitions of humour, which repeated by the lips of others seemed to lose all their aroma. But nothing so marked his character as his evangelical piety. It was the opinion of his colleague [Archibald Alexander], that in this Dr. Miller steadily grew, till the very last. He loved the cause of his Master, and was unwearied in his endeavours to promote it.

Though he was a gifted scholar, teacher, and preacher, it was Miller's Christian character that made him such an effective mentor of theological students and a valued faculty member at Princeton seminary.

5

OLD PRINCETON AND THE MINISTRY: SAMUEL MILLER'S *THE RULING ELDER* AND *LETTERS ON CLERICAL MANNERS AND HABITS*

I think him [Samuel Miller] one of the most conscientious and pious men I ever knew.

—James W. Alexander

The importance of the union of piety and learning in the holy ministry, is one of those radical principles of ecclesiastical wisdom, which the experience of ages has served more and more to confirm.

—Samuel Miller

Ought not the subject of church government generally . . . to be more attended to and better understood, than it commonly is among our brethren[?]

—Samuel Miller to Ashbel Green, May 13, 1805

Theological training at Old Princeton focused on biblical, theological, and historical studies. Apart from attention given to preaching and Presbyterian church polity, its focus was not oriented toward "job training" for pastoral ministry.

This does not mean that the theologians of Old Princeton were unconcerned about the state of church life and pastoral ministry in the churches. Samuel Miller's writings on pastoral ministry illustrate the Princeton theologians' concern for healthy church life and the high view they placed on local church ministry. This chapter will summarize key portions and themes from two of Miller's books on local church ministry: *The Warrant, Nature, and*

AN

ESSAY,

ON THE

WARRANT, NATURE AND DUTIES

OF THE OFFICE OF THE

RULING ELDER,

IN THE

PRESBYTERIAN CHURCH.

BY SAMUEL MILLER, D. D.

PROFESSOR OF ECCLESIASTICAL HISTORY AND CHURCH GOVERN-
MENT IN THE THEOLOGICAL SEMINARY
AT PRINCETON, N. J.

SECOND EDITION.

NEW-YORK:
JONATHAN LEAVITT.

BOSTON:
CROCKER & BREWSTER.

1832.

5.1 Title Page of Samuel Miller's *Ruling Elder.*

Duties of the Office of the Ruling Elder and *Letters on Clerical Manners and Habits.*

Samuel Miller and *The Ruling Elder*

Samuel Miller published *An Essay on the Warrant, Nature, and Duties of the Office of the Ruling Elder, in the Presbyterian Church* in 1831 after many years of both pastoral and academic experience. With Episcopal clericalism primarily in the background, Miller defended in this book his understanding of the American Presbyterian form of church government through biblical, historical, and practical arguments. His book immediately became a standard on the subject of eldership within American Presbyterianism. While Charles Hodge, James H. Thornwell, and others would later disagree with Miller and with each other about details within the Presbyterian system, Miller became, in the words of one Leroy Halsey in 1868, "perhaps more than any other man the recognized authority of the Presbyterian Church in all matters relating to her polity and order."

The Warrant for Ruling Elders in the Churches

Miller firmly believed that Presbyterianism was the binding form of church governance "laid down in Scripture," and yet he did not believe that "any particular form of government is in so rigorous a sense of *divine right*, as to be *essential* to the *existence* of the Church." Many, perhaps, might undervalue the necessity of promoting a particular form of government, but Miller asserted that "it is plain, from the word of God, as well as from uniform experience, that the government of the Church is a matter of great importance; that the *form* as well as the *administration* of that government is more vitally connected with the peace, purity, and edification of the Church, than many Christians appear to believe."

Miller's main goal in *The Ruling Elder* was to defend and elevate the office of "ruling elder" in the churches. Ruling elders, as Miller understood them, are one of the "three classes of officers" in the church, along with teaching elders (also called bishops, ministers, or pastors) and deacons. Ruling elders are those who are set apart from among their congregations to work diligently with "those who 'labor in the word and doctrine' [i.e., pastors or teaching elders] in inspecting, counseling, and watching over the 'flocks' respectively committed to their 'oversight in the Lord.' " Miller expressed his concern that the office of ruling elder had fallen to a low state in the churches, and he pressed his view that a godly and active "bench of ruling elders" was essential for healthy church governance and healthy church life. According to Miller, "the laws which Christ has appointed for the government and edification of his people, cannot possibly be executed, without such a class of officers [i.e., ruling elders] in fact, whatever name they may bear."

Miller believed that the office and authority of ruling elders is grounded first and foremost upon explicit scriptural teaching and practice. He found the plurality of elders taught in passages such as Acts 14:23; James 5:14; Titus 1:5; and Hebrews 13:16. He also found the office of ruling elder taught by the collective consideration of passages such as Romans 12:6–8; 1 Corinthians 12:28; and 1 Timothy 5:17, as well as by the archetypal pattern set for the churches in the Jewish synagogues. Miller believed that there is strong historical support for the office of ruling elders as well. Starting with "the Old Testament economy in general" and the Jewish synagogues, Miller traced the historical origin and precedent for ruling elders through to the churches of his day. Separate chapters and extended discussions are devoted to the history and practice of eldership in the Old Testament, the New Testament, the early church period, the "Dark Ages," the Reformation period, and the seventeenth and eighteenth centuries. Miller's historical survey finds that the essentials of elder plurality and the office of ruling elder were well established in the early church period; preserved by the Waldensians, Albigensians, and the Bohemian Brethren in the Middle Ages; and reestablished by the Reformers. In his chapter on the "Testimony of Eminent Divines Since the Time of the Reformers," Miller also quotes from a number of non-Presbyterian theologians such as John Owen, Richard Baxter, Thomas Goodwin, Thomas Hooker, John Cotton, Cotton Mather, and Increase Mather to show their overall agreement with his basic position, namely, that the office of ruling elder is essential to the governance of the church and is distinct from the office of pastor or teacher.

Miller also believed that the service of ruling elders in the churches is warranted by its practical necessity. By whatever name they may be called, Miller believed that ruling elders are absolutely critical in the churches to assist pastors in spiritually shepherding and ministering to the needs of individuals in the church. In his words:

Besides the preaching of the gospel, and the administration of the sacraments, there is very much to be done for promoting the order, purity and edification of the Church, by the maintenance of a scriptural Discipline. . . . the best interest of every ecclesiastical community requires, that there be a constant and faithful inspection of all the members and families of the Church; that the negligent be admonished; that wanderers be reclaimed; that scandals be removed; that irregularities corrected; that differences be reconciled; and every proper measure adopted to bind the whole body together by the ties of Christian purity and charity. . . . [It is] vitally important that there be added to the labors of the Pulpit, those of teaching "from house to house," visiting the sick, conversing with serious inquirers, catechizing children, learning as far as possible the character and state of every member, even the poorest and most obscure, of the flock, and endeavouring, by all scriptural means, to promote the knowledge, holiness, comfort and spiritual welfare of every individual.

Miller believed that, on their own, pastors are insufficient to spiritually shepherd and nurture the flock of God and that it is impractical to expect a pastor to perform "the whole work of inspection and government over a congregation of ordinary size." According to Miller:

Besides the arduous work of public instruction and exhortation, who shall attend to all the numberless and ever-recurring details of inspection, warning and visitation, which are so needful in every Christian community? Will any say, it is the duty of the Pastor of each church to perform them all? The very suggestion is absurd. . . . He cannot perform what is expected from him, and at the same time so watch over his whole flock as to fulfill every duty which the interest of the Church demands. He must "give himself to reading;" he must prepare for the services of the pulpit; he must discharge his various public labors; he must employ much time in private, in instructing and counseling those who apply to him for instruction and advice; and he must act his part in the concerns of the whole Church with which he is connected.

Miller quoted from John Owen's *True Nature of a Gospel Church*, which makes the same point. Owen says,

> It is a vain apprehension . . . to suppose that one or two teaching officers in a Church, who are obliged to give themselves unto the word and prayer, to labor in the word and doctrine, to preach in and out of season—should be able to take care of, and attend with diligence unto, all those things that do evidently belong unto the rule of the Church.

Pastors need faithful elders to assist them in shepherding the church by serving in a more private and individualized way. Their work, then, should consist primarily in visitation, in spiritually examining each individual, and in giving individualized admonition, encouragement, warning, and instruction. Ruling elders should also exercise leadership, together with the pastor, in examining candidates for membership, enacting church discipline, and in removing members. They are to assist the pastor in "counsel and in government" and in "inspecting and ruling the flock of Christ."

Miller believed it was undesirable for churches to entrust all spiritual leadership and spiritual authority to one individual. Pastors should not possess sole spiritual authority and oversight of the flock, for this had proven historically to lead to the abuse of the people of God. "Ministers," according to Miller, "are subject to the same frailties and imperfections with other men," including the sinful tendency toward "the love of preeminence and of power." Entrusting all spiritual authority to one man alone, Miller believed, had historically led to "Prelacy" and then to "Popery" which "enslaved the Church of Christ." It was unwise to make one man a "despot" over a whole church, and because of man's sinful tendencies, Miller believed that God designed each local church to have a plurality of elders:

> We have no example in Scripture of a Church being committed to the government of a single individual. Such a thing was unknown in the Jewish Synagogue. It was unknown in the apostolic age. And it con-

tinued to be unknown, until ecclesiastical pride and ambition introduced it, and with it a host of mischiefs to the body of Christ. In all
the primate churches we find a plurality of "Elders."

The protection of the church from the abuse of spiritual "despotism"
was yet another reason why Miller believed that the robust presence
of ruling elders was warranted.

The Role of Ruling Elders

Miller was not opposed to setting pastors apart from ruling elders
and giving them a distinct position of spiritual leadership in the
churches. While he believed that spiritual leadership should be
exercised by a plurality of elders, he also believed it was necessary
to distinguish between the role of a teaching elder (i.e., pastor) and
that of the ruling elder. He felt that a clear distinction in roles was
important for a number of reasons. First, pastors require special
education and training for the work of preaching and public ministry
that most ruling elders are not able to acquire. Also, the special
public duties of pastors require them to be protected from all the
harried demands of shepherding and caring for each individual
church member. According to Miller, how else would they be able
to "give themselves to reading" unless assisted in ministry by elders
from the congregation? Furthermore, he believed that most churches
in his day would not be able to financially support more than one
pastor. If no distinction is to be made among the elders, Miller
argued, all would need to be paid equally. Finally, Miller believed
that if all elders in the church were viewed as equally authorized to
preach and teach publically, the net effect would be to "degrade,
and ultimately to prostrate the [pastoral] ministry." If all elders in
the church are viewed as equally equipped and authorized to preach,
the standards for the preaching ministry would need to be lowered
to accommodate the ruling elders, most of whom would be without
formal training. For these reasons, Miller believed it was necessary
to make a clear distinction between pastors (i.e., teaching elders)
and ruling elders, with teaching elders held to a much higher standard for preparation and training and given a greater responsibility
for the public ministries of the church.

While pastors alone are entrusted with preaching, teaching, and administering the sacraments, ruling elders are to join with the pastor in governing and "ruling" over the church, seeing to its spiritual peace, order, and prosperity. As "Justices of the Peace" are given authority to keep peace and order in "the civil community," in a similar fashion pastors and the elders are given authority from God to keep peace and order in the churches. Unlike political authorities, however, the only power at their disposal is the "moral power" of their office. Just as teaching elders serve in the authority of Christ, so too do ruling elders, and the church is required by God to recognize their authority in matters of spiritual discipline and oversight, in accordance with Hebrews 13:17.

Given their position of spiritual authority and oversight, ruling elders are to work with the teaching elders in leading and regulating the life of the church. According to Miller, "the particular department assigned to the Ruling Elder is to co-operate with the Pastor in spiritual inspection and government." Some of this work will be done informally with individual members of the church, and other aspects of this work will be done in a formal capacity, when official church judgments and discipline need to be carried out. Miller's ideal was to see in every church

> a body of grave, pious and prudent men, associated with the Pastor; chosen out of the body of the Church members, carrying with them, in some measure, the feelings and views of their constituents, capable of counseling the Pastor in all delicate and doubtful cases, counteracting any undue influence, or course of measures into which his partiality, prejudice, or want of information might betray him, exonerating him at once from the odium, and the temptation of having all the power of the Church in his own hands; conducting the difficult cases which often arise in the exercise of discipline with the intelligence, calmness, and wisdom which cannot be expected to prevail in a promiscuous body of communicants.

Apart from duties in their "collective capacity," ruling elders are to engage in a wide variety of tasks with a view to "constantly edifying the body of Christ." They are to "have an eye of inspection and care over all the members of the congregation" and to "cultivate a universal and intimate acquaintance . . . with every family of the flock." It is also their duty to instruct those under conviction regarding their eternal estate and to "admonish, in private, those who appear to be growing careless." Further, it is their duty

> to visit and pray with the sick, . . . to assist the Pastor in maintaining meetings for social prayer, . . . to instruct the ignorant; to confirm the wavering; to caution the unwary; to reclaim the wandering; to encourage the timid; to excite and animate all classes to a faithful and exemplary discharge of duty. It is incumbent upon them to consult frequently and freely with their Pastor, on the interests of the flock committed to their charge; to aid him in forming and executing plans for the welfare of the Church; to give him from time to time, such information as he may need, to enable him to perform aright his various and momentous duties; to impart to him, with affectionate respect, their advice; to support him with their influence; to defend his reputation; to enforce his just admonitions; and in a word, by every means in their power, to promote the comfort, and extend the usefulness of his labors.

With these spiritual responsibilities given to ruling elders, Miller did not believe it was proper to refer to them as "lay elders," since this would put too great a distinction between them and the pastor: "so far as the distinction between Clergy and Laity is proper at all, it ought not to be made the point of distinction between these two classes of Elders."

The Qualifications, Election, and Ordination of Ruling Elders

Miller's *The Ruling Elder* gives a number of details regarding the selection and commissioning of ruling elders in the churches. Miller asserted that churches must be careful in the selection of elders and that elders must clearly meet certain qualifications. The foundational criteria for choosing ruling elders, Miller believed, is found in the Pastoral Epistles. Miller asserted that the elder qualifications in 1 Timothy and Titus are equally applicable to teaching elders and ruling elders. With these passages in view, Miller elaborated on a number of qualities that ruling elders should have. First and foremost, a ruling elder ought to be a man of "unfeigned and approved piety."

He must possess a "cordial and decisive attachment to the service of the Church," which expresses itself in an "ardent zeal and a spirit of importunate prayer." Next, a ruling elder must possess "good sense and sound judgment," as well as "eminent prudence," which Miller defines as nothing other than "practical Christian wisdom." A ruling elder must also be "sound in the faith and well informed in relation to gospel truth." Elaborating on this, Miller says,

> although all Elders are not expected to be profound theologians, any more than all ministers; yet that the former, as well as the latter, should have a general and accurate acquaintance with the gospel system, and be ready to defend its leading doctrines, by a ready, pertinent, and conclusive reference to scriptural testimony, and thus be able to "separate between the precious and the vile," in theory as well as in practice, is surely as little as can possibly be demanded of those who are placed as leaders and guides in the house of God.

Finally, a ruling elder must be "a man of public spirit and enlarged views" and possess "a good report of them that are without." Miller did not believe that elders in the church necessarily need to be "aged persons," but that "young men, if otherwise well qualified, may with propriety be appointed Elders to assist in ruling the Church of God."

Miller also believed, in line with the declaration of the 1829 Presbyterian General Assembly, that ruling elders are "the representatives of the people, by whom they are chosen." In his mind, each pastor should have

> associated with him, a body of pious, wise, and disinterested counselors, taken from among the people; acquainted with their views; participating in their feelings; able to give sound advice as to the wisdom and practicability of plans which require general co-operation for carrying them into effect; and able also, after having aided in the formation of such plans, to return to their constituents, and so to advocate and recommend them, as to secure general concurrence in their favor.

Ruling elders are elected by the congregation to be their representative overseers and disciplinarians, so that "the discipline lawfully exercised by them [i.e., the elders] is the discipline exercised through them by their constituents, in whose name, and by whose authority [under Christ] they act in all that they do." Miller believed strongly in the principle of representation, and believed that it was a kind of "universal principle" in governance for both the civil society and the church. Since the members of a local church have a voice in the leadership and oversight of the church through the ruling elders, their representatives, the congregation should elect the ruling elders whom they deem fit to serve in this way. Miller believed that candidates for eldership may be either nominated by the existing elders or in some cases chosen by them directly, and yet he believed that it seemed "more in harmony with the general spirit of Presbyterian Church government, and certainly with the prevailing character of our institutions, to refer the choice, where it can conveniently be done, after due consultation and care, to the suffrages of the members of the Church."

Miller believed that a church's ruling elders should also be ordained and formally set apart for their role after being chosen by the church. While ordination does not impart "any direct influence, either physical or moral, to him who receives it," it is the formal and official act "by which a man is pronounced, declared and manifested, to be actually put in possession of the office to which he has been chosen." Miller pointed to the scriptural practice of setting something or someone apart through the "laying on of hands," and he believed that both ruling elders and teaching elders should be set apart in this same way. Miller admitted that he had "long deplored" the practice of the Presbyterian churches in this matter, for they would commonly set apart teaching elders with "the laying on of hands" but would omit this expression for the ordination of ruling elders. While Miller did not consider "the laying on of hands" to be an absolute necessity for the act of ordination, he did argue at length for the practice and believed that much good could come of restoring it. The chief benefit of doing so would be to give "warranted and appropriate honor to a class of officers too long deprived of their due estimation and authority."

Miller's *The Ruling Elder* in Perspective

Samuel Miller wrote *The Ruling Elder* to elevate the office of ruling elder in the Presbyterian churches. He believed that ruling elders are essential for the governance and health of every local church and are instituted by God to assist the pastor(s) in giving spiritual oversight of a local church. He also held that they were given as safeguards for the churches against both "clerical ambition" and the "tyranny" of "an excited, infuriated popular assembly."

Not all segments within American Presbyterianism accepted the positions and language contained in *The Ruling Elder*. With James Henley Thornwell and Charles Hodge each making their own modifications upon the language of governance that Miller set forth, the polity of Northern and Southern Presbyterian churches would develop in slightly different directions. Northern Presbyterianism was comfortable following Miller in designating teaching elders and ruling elders as two different "classes of officers," while Southern Presbyterianism preferred to unite the two into the same "class" and distinguished teaching elders from ruling elders only by gifts, calling, training, and function. Thornwell himself believed that designating two classes of elders would lead to a form of clericalism that would mimic Episcopalianism and be unhealthy for the church. Charles Hodge's *What Is Presbyterianism?* largely followed Miller's position on the distinction between teaching and ruling elders, though Hodge insisted that ruling elders should be understood as "laymen" and teaching elders alone as "clergy." Hodge believed that by not making this distinction, the unique office and function of "ministers" (i.e., pastors) would be subverted. This point aside, Hodge would write: "We do not differ from Dr. Miller as to the nature of the office of ruling elder. . . . As to the importance, nature, and divine institution of the office, we are faithful to his instructions." Even where variation existed among the Princeton theologians, the main outlines of Miller's ruling eldership were largely followed and upheld among them.

Samuel Miller and *Letters on Clerical Manners and Habits*

Miller wrote *The Ruling Elder* to elevate the office of ruling elder, and he wrote his *Letters on Clerical Manners and Habits* in 1827 to elevate the office of pastor. Miller's son and biographer stated that this treatise was perhaps the most popular and widely circulated production from his pen, if we except his tracts on Presbyterianism and Baptism. It had no doubt occupied his thoughts, more or less definitely, for a number of years; and the subject which it unfolded had, evidently, been with him a life-long and favorite study. His observation of successive classes of students in the Seminary had, certainly, deepened all his impression of the importance of much more attention to this subject, on the

LETTERS

ON

Clerical Manners and Habits:

ADDRESSED TO

A STUDENT

IN THE

THEOLOGICAL SEMINARY,

AT PRINCETON, N. J.

BY SAMUEL MILLER, D.D.

Professor of Ecclesiastical History and Church Government, in the said Seminary.

SECOND EDITION.

NEW YORK:

PUBLISHED BY G. & C. CARVILL.

1827.

5.2 Title Page of Miller's *Letters on Clerical Manners.*

part especially of ministers of the Gospel, than they usually gave, or considered needful.

Miller himself paid close attention to his own personal bearing and demeanor as a minister of the gospel, and by careful study had attained polished manners and gentlemanly dignity to commend his own ministry to others. Feeling that ministerial deportment is important, Miller addressed this volume of letters to an unnamed seminary student training for the ministry. While these letters are at times entertaining, they also contain a wealth of material for young theological students and pastors to consider for the development of good ministerial "manners" and "habits."

Clerical Manners and Demeanor

Miller believed that "the manners of a clergyman" ought "perceptibly to differ" from others' in society, even those of "a well-bred man of a secular profession." Clergymen, according to Miller, ought to "bear a stamp, in a variety of particulars, characteristic of the hallowed spirit and sacred office with which they are connected." Clerical manners are especially important for ministers of the gospel for a wide variety of reasons. Some ministers might unwittingly do great detriment to their ministries and to the cause of Christ through "a few ridiculous foibles or inadvertent habits." On the other hand, good manners can provide a hearing and a platform for ministry to certain individuals with whom social graces are important. In his words:

> The idea that the manners of any one ought to be left to take care of themselves is a miserable delusion. As long as we are bound, every hour, to "consider our ways," and, "whether we eat or drink, or whatever we do, to do all to the glory of God," it will be incumbent upon persons, of all ages and stations, to endeavor in all things, even the minutest, to "order their conversation aright." But for a minister of the gospel, who stands continually as a "watchman," and a "defender," on "the walls of Zion;" and who is acting every hour, not only for himself, but also for the church of God;—for him to doubt whether habitual care as to every word, and look, and action, is incumbent on him, is indeed strangely to misapprehend his obligations.

All in all, it was Miller's belief that clerical manners universally have "more influence [upon others] . . . than is commonly imagined."

Miller believed that many candidates for ministry naturally neglect the study of clerical manners in the course of their ministerial preparation and look down upon all exhortations on clerical manners out of prejudice and pride. According to Miller, "I am aware that many worthy men entertain strong prejudices against all formal precepts or exhortations on the subject of manners and are ready to consider them as worse than useless." These prejudices, Miller stated, often arise from ignorance or a proud "affectation of singularity, which prompts them to delight in those manners which are strange and peculiar, and to look with a sort of contempt on all rules of behavior." More people, however, revolt from the discussion of clerical manners, thinking that such a discussion will encourage one in sanctimonious artificiality, affectation, and hypocrisy. Nothing could be further from Miller's intent:

> It is by no means my purpose to recommend those starched, artificial, formal manners, which display constant effort and constraint; or those ostentatious, splendid, and gracefully refined manners, which are formed upon mere worldly principles; which qualify their possessor to make a distinguished figure in a ball-room, or at the levee [public court assembly] of a great man, and which manifest that he has studied Chesterfield more than his Bible. . . . my object is to recommend those manners which become the Christian gentleman; which naturally flow from the meekness, gentleness, purity, and benevolence of our holy religion; and which both the precepts and examples of the Bible equally recommend.

While good manners are no substitute for genuine godliness and piety, they will help a minister "appear, what [he] ought to be, —a pious, benevolent, amiable man; respectfully attentive to the welfare and comfort of all around you; and seeking habitually and supremely, to promote the best interest of mankind." Such manners can only be attained as the outgrowth of genuine love, humility, and purity of heart. Miller viewed them as "the drawing out of [the Christian] principle [in the heart] into all the practical duties of life," a process which "requires assiduous and laborious culture . . . unceasing self-denial, prayer, and watchfulness."

Miller believed that appropriate manners and demeanor for a minister of the gospel could be summed up under six characteristics. First, pastoral demeanor should be marked with an air of dignity. Miller explains that by dignity he means "that happy mixture of gravity and elevation in human deportment, which evinces a mind habitually thoughtful, serious, and set on high things." It is "an air and manner" opposed to "levity," "jesting," "groveling," and "to every species of lightness or volatility." To maintain one's dignity as a minister, one must avoid or withdraw from "light, frivolous company or where frivolous engagements are going on." One must also avoid "angry contention," pettiness, and any other thing which will bring disrepute upon one's self and one's ministry. Miller quoted William Jay on this point as saying: "There is something defective, especially in a minister, unless his character produces an atmosphere around him, which is felt as soon as entered. It is not enough for him to have courage to reprove certain things; he should have dignity enough to prevent them."

Second, a minister of the gospel should exhibit gentleness, which Miller describes as "that habitual mildness of disposition and softness of manner, which carefully guard against everything, in speech or behavior, adapted unnecessarily to offend or to give uneasiness." Miller says that this kind of gentleness is "opposed to every kind of harshness or undue severity, and forms a deportment calculated to conciliate and attract all to whom it is manifested." Such gentleness exists alongside of courage and conviction and is not to be confused with "that tame, passive spirit, which knows not how to deny the most unreasonable request, or to resist the most unjust encroachment." In fact, gentleness in a minister should be mixed with strength and decisiveness. In his words:

> You will never accomplish much, either in study or in action, without a large share of what may be called decision of character. By this quality, I mean that bold, steady, persevering firmness of purpose and ardour of pursuit, which stand opposed to timidity, indolence and irresolution:—that unwavering confidence in the rectitude and importance of his pursuit, which prompts a man to press forward in it, with

a constancy which nothing can shake; with a courage, which nothing can intimidate; and with a resolution which nothing can divert. This decision of character appeared pre-eminently, in Luther, in Calvin, in Wesley, in Whitefield, in Howard, and in many other men, whose history and services will readily occur to your recollection.

Third, a minister should cultivate condescension toward the lowly, by which he treats "the poor, the deserted, the friendless, [and] the afflicted" with "benevolent respect" and "a readiness to serve them to the utmost of his power." Fourth, a minister should exhibit "affability," or what we may call approachability. An affable minister will have "the happy talent of conversing pleasantly and courteously, and of placing everyone in conversation with him perfectly at his ease." According to Miller, "the opposites of this quality are coldness, haughtiness, habits of taciturnity, [and] . . . everything in manner that is adapted to repel, or to prevent freedom and comfort of approach." Fifth, a minister should possess the kind of "reserve" that stands "opposed to excessive and unseasonable communications." Miller wisely notes that "Affability is good, is important; but incessant and indiscriminate talkativeness will soon reduce in public esteem, and entangle in real difficulties, the official man who allows himself to indulge it." Finally, a minister should possess "uniformity" in his character, whereby he treats individuals in a consistent manner from day to day and also treats all in a relatively consistent manner.

Specific Manners and Habits

After outlining his general points on clerical manners in his first two letters, Miller addressed particular manners, habits, and situations in the following twelve letters. In his discussion of specific points, Miller's advice is at times dated and amusingly situated in the peculiarities of nineteenth-century American culture. Miller himself recognized that his advice on appropriate clerical manners is "founded, in general, on Christian principle," but is also in part, "the result of conventional agreement among well-bred people [of the early nineteenth century!]." As cultural conventions have changed quite significantly since this book was written, so too have expectations of appropriateness in manners shifted over time. Readers should bear this in mind when considering the specific advice that Miller gives.

Miller first addressed a wide variety of "offensive personal habits" which a minister of the gospel should avoid in order not to bring disrepute upon his ministry. Such habits include "boisterous laughter," slouching, intemperate use of alcohol, and bad hygiene. Numerous other habits are mentioned, some of which, as Miller realized, "may excite a smile," including the "cutting or cleaning [of] their nails before company," "the practice of picking the teeth while seated at table," and "the habit of tilting your chair back, while you are sitting upon it, so as to rest only on its two hinder legs." All "slovenly habits of whatsoever kind" are to be avoided, and Miller held up the model of the "characteristically neat" George Whitefield, who was "accustomed to say, that 'a minister ought to be without *spot.*'" Miller also quotes Adam Clarke, who considered "a negligence of cleanliness in a minister of the gospel, as not only disgusting, but as very closely allied to moral delinquency."

Miller next addresses the subject of "conversation," an area which is especially important for ministers who must spend a "large portion" of their time in ministry conversing with others. He gives forty-five different points of instruction to encourage good conversation skills, with the goal that ministers' conversation might further their ministry and be edifying to others. Miller states that a minister should neither be too talkative nor too silent in the company of others. He should neither be a gossip or a "newsmonger." He should cultivate the habit "of paying close attention to the individual with whom you are conversing." He should also develop habits of using good eye contact, of avoiding unnecessary conflict, and of avoiding "levity," "buffoonery," "the recital of low, vulgar anecdotes," and any other thing that displays a lack of seriousness and self-respect.

After his letter on conversation in general, Miller wrote another that deals specifically with "religious conversation." Under this topic Miller has another twenty-six points of counsel for how ministers might "introduce the great subject of religion in an easy, seasonable, and acceptable manner in the daily intercourse of society." Miller believed that many err in this regard in supposing that "religious conversation must be introduced on all occasions, and in all companies, indiscriminately, whether the time, the character of the persons present, and the circumstances, favor it or not." He also believed that some err in thinking that "the same methods of introducing and maintaining religious conversations are equally adapted to all persons, and all occasions." Though acknowledging that the ability to converse in a natural and easy manner is something of "a natural talent," Miller believed that all ministers of the gospel should strive to grow in this area and to introduce "religious conversation" whenever a good opportunity arises. He further believed that ministers should also initiate "religious conversation" in a regular practice of "visiting" the homes of his church members, both for formal "pastoral visits" and for social calls. Twenty-five further additional points are addressed to this subject, including such directives as: "Be careful to extend [visits] to the poor as well as to the rich," "visit the sick," and "guard against a formal, task-like mode of performing [pastoral visits]."

In the following letters, Miller addressed the topics of "habits in the seminary," "habits in the study," and "habits in the lecture hall." Miller believed that seminary students could profit greatly from the special opportunity of being gathered together with other theological students if only they would diligently pursue the potential benefits of their setting. Great gain in seminary is to be had by exerting due effort to "cultivate special friendship with such fellow-students" that are likely to be of spiritual and personal encouragement. "A little circle of three, four, or five of these intimate friends" can prove invaluable for the seminary experience. Miller warned students not to be "too much in society with [one's] fellow students," and yet he also encouraged the students "to be much in the habit of conversing with [one's] fellow students respecting [their] studies." As the last of twenty points of counsel for seminary students, Miller encouraged seminarians to "at the close of each day, and especially every week, call yourself to a solemn account for the manner in which you have spent that day or week." In addressing "habits in the study," Miller encouraged seminarians and ministers to grasp "the infinite importance of theological science" and to "strive to acquire the habit of close and fixed attention in study." Study should be engaged "with a devout spirit" which seeks "the aid of the Holy Spirit in study." After giving "much labor" to study, the student of God's Word should put his knowledge on "all important subjects . . . to the test of writing" to see how clear and accurate his knowledge actually is. After giving twenty-nine points of counsel on "habits in the study," Miller moves on to "habits of the lecture room" and gives seventeen further points of public etiquette and counsel, with seminary students again in mind.

Miller's next set of letters give detailed counsel to pastors regarding "habits in the pulpit and in the house of God" and "conduct in church judicatories." The twenty-four points of counsel under the first of these headings can be considered as practical accompaniment to a more regular course of instruction on homiletics. According to Miller, a minister's preaching is "the most important part of his public work" and the preacher's "whole deportment ought to correspond with the gravity and solemnity of his message." Miller goes on to state, "on the one hand, everything like pomp, ostentation, or mock dignity should be avoided as hateful; on the other, all coarseness, levity, or vulgarity—everything that borders on the ludicrous, or the want of real dignity, ought to be shunned with no less care." Miller exhorts preachers to pay careful attention to their demeanor and conduct both before and after preaching. He also encourages ministers to be careful not to weary their listeners by the length of their sermons:

> Guard against making your public services too long. The opposite to this advice is a fault which often occurs, and which is always unfriendly to edification. Whenever weariness begins, edification terminates. It was well said by Whitefield, that a sermon of more than an hour long, though preached by an angel, would appear tedious, unless the hearers were angels too.

Most importantly, Miller urges preachers to:

> Go from your knees to the pulpit. The more thoroughly your mind is steeped, if I may be allowed the expression, in the spirit of prayer, and of communion with God, when you ascend the sacred desk, the more easy and delightful will it be to preach; the more rich and spiritual will your preaching be; the more fervent and natural your eloquence; and the greater the probability that what you say will be made a blessing.

Miller gives preachers this rule as the one which "unspeakably outweighs all the rest in importance" regarding pulpit eloquence: "go to the sanctuary with a heart full of your subject; warmed with love to your Master, and to immortal souls; remembering too, that the eye of the Master is upon you; and that of the sermon which you are about to deliver, you must soon give an account before his judgment-seat." Miller likewise exhorts ministers to be conscientious, dignified, humble, and spiritually minded in "church judicatories," or deliberative assemblies, and he gives a further twenty-six points of practical counsel regarding such assemblies.

Miller continues by addressing the issue of "female society" and marriage, stating that a pastor's treatment of women requires great "wisdom, fidelity, prudence, and Christian delicacy." A minister of the gospel should strive to "conciliate the esteem and to acquire and maintain the unlimited confidence of his female parishioners." If he cannot do this, he will neither be "very acceptable or very useful" in his ministry. Using Whitefield and Wesley as examples, Miller asserted that "there are some clergymen who ought never to marry," and yet "in general, every settled minister should consider it as his duty as well as his privilege, to be a married man." Regarding the choice of a wife, Miller counsels ministers, among other things, to "be not in too much haste" and to seek "constant divine direction" in the choice of a spouse. Once married, a minister must take care "to set an edifying example of conjugal excellence." Says Miller: "As a clergyman ought to be the most pious man in his parish; to go before all his people in the exemplification of every Christian grace and virtue; so he ought to make a point of being the best husband in his parish, of endeavoring to excel all others in affection, kindness, attention, and every conjugal and domestic virtue." A married minister must also give "serious attention" to the conduct of his wife and daughters, so that they might not bring reproach upon his ministry through flamboyance, immodesty, and indiscretion. Regarding other women in the church and community, a minister must "exercise great delicacy in conversing with females" and treat all forms of contact and interaction with them "in the most scrupulous" manner.

Miller concluded his book of letters with counsel and directives regarding a minister's "dress," "style of living," "pecuniary concerns," and a wide variety of miscellaneous matters, including brief words about punctuality, recreation, and popularity. As Paul instructed the church to do all things "decently and in order," it was Miller's firm belief that every aspect of a minister's life ought to be ordered in such a way that the gospel of Christ and the truth of God are adorned and commended to the sentiments and sensibilities of men, as well as to their minds and hearts.

Clerical Manners in Context

Miller's concern to elevate the pastoral office and position can be understood as a response to the rising tide in his day of democratic egalitarianism in both the church and society. Miller's son and biographer stated on the subject of clerical manners,

> There can be no doubt, that democratic ideas, democratic institutions and democratic usages have tended to lower, in this country, the standard of personal refinement and good manners, and to discourage the cultivation of elegant and polite habits. A proper reaction against the unnatural restraints, the burdensome etiquette, the heartless formalities, the puerile conceits and niceties, the hollow pretences and fictions, of courts and aristocratic saloons, has gone, however, to the extreme of depreciating the true gentleness, and that Christian deference to the feelings of others, of which fashionable politeness has been rightly characterized as only an imitation, or imperfect copy. Refined manners are the natural outgrowth of morals and religion, and to exhibit and cultivate them in their proper connexion and relation is the best means of eradicating the spurious and unwholesome offsets of worldliness and unbelief.

The theologians of Old Princeton firmly believed that the reputation and spread of the gospel required its ministers to occupy positions of respect both in the church and outside of it, and the cultivation of "clerical manners and habits" was one important way in which ministers were to set themselves apart and uphold the dignity of the truth of Christ in the world.

Conclusion

Samuel Miller's many writings highlight the Princeton theologians' concern with church governance and pastoral ministry in the churches. His *The Ruling Elder* sought to defend and elevate the office of elder in the churches, while his *Letters on Clerical Manners and Habits* called pastors to elevate their own office through dignified manners and appropriate pastoral demeanor. Ministry, for the professors of Old Princeton, was more than a matter of performing the varied pastoral tasks of exegesis and preaching. They understood that the calling to shepherd souls and to handle the truth of God in public is a calling that involves the entire conduct, character, and personality of an individual and requires the greatest sensitivity and practical wisdom in all interpersonal affairs. Miller's commitment to order, decency, and propriety in the churches was shared by his colleagues at the seminary, and it left its mark on those who were trained for ministry at Old Princeton.

6

CHARLES HODGE

Charles Hodge was, in my opinion, the most attractive all-around Princeton theologian, especially for the ways in which he brought together thoughtful assertion of classical Christian orthodoxy, especially from Reformed confessions, and heart-felt promotion of pious trust in God.

—Mark Noll

The more we use Hodge, the more we value him. This applies to all his commentaries. . . . With no writer do we more fully agree.

—Charles Spurgeon

When Archibald Alexander was inaugurated as the first professor of Princeton Seminary in the summer of 1812, present in the church was "a boy of fourteen, lying at length on the rail of the gallery listening to the doctor's inaugural address and watching the ceremony of investiture." The boy's father had died when he was yet an infant, leaving his mother to care for him and his two-year-old brother. While this boy had been raised in the Christian faith by his mother and catechized by his pastor, Ashbel Green, few would have imagined that he would someday overshadow both Alexander and Miller and be the foremost systematic theologian of the seminary.

Charles Hodge would become, in fact, one of the foremost theologians in America. Through his theological publications he would vigorously defend the doctrines of the Presbyterian and Reformed tradition against a host of rising alternatives. Through his seminary professorship he would leave his mark upon thousands of clergymen who would branch out to serve far beyond his own denomination. As a devoted churchman, he would carefully engage and comment on the Presbyterian church's internal disputes and conflicts. As the founding editor of the famous *Princeton Review*, he would help shape the discussion of not only theological and ecclesiastical issues, but also social and political issues as well. His devotion to piety and learning would carry forth the dual emphasis that defined Old Princeton, and his attractive Christian character and careful work as a scholar would win him the respect of even those with whom he disagreed.

FIG. 6.1

Timeline of Charles Hodge's Life

December 27, 1797	Born in Philadelphia, Pennsylvania.
1812	Began studies at the College of New Jersey in Princeton.
1816	Began studies at Princeton Theological Seminary.
1819	Licensed to preach by the Philadelphia Presbytery.
1819–20	Missionary in Pennsylvania and New Jersey.
1820	Made instructor of biblical languages at Princeton Theological Seminary.
1821	Ordained by the New Brunswick Presbytery.
1822	Made professor of Oriental and biblical literature.
1825	Started the *Biblical Repertory* (later named *Biblical Repertory and Princeton Review*, etc.)
1826–28	Study abroad in Europe.
1834	Awarded the doctor of divinity degree by Rutgers University.
1835	Published *Commentary on the Epistle to the Romans*.
1840	Made professor of exegetical and didactic theology.

1854	Made professor of exegetical, didactic, and polemic theology.
1861–65	United States Civil War.
1864	Awarded the LL.D. degree by Washington College.
1871–73	Published his *Systematic Theology*.
1872	Celebrated his Golden Jubilee as a professor.
June 19, 1878	Died in Princeton, New Jersey.

The Making of a Professor

Charles Hodge was born into a caring Christian family in Phila-delphia and grew up without a father. Hodge's father, Hugh Hodge, who had died in 1798 when Hodge was only six months old, was a physician who had descended from Scotch-Irish immigrants. His mother, Mary, was from Boston and had descended from French Huguenots. Though widowed with two small children, Hodge's mother raised Charles and his older brother with great care and patiently instructed them in the things of God. According to Hodge, "To us she devoted her life. For us she prayed, labored and suffered. . . . She took us regularly to church, and carefully drilled us in the Westminster Catechism." Charles was especially close to his brother Hugh, of whom he would say, "My brother was far more than a brother to me. Although only eighteen months my senior, he assumed from the first the office of guard-ian. He always went first in the dark. I never slept out of his arms until I was eleven or twelve years old." Hugh Hodge would become a physician, just like his father and namesake, and he and Charles would enjoy a close relationship until Hugh's death in 1873. The family in Philadelphia also enjoyed the close care of their pastor, Ashbel Green. Green married Hodge's parents, baptized him and his brother, delivered the eulogy at the grave of his father, and listened to him recite the catechism.

Hodge's mother sacrificed greatly so that he and his brother might have the best education possible. Most of her income as a widow had come from the Hodge family properties along the wharf of Boston. When the war of 1812 brought about a shipping embargo, the family income suddenly dried up. Hodge would later recall that during this time

> our mother's income was almost entirely cut off. This was the time
> we were preparing for college. Instead of putting her children off her
> hands, and leaving them to provide for themselves, by sacrificing all
> she had, by the most self-denying economy, and by keeping boarders,
> she succeeded in securing for them the benefits of a collegiate and
> professional education, at her expense and without loss of time.

Hodge's mother moved the family to Princeton in 1812 so that some of the costs of an education there would be lessened. Hodge and his brother entered the College of New Jersey in the fall of 1812, just a few weeks after Ashbel Green came to be its president. Green's ministry to Hodge which began in Philadelphia now continued, only this time as a teacher. Green taught Hodge's courses in Bible, *belles-lettres* (composition), moral philosophy, and logic. Philip Lindsley taught Hodge in Greek and was very kind and patient with him, for Hodge had only taken up Greek a few months before entering the college. Another person to show kindness to Hodge was Archibald Alexander, who had noticed him within the first few weeks of his studies at Princeton. After witnessing Hodge struggle with his Greek exercises, Alexander developed an interest in him, and in the words of Hodge: "He never failed to notice me when I crossed his path [from then on]." Alexander also began to take Hodge on his preaching trips into the countryside.

While Ashbel Green taught a number of the college courses, "the religious culture of the students" was his main concern. He preached regularly in the college chapel on Sunday mornings, lectured every Thursday evening, and made the study of the Bible a regular part of the college curriculum. He was joined in these efforts by Archibald Alexander and Samuel Miller, who began preaching and lecturing regularly to the college students as well. As these efforts progressed, a revival broke out in the winter of 1814–15, touching the lives of many of the students, Hodge being one of the first. In Hodge's estimation, around thirty of the one hundred students had come to be "really changed" by the gracious work of God. As a result of this revival, Hodge made a public profession of his faith and joined the Presbyterian church in Princeton in the early months of 1815.

After Hodge graduated from the college in September of that same year, he and his mother returned to Philadelphia so that he might recover from an exhausting final phase of his studies. While convalescing under the care of his mother and physician brother, and while occupying himself with a course of "general reading," Hodge confirmed his desire to return to Princeton to study at the seminary and to prepare for the ministry. Before returning to Princeton to begin his studies in the fall of 1816, Hodge accompanied Archibald Alexander on an extended preaching tour through Virginia. This trip only deepened his respect and affection for his mentor. As a student at the seminary, Hodge would pursue his study under Alexander and Miller for the next three years.

Toward the end of his seminary course, Alexander suddenly posed the question to Hodge, "How would you like to be a professor in the Seminary?" It was something that Hodge had not before considered, but he was immediately open to the idea. He followed Alexander's advice and returned to Philadelphia after his graduation in the fall of 1819 to begin a serious study of Hebrew, with the possibility of teaching it at the seminary. In the midst of this study, Hodge was also licensed to preach by the Presbytery of Philadelphia, and he took up regular Sunday preaching at varied places as a "missionary" for the next several years. After the General Assembly granted the seminary professors permission to hire "an assistant teacher of the original languages of Scripture," they offered Hodge a one-year appointment, which he began in the fall of 1820. Hodge continued teaching Greek and Hebrew on a temporary basis until he was hired as a professor in the fall of 1822.

When Hodge was inaugurated as the professor of Oriental [i.e., Middle Eastern] and biblical literature in 1822, the dual Old Princeton emphasis on learning and piety had already impacted Hodge's approach to the study of Scripture. For his inaugural address, Hodge chose "the importance of piety in the interpretation of Scripture" as his subject. In this address, he asserted that "the moral qualifications of an interpreter of Scripture [are all subsumed] in piety; which embraces humility, candor, and those views and feelings which can only result from the inward operation of the Holy Spirit." Far from adopting a barren intellectualism or a rationalistic approach to the interpretation of Scripture, Hodge was already stressing the importance of inward piety for the interpreter, a point he would later emphasize in his *Systematic Theology*:

> The Scriptures are to be interpreted under the guidance of the Holy Spirit, which guidance is to be humbly and earnestly sought. The ground of this rule is twofold: First, the Spirit is promised as a guide and teacher. He was to come to lead the people of God into the knowledge of the truth. And secondly, the Scriptures teach that "the natural man receiveth not the things of the Spirit of God: for they are foolishness unto him; neither can he know them, because they are spiritually discerned" (1 Cor. 2:14). The unrenewed mind is naturally blind to spiritual truth. His heart is in opposition to the things of God. Congeniality of mind is necessary to the proper apprehension of divine things. As only those who have a moral nature can discern moral truth, so those who are spiritually minded can truly receive the things of the Spirit.

Hodge understood the moral and spiritual nature of Scripture, and this understanding marked his approach to exegetical and theological scholarship.

Trip to Europe

As a professor of biblical studies, Hodge recognized his need to stay abreast of the critical trends with regard to the Bible that were developing outside of America. Specifically, he saw the need to become more acquainted with German higher criticism of the Scriptures, not so much to profit directly from such knowledge, but in order that he might refute these approaches that were finding their way more and more into the American scene. In 1821 he had started a "Society for Improvement in Biblical Literature" in Princeton, and in 1825 he began a quarterly journal called *The Biblical Repertory*, which he described as "A Collection of Tracts in Biblical Literature" produced "to assist ministers and laymen in the criticism and interpretation of the Bible." Hodge began this journal "from the conviction of the importance of Biblical studies, and from the desire of exciting greater interest in their cultivation." The *Biblical Repertory* consisted largely of translations and reprinted articles. Through all these means, Hodge was attempting to develop his own linguistic abilities and to become more familiar with current issues in biblical criticism and interpretation.

It became clear to Hodge in the summer of 1826 that what he really needed was to spend two years of uninterrupted study in Europe in order to improve his abilities as a professor and interpreter of Scripture. Alexander and Miller agreed with him and wrote the following appeal to the seminary trustees on his behalf:

> Rev. Mr. Hodge . . . has been for a considerable time past under a deep impression that he needed further advantages of leisurely study, particularly in some of the higher departments of Biblical criticism, and the auxiliary branches of knowledge. These advantages he is persuaded he can never hope fully to enjoy, unless he shall be enabled to retire for a time from the discharge of his duties in the Seminary, and to obtain access to those richly furnished libraries and those eminently skilled and profound masters of Oriental Literature of whose assistance he cannot avail himself in his present situation.

Hodge's "present situation" involved a demanding load of seminary instruction, as well as the necessities of caring for a young family. Hodge had married Sarah Bache, a great-granddaughter of Benjamin Franklin, in 1822, and the two had been blessed with two small children. The Hodges would go on to have eight children altogether. Hodge considered bringing his family with him to Europe, but in the end decided that the two years would be better and more affordably spent with his family residing in Philadelphia with his mother and brother.

Hodge departed on his European trip in the fall of 1826, and he would not return to Princeton until almost two years later. After being at sea for twenty-five days, Hodge arrived safely in Europe, and he wrote from Paris his initial impressions of Europe to Archibald Alexander:

> The moment you set your foot on land you see you are in the old world. The houses are antiquated in their appearance in the

extreme. The streets are narrow, destitute of side-walks and dirty. The people are poorly dressed, clattering along on wooden shoes, none of the women (at least the poorer ones) wearing bonnets, but in place of them a singular kind of cap. You soon see also, that the land is France. We had not walked far before we heard the violin, and discovered singing and dancing going on one side of the way, while on the other people were praying on their knees at the door of a chapel.

After staying in France for a number of months studying French, Arabic, and Syriac, Hodge arrived in Germany, where he was introduced to German Bible scholars Wilhelm Gesenius, August Tholuck, Ernst Wilhelm Hengstenberg, Ludwig and Otto von Gerlach, and numerous others. With some of the more evangelical scholars, such as Tholuck and Hengstenberg, Hodge would develop a life-long friendship. Even so, Hodge was not at all impressed with the reigning theologies and philosophies he encountered in Germany, those of Friedrich Schleiermacher and G. W. F. Hegel. Hodge had the opportunity to hear the preaching of the celebrated Schleiermacher in Berlin, but his experience left him underwhelmed. He recorded the following after hearing him preach: "I went to hear Schleiermacher, not knowing of any more evangelical preacher who had service in the morning. The sermon was peculiar. The words were Biblical, but the whole tenor so general, the ideas so vague and indefinite, that it was impossible for me to understand exactly what he meant." Hodge respected Schleiermacher's piety and "reverence for Christ" but believed his system of doctrine was to be rejected as mystical, unscriptural, and tending toward pantheism.

While Hodge was in Germany, some of those he left behind in America were anxious about his intellectual and spiritual well-being. By this time Archibald Alexander believed that Hodge would someday be the "senior Professor" of the seminary, and he was concerned for the preservation of Hodge's evangelical spirituality and belief. He wrote to him in the summer of 1827:

The air which you breathe in Germany will either have a deleterious effect on your moral constitution, or else by the strength of faith required to resist its effects your spiritual health will be confirmed. I pray God to keep you from the poison of Neology! I wish you to come home enriched in Biblical learning, but abhorring German philosophy and theology. I have been paying attention to Kant's philosophy, but it confounds and astonishes me.

A few weeks later he would again write:

> I feel anxious to hear from you, to know how you are, and what progress you make in the literature of Germany. . . . It will be worthwhile to have gone to Germany to know that there is but little worth going for. It will at any rate place you on a level with the other traveled literati of this country. But whatever you may gain of literature and knowledge of the world, I hope and pray that you may not lose any thing of the love of the truth and spirituality of the mind. On many accounts we miss you very much.

Hodge would remain steadfast in the views he had taken with him from Princeton. His acquaintance with German rationalism and Romantic philosophies solidified him and gave him confidence in his own view and abilities to answer critical approaches to Scripture. Hodge wrote to Alexander of the fixedness of his positions while yet in Europe, and upon hearing this word, Alexander would reply with elation: "I rejoice to learn that you live in an infected atmosphere, without being yourself infected."

Hodge returned from Europe in the fall of 1828 not only unmoved in his theology but also with a deepened appreciation for the importance of godliness in biblical interpretation. Hodge opened the new school term that fall with an address to the students on three "practical truths which the circumstances of foreign states and countries had deeply impressed upon his own [views]." After reflecting on "the great importance of civil and religious liberty" and the need to improve the state of religious instruction in America's common schools, Hodge reflected on the connection between one's moral character and one's theological beliefs. After seeing the spiritual barrenness produced by German rationalists, he had become further convinced that "Holiness is essential to the correct knowledge of divine things and the great security from error." He went on to warn the students: "Beware of any course of study which has a tendency to harden your hearts and deaden the delicate sensibility of the soul to moral truth and beauty." The prayers of Alexander had been answered, for Hodge's time in Europe had made him more a man of Old Princeton than ever.

A Flourishing Theologian

As the professor of Oriental and biblical literature from 1822 to 1840, Hodge taught courses on Hebrew and related languages, Old Testament interpretation, Greek exegesis, and New Testament interpretation. He also prepared courses on biblical criticism, hermeneutics, biblical geography, and some exegetical classes on individual books of the Bible. He frequently preached in local churches during these years, writing out his sermons in full and preaching them with warmth and effectiveness. Hodge also labored in these years to produce an exegetical and doctrinal *Commentary on the Epistle to the Romans* (1835). Because he suffered at this time from a debilitating affliction in his right leg and hip, most of this commentary was written while Hodge was "stretched horizontally on a couch, and his right limb often bound in a steel-splint." While this affliction left him almost entirely homebound for three years, the commentary he produced demonstrated Hodge's great ability for handling the linguistic, exegetical, and doctrinal issues found in the interpretation of Scripture.

In 1829 Hodge changed the scope of the *Biblical Repertory* to cover a broader range of theological and ecclesiastical issues. Its broader purpose would now be

> to bring under strict, impartial review the philosophy and literature of the time, and show their influence, whether for good or evil, on biblical interpretation, systematic theology, and practical religion, in doing which it will be necessary to correct and expose the error of founding religious doctrines on isolated passages, and partial views of Bible truth, or forcing the Scriptures to a meaning which shall accord with philosophical theories.

It would also aim to sharpen "facilities for a right understanding of the divine oracles," "to notice and exhibit the dangers of the particular form of error prevailing in the [present] period," "to present the history of religious doctrine and opinion," and "to consider the influence of different principles of ecclesiastical polity on piety, morals, literature, and civil institutions." To mark this expanded focus, the journal's name was changed to the *Biblical Repertory and Theological Review*. The editorship of the journal was also expanded to an "association of gentlemen," which included the three seminary professors Hodge, Alexander, and Miller; James Carnahan, John Maclean, and Albert Dod from the College of New Jersey; and Archibald Alexander's two sons, James W. Alexander and Joseph Addison Alexander. Over time the *Repertory* would change its name to the *Biblical Repertory and Princeton Review* (1837), the *Presbyterian Quarterly and Princeton Review* (1872), and finally to the *Princeton Review* (1877). Hodge was the primary editor of the journal for all practical purposes, until he was joined by coeditor Lyman Atwater in 1856. Besides the work of soliciting and editing contributions from others, Hodge would contribute more than 130 substantial articles to the journal covering a wide range of topics. Many of the theological controversies that Hodge was involved in over the course of his career were also played out in the pages of the *Princeton Review* for all to see.

Hodge labored at writing, preaching, and teaching in Princeton all the while tending to his wife and eight children, the last of whom was born in 1840. He had a home built close to the seminary's main building, and his study became the meeting place for the seminary's faculty and "the association of gentlemen" who edited the *Princeton Review*. His family life blended in seamlessly with his professional duties, and his young children were frequently found in his study as well. Archibald Alexander Hodge, his firstborn son, recounted as his father's biographer how Hodge allowed his young family full access to him in his study:

[Hodge's children] were at every age and at all times allowed free access to him. If they were sick, he nursed them. If they were well, he played with them. If he were busy, they played about him. His study had two doors, one opening outward towards the Seminary for the convenience of the students, and a second one opening inward into the main hall of the home. Hence his study was always the family thoroughfare, through which the children, boys and girls, young and old, and after them the grandchildren, went in and out for work and play. When he was too lame to open the door, and afterwards when he was too busy to be interrupted by that action, he took the latch from the doors, and caused them to swing in obedience to gentle springs, so that the least child might toddle in at will unhindered. He prayed for us all at family prayers, and singly, and taught us to pray at his knees with such soul-felt tenderness, that however bad we were our hearts all melted to his touch.

During later years he always caused his family to repeat after him at morning worship the Apostles' Creed, and a formula, of his own composition, professing personal consecration to the Father, and to the Son, and to the Holy Ghost. But that which makes those days sacred in the retrospect of his children is the person and character of the father himself as discovered in the privacy of his home, all radiant as that was with love, with unwavering faith, and with unclouded hope.

Some of his children would also recollect the image of Hodge "walking up and down his study singing devotional hymns" as he blended devotion into his studies as well.

In 1840 Hodge gave up the professorship of Oriental and biblical literature to become the professor of exegetical and didactic theology. This meant that Hodge's teaching focus would shift from the exegesis and interpretation of Scripture to the theology that was built upon it. This change in positions was brought on by Archibald Alexander's advancing age and his inability to continue teaching these subjects at the level he had done previously. The idea of changing positions was not something that originally appealed to Hodge. He confided to his brother Hugh that: "I would give five thousand dollars, if I had them, to be let off [the proposed change in positions]. The new arrangement knocks all my plans in the head, and will increase my *official* labors for years to come fourfold. . . . I live in great hopes that it will fall through without any agency of mine. And then I shall have a clear conscience as well as a merry heart." Despite Hodge's initial dread, the professorship of theology was something that suited him very well. Like his predecessor, Hodge had his students do extensive work in the Latin text of Francis Turretin's *Institutes of Elenctic Theology*, until this text was eventually replaced by his own *Systematic Theology* toward the end of his life. Hodge's former position was taken over by Joseph Addison Alexander.

Hodge produced a variety of books that extended beyond his primary calling as a theologian. Even as a professor of theology, Hodge continued to give his course of exegetical lectures on the Pauline Epistles. Some of these lectures were eventually expanded into printed commentaries: *Commentary on the Epistle to the Ephesians* (1856), *An Exposition of the First Epistle to the Corinthians* (1856), and *An Exposition of the Second Epistle to the Corinthians* (1857). Hodge also wrote a massive two-volume *Consti-*

tutional History of the Presbyterian Church in the United States of America (1839–40), which his son A. A. Hodge says "was for him the least natural and most laborious work he ever undertook." He wrote this history of Presbyterianism in colonial America to shed light on the Old School–New School conflict and division of 1837–38. He also wrote this work "to exhibit the true character of our Church; to show on what principles it was founded and governed; in other words, to exhibit historically its constitution, both as to doctrine and order." Hodge's contention in this work was to show the historic link between American Presbyterianism and Scottish Presbyterianism and to assert the need for Presbyterian pastors to subscribe to the system of doctrine contained in the Westminster Confession of Faith and Catechisms. Hodge also published a small book in 1841 called *The Way of Life*, which systematically set forth the doctrine of salvation for a popular audience. Topics in this book include: the Scriptures as the Word of God, conviction of sin, justification, faith, "profession of religion," and "holy living." This book was originally published by the American Sunday School Union and proved to be immensely popular. It was immediately reprinted in Europe and translated into a number of languages around the world. Although Hodge was now a Princeton theologian, he was also spreading the simple truths of the gospel to an audience far beyond the lecture halls of Old Princeton.

FIG. 6.2

Selected Works of Charles Hodge

Commentary on the Epistle to the Romans, 1835

The Constitutional History of the Presbyterian Church in the United States of America, 1839–40

The Way of Life, 1841

What Is Presbyterianism?, 1855

Commentary on the Epistle to the Ephesians, 1856

An Exposition of the First Epistle to the Corinthians, 1856

An Exposition of the Second Epistle to the Corinthians, 1857

Systematic Theology, 1871–72

What Is Darwinism?, 1874

Conflicts

Hodge's teaching and writing did not take place in a climate of ecclesiastical peace and stability. His career at Princeton unfolded amidst conflict and division, and much of his writing grew out of the doctrinal and ecclesiastical conflicts within his own denomination. Hodge and other Princeton theologians wrote at length in the *Princeton Review* against the theology of the "New School" Presbyterians, an assorted group that had been influenced by the "New Haven Theology" of Nathaniel Taylor and other New England Congregationalists. Taylor's theology developed out of the "New Divinity" promoted by Samuel Hopkins and the Edwardsean Congregationalists of New England and was a significant deviation from the Reformed theology found in the Westminster Confession and the Congregationalists' Savoy Declaration. Taylor himself came to deny the doctrine of original sin, as well as the imputation of Adam's sin to his descendants. Taylor also abandoned the Reformed understanding of the atonement and of regeneration as well. His views were influential on Congregationalist professor Moses Stuart at Andover Theological Seminary and Albert Barnes, a Presbyterian pastor in Philadelphia and a graduate of Princeton Seminary. Both Stuart and Barnes published commentaries on Romans before Hodge, and he responded at length to their deviations from Reformed orthodoxy. Hodge also wrote a number of articles for the *Princeton Review* that addressed various forms of New England theology and the views put forth by New School Presbyterians, including: "Regeneration and the Manner of its Occurrence" (1830), "Review of an Article in *The Christian Spectator* on Imputation" (1830), "Doctrine of Imputation" (1831), "Remarks on Dr. Cox's Communications" (1831), "The New Divinity Tried" (1832), "Stuart on Romans" (1833), "Barnes on the Epistle to the Romans" (1835), "Clap's Defense of the Doctrines of the New England Churches" (1839), and "Beman on the Atonement" (1845).

As the division between the Old School and New School Presbyterians began to take shape, Hodge and his colleagues at Princeton tried to prevent schism, even while their doctrinal views were decidedly with the Old School. Hodge disagreed with many Old School Presbyterians' harsh tactics for confronting the New School party, even though the Old School was led by individuals with close ties to Princeton Seminary such as Ashbel Green and Robert J. Breckinridge. When the Old School leaders drew up their "Act and Testimony" document in 1834 in an attempt to decisively remove the New School elements from the denomination, Hodge disagreed with this "extra-constitutional method" and advocated a more gradual and moderate approach. He laid out his "moderate Old School" approach in his "Act and Testimony" (1835) and "State of the Church" (1838) articles.

Another form of theology which engaged Hodge's attention was the Mercersburg Theology of John Williamson Nevin and Philip Schaff. Nevin was a former student of Hodge and had replaced him as a professor temporarily while Hodge was in Europe. While a professor at a German Reformed seminary in Mercersburg, Pennsylvania, Nevin, along with Schaff, attempted to combine certain elements of German theology and philosophical idealism into an ecumenical form of theology that elevated the church and the sacraments in a direction akin to Roman Catholic thought. Hodge addressed Mercersburg Theology in his "Schaff's Protestantism" (1845) and "Doctrine of the Reformed Church on the Lord's Supper" (1848) articles. Hodge also wrote extensive criticisms of the innovations of other American theologians, including Horace Bushnell, Charles Finney, and Edwards Amasa Park. In addition, he wrote critiques of the Oxford Tractarians. In all of these engagements, Hodge sought to defend the traditional doctrines set forth in the Westminster Confession of Faith.

Hodge also aired his differences with fellow Old School Presbyterians and contended for points of doctrine and polity he felt were important within his own circles. Old School Presbyterians had a number of disagreements among themselves over the course of Hodge's career. They disagreed, for example, regarding the best way to spread religious instruction to the next generation of Americans, with Hodge supporting the Presbyterian effort to build parochial schools in the period from 1840 to 1870. James Henley Thornwell of South Carolina opposed Hodge on this point and believed that Presbyterian churches should encourage their members to work within the public school system to help provide suitable Christian instruction.

This was only one of many ecclesiastical disagreements that Hodge had with Thornwell. Hodge aired many of them in his annual review article of the Presbyterian General Assembly. He began writing these articles in 1835 and continued each year almost without fail until the year of his death.

Hodge debated Thornwell on numerous matters of church polity for the better part of twenty years. Their disagreements in this area revolved around three main issues. First, Hodge believed that ruling elders, as representatives of the congregation, were to be considered as part of the laity and held in clear distinction from pastors (teaching elders), while Thornwell believed that ruling elders and pastors occupy the same office. On this point, both Hodge and Thornwell believed that the position of the other seriously compromised the congregation's "representative" role in its own governance. Second, Hodge believed that voluntary societies operating outside the direct governance of the church were helpful and useful, while Thornwell felt they posed a threat to Presbyterian governance. Finally, Hodge believed that Roman Catholic baptisms were valid, arguing from the historic practice of the Reformed churches, while Thornwell believed that Roman Catholic baptisms were not valid, arguing from his doctrine of the church. Thornwell believed that the Roman Catholic churches had become "so degenerated, as to become no churches of Christ, but synagogues of Satan" (*Westminster Confession of Faith*, 25.5) and that those who converted from Roman Catholicism to Presbyterianism should yet be baptized. Hodge on the other hand believed that the Roman Catholic Church was yet "part of the visible Church" and its baptisms were valid, even though he considered its doctrines "perverted and overlaid" with error. These disagreements between Hodge and Thornwell sometimes took on more rancor than might be expected. Feeling that Old School Presbyterianism needed a voice to rival Hodge's *Princeton Review*, Thornwell launched a theological journal friendly to his ecclesiastical perspectives called the *Southern Presbyterian Review*, which ran from 1847–85.

Hodge and Thornwell's disagreements reached their height over the issue of slavery. Hodge tried to adopt a middle ground position between the abolitionists on the one hand and the Southern supporters of slavery on the other. Hodge took up the issue in his 1836

Princeton Review article "On Slavery" and followed with a number of other articles, including "West India Emancipation" (1838), "Abolitionism" (1844), and "Emancipation" (1849). In his first article, Hodge blamed abolitionists for inflaming divisions and encouraging the support of slavery itself by their blanket condemnation of slaveholders:

> It was not long since the acknowledgement was frequent at the South, and universal at the North, that it [slavery] was a great evil. . . . How altered is the present state of the country! Instead of lamentations and acknowledgements, we hear from the South the strongest language of justification. And at the North, opposition to the proceedings of the antislavery societies seems to be rapidly producing a public feeling in favor of slavery itself. . . . What has produced this lamentable change? . . . By far the most prominent cause is the conduct of the abolitionists.

Hodge believed that abolitionists like William Lloyd Garrison went way beyond Scripture in their blanket condemnation of slaveholding and that it was possible to distinguish between slavery *abstractly considered* and slavery as it exists in any particular setting: "We must distinguish between slavery and its separable adjuncts; between the relation itself and the abuse of it; between the possession of power and the unjust exercise of it." With its racism and cruelty, however, Hodge did believe that Southern slavery was a great evil. This position put him at odds with the position eventually adopted by Thornwell and Southern Presbyterian leader Benjamin Morgan Palmer, who came to defend Southern slavery as a positive social good. In distinction from the abolitionists, Hodge believed that slavery could best be eliminated through gradual and peaceful means. He summarized his position as follows:

> How did they [Christ and the apostles] treat it? Not by denunciations of slaveholding as necessarily and universally sinful. Not by declaring that all slaveholders were menstealers and robbers, and consequently to be excluded from the church and the kingdom of heaven. Not by insisting on immediate emancipation. Not by appeals to the passions of men on the evils of slavery, or by the

adoption of a system of universal agitation. On the contrary, it was by teaching the true nature, dignity, equality and destiny of men; by inculcating the principles of justice and love; and by leaving these principles to produce their legitimate effects in ameliorating the condition of all classes of society.

Hodge referred to his position of gradual emancipationism as "the gospel method of extinguishing slavery," which he believed would be brought about through the spread of gospel truth to all parts of society. According to Hodge, the "natural and peaceful mode of [slavery's] extinction is the gradual elevation of the slaves in knowledge, virtue and property to the point at which it is no longer desirable or possible to keep them in bondage. Their chains thus gradually relax, until they fall off entirely. It is in this way that Christianity has abolished both political and domestic bondage, whenever it has had free scope." He stated his position further in his commentary on Ephesians:

> The Bible method of dealing with this and similar institutions is to enforce on all concerned the great principles of moral obligation, assured that those principles, if allowed free scope, will put an end to all evils both in the political and social relations of men. . . . The result of such obedience, if it could become general, would be, that first the evils of slavery, and then slavery itself, would pass away as naturally and as healthfully as children cease to be minors.

With the abolitionists on one side and Southern Presbyterians like Thornwell on the other, Hodge and the faculty of Old Princeton sought to occupy a shrinking middle ground on the issue of slavery that few were ultimately pleased with but themselves.

When Civil War broke out in 1861, Hodge hoped his middle ground position could keep the Old School Presbyterians from dividing. With the union of the country unraveling, Hodge published his article "The State of the Country" (1861) in the *Princeton Review* to argue against secession and national division. Thornwell quickly published a rebuttal to Hodge's article, defending secession in the *Southern Presbyterian Review*. When the General Assembly passed the "Gardiner Spring Resolutions" in the spring of 1861, declaring the loyalty of the Old School Presbyterians to the federal government, Hodge lodged a formal protest. While he agreed with those in the majority that individual states did not have the right to secede, he did not think that the Presbyterian church should take a stand on the political questions involved or force out from its ranks those in the South who could not agree. After Thornwell led the Southern Presbyterians to separate in 1861, and as the horrors of war ravaged the nation, Hodge threw off his position of neutrality and openly expressed in an 1863 *Princeton Review* article his "moral duty" of loyalty and allegiance to "the national government in Washington, of which Abraham Lincoln is the constitutional head." In promoting the Northern cause, Hodge went further and stated: "Confident in the justice of the national cause, assured that God is on our side, we are bound not to despond. We should remember that we are acting for generations to come; that the fate of the country, and, in large measure, of Christendom, hangs on the issue of this conflict." The progress of the war moved Hodge to speak on behalf of the Northern cause with religious conviction. When the war ended, Hodge wrote in the *Princeton Review* in July 1865 with increasing moral passion and certainty that God had been on the side of the Union all along, stating: "Rebellion is a great crime . . . and the rebellion of the South was wanton and wicked." The force of war had moved Hodge away from his original position of moderation and mediation toward religious convictions in favor of the North.

The conflict over slavery and national union was profoundly significant in Hodge's career, and yet this conflict was only one of the many between Hodge and New School Presbyterians in the North and Thornwell and other Old School Presbyterians in the South. In all his theological and ecclesiastical conflicts, Hodge sought to argue for moderate Old School positions that avoided innovations and extremes and were faithful to the historic positions of the Reformed tradition. Even so, the positions forged by Hodge and the Princeton theologians in these contests were clearly shaped by the theological, ecclesiastical, and political context of nineteenth-century America.

The Celebrated Professor

In 1872 a great crowd from across the nation gathered in Princeton to celebrate the completion of Hodge's fiftieth year as a professor at Princeton seminary. A large number of Hodge's former students were in attendance, as were many representatives from other seminaries. Letters were presented to Hodge from around the world, including one from the theological faculties of the colleges of the Free Church

6.3 In his over fifty years of teaching at the seminary, Charles Hodge taught more than three thousand students.

of Scotland. Hodge had cherished the work and friendship of many Scottish Free Church theologians such as George Smeaton, Patrick Fairbairn, and especially William Cunningham. In this letter these theologians proclaimed that "we look on you as one of the chief instruments raised up by the Head of the Church, in these times of doubt and contention, for maintaining in its purity the faith once delivered to the saints." Numerous speeches were given at this celebration which similarly honored the senior professor of Old Princeton. Hodge referred to this celebration as "the apex of my life." He was seventy-four years old at the time. The seminary had been in existence for sixty years, and Hodge had been a professor at the seminary for fifty of them.

Hodge would continue serving as a professor for six more years. Before his death at the age of eighty in 1878, Hodge would serve as an instructor for more than three thousand students. He had been a spiritual father and counselor to many students preparing for the ministry, instructing them in the classroom, meeting them in his study, and speaking to them on practical Christian living every Sunday afternoon at the "Sabbath Afternoon Conferences." The outlines of Hodge's "Conference Sermons" were published just after his death in 1879. As a fitting capstone to his publishing career, his three-volume *Systematic Theology* appeared in 1871–72. Apart from a small book against atheistic evolution called *What Is Darwinism?* (1874), his *Systematic Theology* was his last major work and the crowning achievement of his long career. While volumes of theological sermons and lectures had appeared in America prior to Hodge's *Systematic Theology*, a text of its scope and magnitude had not yet been published by an American theologian. Hodge had hoped to add a fourth volume devoted to the subject of ecclesiology, but decided to forgo it after completing three volumes. One of Hodge's students, William Durant, received his permission to pull together and arrange into systematic order Hodge's writings on ecclesiology from articles he had already written for the *Princeton Review*. This appeared in 1878 as *Discussions in Church Polity*. Another student helped Hodge produce an index to his *Systematic Theology*, thus completing the publications of a celebrated theologian.

Conclusion

When Hodge died peacefully in his Princeton home on June 19, 1878, the seminary deeply felt the loss of the one who had become "its Patriarchal head." Princeton seminary had only had two theology professors, and Hodge had followed faithfully in the path laid out for him by his predecessor Archibald Alexander. While maintaining the spiritual warmth of Alexander and the Old Princeton devotion to "vital piety," Hodge surpassed Alexander as an interpreter of Scripture and as a theologian. The production of his *Systematic Theology* gave Old School Presbyterianism a systematic theology text devoted to the exposition and defense of Reformed orthodoxy against a host of alternative theologies and beliefs. Hodge had also advanced the seminary as an institution of theological and cultural engagement through his celebrated *Princeton Review*. Even with these advancements, Hodge led Old Princeton to maintain its original concern for the piety of its students and the spirituality of the church.

7

OLD PRINCETON AND THE CHURCH: CHARLES HODGE'S *PRINCETON REVIEW* ARTICLES ON THE CHURCH

He has carried it [The Princeton Review] *as a ball-and-chain for forty years, with scarcely any other compensation than the high privilege and honour of making it an organ for upholding sound Presbyterianism, the cause of the country, and the honor of our common Redeemer.*

—Charles Hodge, speaking in 1865 of himself and his editorship of the *Princeton Review*

It is beyond all question the greatest purely theological review that has ever been published in the English tongue, and has waged war in defence of the Westminster standards for a period of forty years, with a polemic vigor and unity of design without any parallel in the history of religious journalism. If we were called to name any living writer who, to Calvin's exegetical tact, unites a large measure of Calvin's grasp of mind and transcendent clearness in the department of systematic theology, we should point to this Princeton Professor. He possesses, to use the words of an English critic, the power of seizing and retaining with a rare vigor and tenacity the great doctrinal turning-points in a controversy, while he is able to expose with triumphant dexterity the various subterfuges under which it has been brought to elude them. His articles furnish a remarkably full and exact repository of historic and polemic theology.

—*The British Quarterly Review* on *The Princeton Review* (January 1871)

While the theologians of Old Princeton produced many important books, the *Princeton Review* was in many ways the true voice of the seminary. The "association of gentlemen" that produced it every quarter published the articles anonymously until 1871, tying the content of the *Review* to no explicit individual in particular. Many associated all of its articles with its main editor Charles Hodge, but Hodge had many capable accomplices as writers for the journal. An index volume published in 1871 provided names and biographical sketches of the authors for most of the articles appearing from 1825 to 1868, but before then, Hodge's *Princeton Review* united a number of voices into an undifferentiated and distinct school of thought. James W. Alexander wrote of the *Princeton Review* in 1854:

> Through good and evil report it has pursued its way, and has con-
> tributed more than any other agency, to make known those opinions
> which belong to what some have chosen to call the Princeton School.
> In times of controversy it has not refrained from a free expression
> of judgment on great questions; and its pages contain ample discus-
> sion of all matters relating to the defense of Calvinism and Presbytery,
> the policy of the Church, the charities of the age, new divinity, new
> philosophy, and new measures, and especially the difficulties which
> preceded, accompanied and followed the division of our ecclesiasti-
> cal body.

As a body of theological work, the *Princeton Review* gives us a detailed display of the thinking of the "Princeton school." It also allows us to understand the ecclesiastical, theological, and historical context in which it flourished.

Of those who contributed to the many *Princeton Review* articles on theological matters, Charles Hodge had the most to say about the theology of the church. Since he never composed a fourth volume on ecclesiology for his *Systematic Theology*, his most important writings on the church are contained in these articles. Hodge's annual review articles of the Presbyterian General Assembly addressed the most debated issues within his own denomination, and many of his articles addressed ecclesiological issues outside of Old School Presbyterianism. This chapter will survey a selection of Hodge's articles and ideas on two of his many ecclesiastical concerns: high church ecclesiology and the relationship between the church and the state.

Charles Hodge on High Church Ecclesiology

Church Hodge wrote a number of articles that addressed the high church ecclesiology that was found in the Church of England's Oxford movement, which was sometimes called the Tractarian Movement after the *Tracts for the Times* series produced from 1833 to 1841. This movement developed into what is now called "Anglo-Catholicism" and was promoted in Hodge's day by John Henry Newman, Edward Bouverie Pusey, John Keble, William Palmer, and others. Hodge believed that the Tractarians raised important ecclesiological questions with significant implications for how one understands what it means to be a Christian.

In 1846 Hodge reviewed Henry Edward Manning's *The Unity of the Church* in an article that appeared under the title "Theories of the Church." Using Manning's work as the backdrop for his discussion, a work he called one of "the ablest productions of the Oxford school," Hodge began by noting that Christianity has appeared under "three characteristic forms" which have battled against each other since the beginning of the church. He called these forms "the Evangelical, the Ritual, and the Rationalistic." Rationalistic Christianity arose with forms of Gnostic and Platonized Christianity in the early church, found later expression in Arminian and Socinian forms, and became predominant in the Church of England in the early eighteenth century. Ritualistic Christianity first developed with the Judiazers, rose to dominance in the Middle Ages, found new expression under Archbishop Laud in the 1600s, and was now being promoted with great energy by the Oxford movement. It was the ritualism of the Oxford movement that had recently "attracted the attention of the whole Christian world" and was "now in obvious conflict" with the evangelical form of religion.

Hodge asserted that the evangelical understanding of the church "necessarily arises out of the evangelical system of doctrine." This system of doctrine emphasizes the saving work of God in the hearts of individuals through the gospel. God supernaturally works in the hearts of individuals to save them out of a state of sin and to spiritually unite them to Christ through a personal and living faith. This spiritual union that believers have with Christ forms the basis for an evangelical understanding of the church. The church, according to Hodge, must first of all be considered as composed of all those who are truly saved and spiritually united to Christ, the head of the church: "To the question, what is the Church; or, who constitute the Church? the Evangelical answer, and must answer, true believers." True believers make up the church, and this is the fundamental starting point of Hodge's evangelical ecclesiology.

When believers who make up a part of the church visibly join together "for the purposes of worship and discipline and [to] have their proper officers for instruction and government," they "appear before the world as a visible body." This body admits individuals into its membership or "communion" by a credible profession of faith, and because it cannot infallibly distinguish between those who are spiritually in Christ from those who are not, it may admit many "who are either self-deceived or deceivers." According to Hodge, then, "many are of the Church who are not in the Church." Some are "real" and some are "nominal," and out of this distinction arises the further distinction between "the invisible and visible church." Hodge stated that the following is "the fundamental principle of the evangelical theory as to the nature of the Church," namely:

> that it consists of true believers, and is visible as they are visible as believers by their profession and fruits, and that those associated with them in external union, are the Church only outwardly, and not as constituent members of the body of Christ and temple of God. In this [principle] is involved an admission of the distinction for which the evangelical contend between the Church invisible and visible, between nominal and real Christians, between true and professing believers.

While a "visible Church is a body of professing believers," the true church is composed of all true believers who are spiritually united to Christ. Distinguishing between nominal and real Christians and between the visible and the invisible church was of central importance to Hodge: "all who really believe the gospel constitute the true Church, and all who profess such faith constitute the visible

Church." Failing to make this distinction was a fundamental error of the Oxford school.

Hodge believed that the Oxford theologians' "ritualist" ecclesiology was ultimately based on a different understanding of what it means to be a Christian. For the ritualist, a Christian is made one through attachment to the *visible* church, which ritualists understand to be the exclusive channel of saving grace. Ritualists elevate the clerical function in the church to that of a priesthood, and they elevate the sacraments to vehicles of saving grace, having "inherent virtue" and "an *opus operatum* efficacy." "The doctrine of the priestly character of the Christian ministry," says Hodge, "is one of the distinguishing characteristics of the Ritual system," as is an elevated view of the sacraments. One is made a Christian, for the ritualist, by attaching oneself to a visible church, by partaking of its sacraments, by submitting to its priesthood, and by participating in its ritualistic and mystical forms of worship. The practical effect of the ritualistic system of salvation is to make "the Church so prominent that Christ and the truth are eclipsed." According to Hodge:

> If the soul convinced of sin and desirous of reconciliation with God, is allowed to hear the Saviour's voice, and permitted to go to him by faith for pardon and the Spirit, then the way of life is unobstructed. But if a human priest must intervene, and bar our access to Christ, assuming the exclusive power to dispense the blessings Christ has purchased, and to grant or withhold them at discretion, then the whole plan of salvation is effectually changed. No sprinkling priest, no sacrificial or sacramental rite can be substituted for the immediate access of the soul to Christ, without imminent peril of salvation.

Because of the different conception of how one becomes a Christian, Hodge understood the debate with the Oxford school to be more than a debate "about externals of religion." The very nature of Christianity itself was at stake.

The high church understanding of ecclesiology also has major implications for Christian experience and spirituality. Whereas the evangelical understanding of the church and of Christianity asserts that "God and Christ are the immediate objects of reverence and love," the ritual system makes "rites, ceremonies, altars, buildings, priests, saints, [and] the blessed virgin intervene and divide or absorb the reverence and homage due to God alone." The effect of this "produces a different kind of religion from that which we find portrayed in the Bible, and exemplified in the lives of the apostles and early Christians." The end of such a system is disastrous to real Christian experience:

> If external rites and creature agents are made necessary to our access to God, then those rites and agents will more or less take the place of God, and men will come to worship the creature rather than the creator. This tendency constantly gathers strength, until actual idolatry is the consequence, or until all religion is made to consist in the performance of external services.

The ritualistic ecclesiology has been detrimental to the gospel throughout the world, and Hodge closed his critique of high church ritualism based on what it has historically produced. According to Hodge, high church ritualism has

> changed the plan of salvation; it has rendered obsolete the answer given by Paul to the question, What must I do to be saved? It has perverted religion. It has introduced idolatry. It has rendered men secure in the habitual commission of crime. It has subjected the faith, the conscience, and the conduct of the people to the dictation of the priesthood. It has exalted the hierarchy, saints, angels, and the Virgin Mary, into the place of God, so as to give a polytheistic character to the religion of a large part of Christendom. Such are the actual fruits of that system which has of late renewed its strength, and which everywhere asserts its claims to be received as genuine Christianity.

Even though the immediate issue with the Oxford school in the 1840s and 1850s was over the nature of the church, Hodge understood that the issues involved were much deeper and older. In his words, "The controversy between Protestants and Romanists, has, in appearance, shifted ground from matters of doctrine to the question concerning the Church. This is, however, only a change in form. The essential question remains the same. It is still a contention about the very nature of religion, and the method of salvation."

Hodge wrote other articles aimed at the Oxford school, including a lengthy one in 1853 called "The Idea of the Church." This article provided an extensive biblical defense of Hodge's main point against the Tractarians, namely, that the church "is not essentially a visible society," but is "the communion of saints, the body of those who are united to Christ by the indwelling of his Spirit." Hodge's understanding of the church was built upon the evangelical priority given to the gospel of justifying grace that comes through personal faith in Jesus Christ.

Sacramentalism and the Mercersburg Theology

Hodge's concern with high church ecclesiology deepened when he saw a form of it emerge in the thinking of his former student, John Williamson Nevin, and in Nevin's so-called "Mercersburg Theology." Nevin felt that the early nineteenth-century American emphasis on revivals and individual religious experience had pushed the church to the periphery, and he sought to recover the church's central importance for Christian experience. Nevin wrote his work *The Mystical Presence* (1846) to be "a vindication of the Reformed or Calvinistic doctrine of the Holy Eucharist," though broader theological issues related to the church and salvation were addressed as well. Hodge responded to *The Mystical Presence* in an 1848 article entitled "The Doctrine of the Reformed Church on the Lord's Supper."

Hodge began his response to Nevin by analyzing different expressions of early Reformed thought on the nature of the Lord's Supper. He stated that discerning the early Reformed position is difficult, since "almost all the Reformed confessions were framed for the express purpose of compromise" with Lutheranism. Preventing "schism between the two branches of the Protestant church" was the "one great object of Calvin's life," and so Calvin also expressed his position on the Lord's Supper in terms intended to conciliate Lutheran thought. The ensuing Reformed tradition as well adopted similarly conciliatory language , so that "while the Reformed held a doctrine which admitted of expression in the language adopted [by them in their confessions], it might be much more simply and intelligibly expressed in other terms." Once union with Lutherans was no longer as vital an issue, Reformed expressions on the Lord's Supper became clearer, such that "no one pretends to misunderstand the language of Turretin and Pictet" on the subject. Hodge asserts that a historical analysis of the development of the Reformed position on the Lord's Supper must take into account the Swiss (or "Zwinglian view") as well as that of Calvin, and he faults Nevin for choosing "to make Calvin the great authority" at the expense of other early Reformed writers on the subject.

In his survey of the tradition, Hodge argued that the Reformed understanding of the Lord's Supper historically put its emphasis on the spiritual reception of Christ that takes place in it through faith. Hodge states that the early Reformed theologians (including the Zwinglians) were unified in believing in the "real presence" of Christ in the Lord's Supper. That is to say, the early Reformed theologians believed that Christ is present in the Lord's Supper not "locally" but "mystically" and "in the mind," and his presence is "apprehended by faith." According to Hodge, the Reformed were united in asserting that there is "a presence of Christ's body in the Lord's Supper; not local, but spiritual; not for the sense but for the mind and to faith; not of nearness, but of efficacy." Christ's body and blood are received in the partaking of the Lord's Supper not by the mouth but "only by the soul . . . by faith . . . [and] by or through the power of the Holy Spirit." Since the feeding upon Christ's body and blood is a spiritual act done in the heart by faith, Hodge stated that Reformed theologians unanimously affirmed that there is no "special benefit or communion with Christ to be had there [in the Lord's Supper] and which cannot elsewhere be obtained." According to Hodge, "what is elsewhere received by faith, without the signs and significant actions, is in the sacraments received in connexion with them." The same grace that comes through the sacrament comes through the gospel, and it is by faith in Christ (with or without the sacrament) that a believer receives his grace. Hodge went on to state:

[The sacraments] are declared to be efficacious means of grace; but their efficacy, as such, is referred neither to any virtue in them nor in him that administers them, but solely to the attending operation or influence of the Holy Spirit, precisely as in the case of the word. . . . [The sacraments'] power, in other words, to convey grace depends entirely, as in the case of the Word, on the co-operation of the Holy Ghost. Hence the power is in no way tied to the sacraments. It may be exerted without them.

The "real presence" of Christ in the sacraments, then, does not make them means of grace in and of themselves, nor do they replace faith as the means by which we receive God's saving grace.

After stating the Reformed understanding of the Supper, Hodge went on in his article entitled "Doctrine of the Reformed Church on the Lord's Supper" to criticize Nevin's overall system of theology, which Hodge viewed as "a radical rejection of the doctrine and theology of the Reformed Church." Nevin's "confessedly mystical" book on the Lord's Supper, according to Hodge, reflected the deep imprint of German liberalism and contained "all the essential features of Schleiermacher's theory" of Christian doctrine. For Nevin, the reconciliation between God and man takes place mystically in the incarnation of Christ (where the divine is joined with mankind) and by extension in the church, which is "the depository and continuation of the Saviour's theoanthropic life itself." For Nevin, it is the visible church which possesses and embodies the reconciliation between God and sinful man, and those who would partake of this reconciliation must receive it through the church. Ultimately, Hodge found Nevin at fault for fundamentally changing the gospel into a different form altogether, locating redemption in the incarnation instead of in the cross and in the church instead of in the heart.

Even though Nevin held to a different view of the church than the Oxford Tractarians, Hodge faulted him for having a similar ecclesiology and understanding of the sacraments. He believed that Nevin was wrong to make the *visible* church all-important in his thinking about the church. He also believed that Nevin was in error "to ascribe to the outward church, the attributes and prerogatives of the mystical body of Christ," an error Hodge considered as "the fundamental error of Romanism" and "the source of her power and of her corruption." Regarding the position taken in Nevin's *The Mystical Presence* on the church and the sacraments, Hodge stated:

Its whole spirit is churchy. It makes religion to be a church life, its manifestations a liturgical service, its support sacramental grace. . . . His book [has] a character as different as can be from the healthful, evangelical free spirit of Luther or Calvin. The main question whether we come to Christ, and then to the church; whether we by a personal act of faith receive him, and by union with him become a member of his mystical body; or whether all our access to Christ is through a mediating church, Dr. Nevin decides against the evangelical system.

Hodge faulted Nevin for deviating from the Reformed tradition in ascribing to the Lord's Supper "a presence and of course a receiving of the body and blood of Christ" that is "to be had nowhere else." Connected with this, Hodge further faulted Nevin for ascribing to the sacraments a mystical power and an efficacy that seemed to him "to lie somewhere between the Romish and the Lutheran view." Hodge quoted Nevin as saying that "grace goes inseparably along with the sign" and that when a believer takes the sacrament it "serves in itself to convey the life of Christ into our persons." Practically speaking, Hodge found that this mystical view of the sacrament amounted to a kind of sacramentalism not much different from that of Roman Catholicism.

Hodge believed that an evangelical and Reformed understanding of the church started with a consideration of those individuals who are spiritually and invisibly united to Christ by the new birth and genuine faith. The salvation of individuals comes prior to their participation in the visible church, and not the other way around. The fundamental ecclesiological error of both Nevin and the Tractarians was in elevating the visible church to a level that virtually destroyed all consideration of an invisible church.

The Church's Relation to the State

Hodge wrote as much in the *Princeton Review* on the church's relationship to the state as he did on high church ecclesiology. While he once stated that the relationship between the church and the state was relatively simple and clear, by the middle of the Civil War he had come to view this issue as an "exceedingly complicated and difficult subject." In the midst of the war Hodge wrote directly on this topic in his 1863 article "The Relation of the Church and State." He began this article with a historical overview of the relationship between the two. Hodge understood the pre-Reformation history of the church to be largely one of corrupting entanglements in political affairs, starting with the conversion of Constantine in 312. The subsequent history of the medieval church, then, was one of conflict and tension as the civil and religious authorities attempted to exert their authority over each other. With the Protestant Reformation came "the rejection of the doctrine of the visible unity of the Church under one infallible head" in the West, and new understandings of the doctrine of the church began to emerge. After surveying Anglican, Lutheran, and Reformed thought on the church's relationship to the state, Hodge described the unique doctrine of church and state that emerged in America. In his mind, the American notion of the state and the church being separate and independent bodies was "of very recent origin" and was unheard of until it gradually became established in the New World. This "novel, yet sound doctrine," says Hodge, rests firmly upon conclusions derived from the New Testament. Hodge argued that only the New Testament should be used to determine this doctrinal question, because one is "not authorized to argue [directly] from the Old Testament economy" on this point, since that economy was "avowedly temporary and has been abolished." While the colonial "New England theory was more that of a theocracy," the public mind of America had begun to affirm universally by the end of the eighteenth century that governing officials are to have no official role in the affairs of the church. Since Jesus in the New Testament assigned responsibility over church matters to the church itself, the state was not to interfere in any way. The church and the state "cannot rightfully interfere in the affairs of the other," since the two "are to be kept distinctive within their respective spheres." This American understanding of the church's relation to the state stood in contrast with the existence of nationalized churches found in much of the Protestant world. Hodge concluded his article by saying: "We have reason to rejoice in the recently discovered truth, that the Church is independent of the State, and that the State best promotes her interest by letting her alone."

Since the church and the state are separate and independent institutions, Hodge believed that it was improper for the church to address or meddle in political affairs. Hodge had already expressed this as his fundamental position four years earlier in his 1859 General Assem-

1863.]   *Relation of the Church and State.*   679

ART. VIII.—*Relation of the Church and State.*

THIS is an exceedingly complicated and difficult subject. There are three aspects under which it may be viewed.

I. The actual relation which at different times and in different countries has subsisted between the two institutions.

II. The theory devised to justify or determine the limits of such existing relation.

III. The normal relation, such as should exist according to the revealed will of God, and the nature of the state and of the church.

Before the conversion of Constantine, the church was of course so far independent of the state, that she determined her own faith, regulated her worship, chose her officers, and exercised her discipline without any interference of the civil authorities. Her members were regarded as citizens of the state, whose religious opinions and practices were, except in times of persecution, regarded as matters of indifference. It is probable that much the same liberty was accorded to the early Christians as was granted by the Romans to the Jews, who were not only allowed, in ordinary cases, to conduct their synagogue services as they pleased, but to decide matters of dispute among themselves, according to their own laws. It is also stated that churches were allowed to hold real estate before the profession of Christianity by the Emperor.

When Constantine declared himself a Christian, he expressed the relation which was henceforth to subsist between the church and state, by saying to certain bishops, "God has made you the bishops of the internal affairs of the church, and me the bishop of its external affairs." This saying has ever since been, throughout a large portion of Christendom, the standing formula for expressing the relation of the civil magistrate to the kingdom of Christ.

According to this statement, it belongs to the church, through her own organs, to choose her officers, to regulate all matters relating to doctrine, to administer the word and sacraments, to

7.1 Charles Hodge's 1863 article on "The Relation of the Church and the State." The identity of the authors of the *Princeton Review* articles were not published until 1871.

bly review article. Here Hodge stated that the church "has nothing to do with the State, in the exercise of its discretion within its own sphere; and therefore has no right to meddle with questions of policy, foreign or domestic. She has nothing to do with tariffs, or banks, or internal improvements . . . She has nothing to do as a Church with secular affairs, with questions of politics or state policy." Where political issues were concerned, the church was to remain silent and strictly nonpartisan. Hodge made these statements in connection with his debate with James Henley Thornwell on the floor of the 1859 Presbyterian General Assembly. Hodge and Thornwell agreed with the "American" doctrine that the church should be independent of and separate from the state, but they differed sharply as to whether the corporate church should speak into the affairs of state which were outside its immediate purview as an essentially spiritual organization. Thornwell had come to the position that the spiritual nature of the church forbade it from making any pronouncements pertaining to any secular or "voluntary associations for various civil and social purposes" outside the church. Thornwell argued that the church *as the church* should only engage in its spiritual vocation, while Christian individuals should feel at liberty to involve themselves in broader societal and political endeavors as they see fit. He argued this point in a speech given before the 1859 General Assembly to persuade the Presbyterian church from giving its approval of the African colonization enterprise.

One might guess that Hodge would be in agreement with Thornwell's position, but in actual fact he was not. Hodge agreed with Thornwell on the essential separation of the church and state, but he disagreed sharply with Thornwell on whether or not the church should speak into public affairs and issues of public concern. He believed that Thornwell's view would "stop the mouth of the Church, and prevent her bearing her testimony to kings and rulers, magistrates and people, in behalf of the truth and law of God." With sharpness in his response, Hodge stated that Thornwell's view was a "poison" to be "dashed away."

Hodge's main point in his 1859 General Assembly review article was to argue that it was the church's duty to speak the truth of God's law in the public arena. The church must speak to the unregenerate, since the church itself was a mixed body, containing many baptized members (i.e., children) of the invisible church and others who are not regenerate. While Thornwell argued for the church's noninvolvement in secular or political affairs based on the "spirituality" of the church, Hodge argued that the church was not as "purely spiritual" as Thornwell was making it out to be. Hodge believed that his view was faithful to the Presbyterian understanding of the mixed character of the church, as opposed to what he called the "extreme" view of John Owen and his branch of Congregational Puritanism.

While agreeing with Thornwell that the church should not be a place of political partisanship, Hodge went on to argue that the church should openly and boldly make formal pronouncements on issues of public morality, all the while avoiding pronouncements on political matters. Hodge stated that the Great Commission gave the church the "prerogative and duty to testify for the truth and the law of God, wherever she can make her voice heard; not only to her own people, but to kings and rulers, to Jews and Gentiles." Where matters of public morality are concerned, the church is to speak freely and boldly as a prophetic voice. According to Hodge:

> They profane the pulpit when they preach politics, or turn the sacred desk into a rostrum for lectures on secular affairs. But they are only faithful to their vows when they proclaim the truth of God and apply his law to all matters whether of private manners or laws of the state. The whole history of the Presbyterian Church in Europe and America is instinct with this spirit. . . . It has never been afraid to denounce what God forbids, or to proclaim in all ears what God commands. This is her prerogative and this is her duty.

Whenever a public matter has both a moral and political bearing, the church is only to speak on the moral aspects of the issue. According to Hodge:

> If at any time, as may well happen, a given question assumed both a moral and political bearing, as for example, the slave-trade, then the duty of the Church is limited to setting forth the law of God on the subject. It is not her office to argue the question in its bearing on the

civil or secular interests of the community, but simply to declare in her official capacity what God has said on the subject.

This distinction between public morality and public policy was central to Hodge's understanding of how the church should engage in public affairs. While it must speak loudly on matters of public morality, it must be careful not to speak at all on matters that are purely political.

Hodge's View of the Church and State Tried

Hodge stated in his 1859 *Princeton Review* article that his distinction between public morality and public policy was clear and easy to make: "the principle which defines and limits the prerogative and duty of the Church in all such cases seems to us perfectly plain." As the Civil War unfolded in the 1860s, however, Hodge would find the position he had first presented as a simple matter put to the test.

When the Presbyterian General Assembly convened in Philadelphia on May 16, 1861, the nation was in a state of open war. Many Southern delegates were absent from the assembly, and those who gathered were deeply stirred by the political crisis gripping the nation. Public pressure mounted for the assembly to make a pronouncement on the secession and the war. The assembly deliberated and eventually passed a series of resolutions known as the "Gardiner Spring Resolutions," named after the minister who moved that the issue be taken up by the assembly. The motion that was ultimately adopted affirmed the Presbyterian church's "obligation to promote and perpetuate . . . the integrity of the United States, and to strengthen, uphold, and encourage the Federal Government." It also proclaimed its "unabated loyalty" to the Constitution. Hodge strongly disagreed with the assembly's action, holding that the Gardiner Spring Resolutions violated the fundamental principle of the church's separation from the state. Hodge and others filed formal protests against the General Assembly's action, arguing that the assembly's course of action essentially divided the church over political issues and effectively forced Southern ministers out of the Presbyterian church by taking a partisan position on a political matter. For Hodge, such a pronouncement was improper because it addressed and took a decided view on a political and Constitutional question, namely, the right of state secession.

Hodge stated in his 1861 review of the General Assembly that "we deny the right of the General Assembly to decide the political question, to what government the allegiance of Presbyterians, as citizens, is due." These words were put in the form of a formal petition that protested the assembly's action. For Hodge, the issue of secession was strictly a matter of Constitutional interpretation and political philosophy. Secessionists believed that their actions were condoned by the nature of the federated makeup of the United States and by the rights their states retained under the Constitution. While many of the Presbyterian clergy in the South were not in support of secession, they believed that their first political duty was to submit themselves to the separate states of which they were a part. Secession and its implications for the residents of the Southern states were purely political questions, and Hodge (sounding like Thornwell in 1859) did not believe that the church had legitimate authority to address this question and make pronouncements upon it as a church. Hodge did not agree with the political views of the secessionists, and he had in fact argued strongly against the right of secession in a January 1861 article in the *Princeton Review* entitled "The State of the Country." Even though Hodge believed that secessionist ideas were producing "manifold absurdities, abnormities, and evils," he did not believe that it was proper for the church to take a side formally and make a pronouncement on a purely political question.

The General Assembly responded to Hodge's protest by referencing Hodge's "State of the Country" article. Hodge himself, the assembly argued, had already waded into the arena of political pronouncements by commenting on the issue of secession in the *Review*, so who was he to criticize the assembly for following suit? Hodge had written in this article that:

> There are occasions when *political* questions *rise into the sphere of morals and religion*; when the rule of political action is to be sought, not in considerations of state policy, but in the law of God. . . . When the question to be decided turns on moral principles; when reason, conscience, and the religious sentiment are to be addressed, *it is the privilege and duty of all who have access in any way to the public ear* to endeavor

to allay unholy feeling, and *to bring truth to bear* on the minds of their fellow-citizens.

The General Assembly believed, against Hodge, that the outbreak of Civil War was just such an occasion that demanded a pronouncement from the church—that the political issue of war was inextricably linked to "moral principles" and was well within the bounds for what was appropriate for it to address. Both Hodge and the General Assembly agreed that "there are occasions when political questions rise into the sphere of morals and religion," but what Hodge chose to view as a matter of politics—Southern secession—the assembly chose to see as a matter of rebellion and sin.

Hodge's consistency with his own position would be challenged as the war unfolded. As the Civil War went on, Hodge seemed more comfortable with making political statements on the war and commending these statements as "moral" positions. In 1863 Hodge wrote an article for the *Princeton Review* entitled "The War" in which he declared:

> None but the frivolous can in this matter be indifferent or neutral. Men must take sides, and they must speak out. Silence is impossible. The feelings of the community do, and must, find expression at the family altar, from the pulpit, the forum, and the press, both secular and religious. The cobweb theories by which some among us attempted to muzzle the Church, speaking through her ministers, her religious journals, and ecclesiastical courts, have been swept away.

In the same article, Hodge commended the "moral duty" of loyalty and allegiance to "the national government in Washington." By the end of the war Hodge spoke on behalf of the Northern cause with religious conviction, and when the nation was still shocked by the news of President Lincoln's assassination, Hodge asserted that God had been on the side of the Union all along, stating: "Rebellion is a great crime . . . and the rebellion of the South was wanton and wicked."

Later in 1865 Hodge defended the "political" approach he had taken in his articles in the *Princeton Review*. He defended his partisanship in an article entitled "The *Princeton Review* and the State of our Country and the Church," stating that the events of the last four years "touched the conscience" and "called forth the discussion of the most important questions concerning the nature of our government." Given the gravity of the national events, Hodge defended how he had involved himself and the *Princeton Review* in political matters:

> Religious papers and ecclesiastical bodies have freely and earnestly expressed their conviction on all topics in the controversy. Even the special advocates of the spirituality of the church, who professed to have washed their hands of all secular concerns, have been the most pronounced in their opinions, and the most vehement and pertinacious in advocating them. It was neither to be expected nor desired that a quarterly journal, like the *Princeton Review*, whose province it is to discuss all questions of general interest, although specially devoted to theological and ecclesiastical subjects, should remain silent in the midst of this universal agitation.

While the *Review* took up political affairs during the war years, Hodge maintained that it had never veered into "party politics" but had only "advocated the national cause on national principles as a great moral and religious duty." Hodge took comfort in the fact that even the Southern Presbyterians who had advocated for the doctrine of the "spirituality" of the church filled their pulpits and religious journals with "political harangues": "If they may, with heart and soul, embrace the Southern cause and advocate Southern principles in the pulpit, in church-courts, and in religious journals, we may do the same for the national cause and national principles."

The Civil War justified incursions into politics by Presbyterian leaders in the North and the South, even among those who held to Thornwell's conception of the spirituality of the church. In the face of war, Hodge was perhaps not able to uphold his distinction between public policy and public morality consistently, but the position he strove to apply on the relation of the church and the state was relatively clear: the state is fundamentally distinct and separate from the church. The church should therefore not get involved in political affairs, but should proclaim the law of God to the world and speak boldly and dutifully on matters of public morality. Hodge attempted to strike a middle ground between Thornwell's more extreme notion of the spirituality of the church, on the one hand, and any course that would entangle the church in civil and political affairs, on the other. To "preach politics" is to "profane the pulpit," he would write. The "sacred desk" is not to be turned into "a rostrum for lectures on secular affairs." And yet at the same time, no one should attempt to "stop the mouth of the Church, and prevent her bearing her testimony to kings and rulers, magistrates and people, in behalf of the truth and law of God."

Conclusion

Charles Hodge's more than 130 articles in the *Princeton Review* give us insight into his thought on the church and the world around him. They also reveal how Hodge's doctrine of the church was shaped by the many political, ecclesiastical, and theological conflicts that pressed heavily upon him. Foundational to his doctrine of the church was his emphasis on the supernatural work of God in saving individuals and drawing them into his invisible church. This spiritual body was not to be overshadowed by other forms of visible society, be they ecclesiastical or civil. As important as the visible church and the state of the nation was to Hodge, the invisible "communion of saints" and the gospel were more important, and his doctrine of the church was carefully constructed to keep the evangelical gospel at the forefront. While Hodge believed the church should not get involved in political affairs, he himself struggled to remain above partisanship in the face of war. His distinction between politics and public morality was certainly tested, illustrating his own mature assertion that the relationship between the church and the state was "an exceedingly complicated and difficult subject."

8

James Waddel Alexander and Joseph Addison Alexander

I never go to Princeton without visiting [the graves of the Alexanders], and I never think of them without having my poor staggering faith in God and in regenerated humanity strengthened. Let us uncover our heads and thank God for them!

—Archibald Alexander Hodge

My son James has always been a sort of walking encyclopedia.

—Archibald Alexander

He [Joseph Addison Alexander] was considered by the young men in the Seminary as a regular prodigy—a perfect polyglot; and they believed he was master of so many tongues that the tower of Babel need never have suspended operations if he had only lived in those early ages and been appointed superintendent of the building.

—Rev. David Teese, Princeton Seminary class of 1837

I regard Dr. Joseph Addison Alexander as incomparably the greatest man I ever knew—as incomparably the greatest man our church has ever produced. His thorough orthodoxy, his fervent piety, humility, faithfulness in the discharge of his duties, and reverence for the Word of God, consecrated all his other gifts. He glorified the Word of God in the sight of his pupils beyond what any man I ever saw had the power of doing.

—Charles Hodge

Archibald Alexander's two sons, James Waddel Alexander and Joseph Addison Alexander, contributed greatly to Princeton Seminary and to the spread of its theology. While Archibald Alexander left the role of leading theologian to his surrogate son, Charles Hodge, his own sons also carried forward the tradition of piety and learning that he had begun. Both were extraordinary scholars and preachers. James excelled as a pastor, preacher, social reformer, author of tracts, and evangelist, while Addison (as he was often called) excelled as a linguist, exegete, and commentator on Scripture. Through tireless labors, both of these brothers spread the Old Princeton tradition to countless others through their teaching, preaching, writing, and service to both the seminary and the broader church.

James Waddel Alexander: Scholar, Preacher, and Writer

James Waddel Alexander was born on March 13, 1804, in Louisa County, Virginia, as the eldest of Archibald Alexander's seven children. He was named after his maternal grandfather, James Waddel, a blind Presbyterian minister famous for his preaching. James grew up under the tutelage of his father, who at the time of his birth was the president of Hampden-Sydney College.

James entered the College of New Jersey in 1817, five years after his family relocated to Princeton. As a college student, he was an average to below-average student who did not apply himself fully to his studies. In a letter to his lifelong friend John Hall, Alexander reflected on his missed opportunities as a college student:

My time spent in college ran sadly to waste; indeed, I cannot look back upon the opportunities of acquiring useful knowledge which I then abused without shame and regret. Like most brainless and self-conceited boys, I undertook to determine that such and such studies were of no importance, and made this an excuse for neglecting them, although the wise of every age have united in declaring their utility. I was foolish enough to suffer almost all my previous knowledge of classical literature to leak out *e cerebro*, and consequently I found myself a much greater dolt when I was invested with the title and immunities of an A. B., than when I entered as a humble Freshman.

Toward the end of his undergraduate studies, Alexander experienced the converting grace of God and "felt able to trust my whole hope and life upon the Lord." This spiritual change gave Alexander a new love of learning and had a profound impact on his studies. After graduating from Princeton College in 1820, he more than made up for what he had neglected as a student with two years of self-study. He mostly studied on his own, but he also devoted "an hour or two each day" to study the Latin and Greek classics with Charles Hodge, who had just become an instructor at the seminary. Hodge would say of James a few months after his death:

> Probably no minister in our Church was a more accomplished scholar. He was familiar with English literature in all periods of its history. He cultivated the Greek and Latin, French, German, Italian, and Spanish languages, not merely as a philologist, but for the treasures of knowledge and of taste which they contain. . . . He was an erudite theologian. Few men were more conversant with the writings of the early fathers, or more familiar with Christian doctrine in all its phases.

Through diligent and lifelong study, Alexander more than made up for what he had missed in his college years.

A few months after his conversion, Alexander came to the conviction that "I never can, in conscience, embrace any other profession [i.e., vocation] but 'the gospel of Christ.'" He entered Princeton Seminary in 1822 even though he questioned his natural abilities and potential for public speaking. Confiding in Hall, Alexander stated, "Though I never can be eloquent, yet God's Spirit may make me a useful preacher." While a student in the seminary, Alexander studied under his father, Samuel Miller, and Charles Hodge. After he completed his seminary training in 1824 he briefly served as a tutor at the College of New Jersey and then

FIG. 8.1

Timeline of James W. Alexander's Life

March 13, 1804	Born in Louisa County, Virginia.
1817	Began studies at the College of New Jersey .
1822	Began studies at Princeton Theological Seminary.
1824	Became a tutor at the College of New Jersey.
1827	Ordained by the Hanover Presbytery.
1827	Became a pastor in Charlotte Court House, Virginia.
1829	Became a pastor in Trenton.
1833	Served as editor of *The Presbyterian* in Philadelphia.
1833	Became professor of rhetoric and *belles lettres* at the College of New Jersey.
1838	Published *The Scripture Guide* with the American Sunday School Union.
1843	Awarded the doctor of divinity degree from Lafayette College.
1844	Became the pastor of Duane Street Presbyterian Church in New York City.
1849	Became professor of ecclesiastical history and church government at Princeton Seminary.
1851	Made his first trip to Europe.
1851	Became the pastor of Fifth Avenue Presbyterian Church in New York City.
1852	Published *Life of the Rev. Archibald Alexander*.
1854	Awarded the doctor of divinity degree from Harvard University.
1857	Made a second trip to Europe.
1858	Published *Discourses on Common Topics of Christian Faith and Practice*.
July 31, 1859	Died in Red Sweet Springs, Virginia.

as a licentiate under the Presbytery of New Brunswick. He was eventually called as a pastor in 1827 in Charlotte Court House in Louisa County, Virginia, in the very church where his father had also served. Alexander labored in this rural setting for four years until he accepted a call in 1829 to serve as the pastor of First Church in Trenton—then the only Presbyterian church in the city.

Alexander quickly excelled as a preacher, in spite of his earlier misgivings about his speaking abilities. He thought a great deal about his preaching and continually refined his method of preparation and delivery. In order for preaching to benefit its hearers in the long run, Alexander believed it should be expositional and full of biblical content. In 1838 Alexander would write: "Hortation seems to me to be the pulpit-error of the age, which has emasculated the church. . . . In this matter of preaching . . . I feel quite earnest, as believing that most of my earlier sermons were constructed on a wrong principle. I would be plain, but O, I wish I had *fed* my hearers with more truth, and given them less harangue." In his final decade of ministry, Alexander expressed his desire to give himself to "plainer, simpler, more instructive preaching." By the end of his life, Alexander's continual efforts to refine his homiletical approach had made him one of the leading preachers of his day. Charles Hodge said of him just after his death:

> The pulpit was his appropriate sphere. There all his gifts and graces, all his acquirements and experiences found full scope. Hence the remarkable variety which characterized his preaching; which was sometimes doctrinal, sometimes experimental, sometimes historical, sometimes descriptive or graphic, bringing scriptural scenes and incidents as things present before the mind; often exegetical, unfolding the meaning of the word of God in its own divine form. Hence, too, the vivacity of thought, the felicity of style, and fertility of illustration which were displayed in all his sermons. . . . He preached Christ in a manner which seemed to many altogether peculiar. He endeavored to turn the minds of men away from themselves, and to lead them to look only unto Jesus. . . . The great charm in his preaching, that to which more than to any thing else

its efficiency is to be referred, was his power over the religious affections. He not only instructed, encouraged, and strengthened his hearers, but he had, to a remarkable degree, the gift of calling their devotional feelings into exercise. . . . [He was] not the first of orators to hear on rare occasions, but the first of preachers to sit under, month after month and year after year.

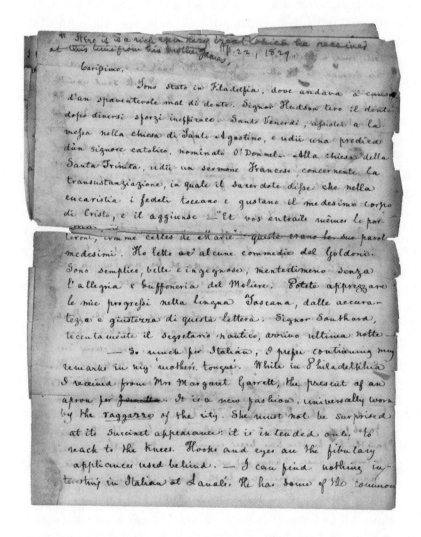

8.2 The Alexander brothers shared a love for words and languages. The first part of this 1829 letter from James to Addison is written in Italian.

Alexander hoped to produce a volume on preaching, and he kept a notebook of "homiletical paragraphs" for such a purpose. After his death in 1859, his brother Samuel Davies Alexander published these paragraphs, along with ten "letters to young ministers" and a few articles that had been published in the *Princeton Review* on the subject of preaching. This collection appeared in 1864 under the title *Thoughts on Preaching*.

Around the time Alexander began his ministry in Trenton in 1829, he became involved in assisting Charles Hodge with the *Princeton Review* and in regularly contributing to its contents. Hodge stated years later: "To no one are the pages of this *Review* more indebted than to the late Dr. James W. Alexander. His communications were always numerous, varied, and instructive. The articles furnished by him were, for the most part, devoted to historical, literary, and practical subjects." The titles of some of Alexander's articles in the *Princeton Review* reveal how wide-ranging his academic interests were: "Pascal's Provincial Letters" (1830), "The Use and Abuse of Systematic Theology" (1832), "Monosyllabic Languages of Asia" (1834), "Civilization of India" (1835), "French Presbyterianism" (1840), "Religious Instruction of the Negroes" (1845), "Life of Hegel" (1848), "Writings of Doddridge" (1857), and "Immediate Perception" (1859). Alexander would contribute more than one hundred articles to the *Princeton Review* over the course of his life.

While in Trenton, Alexander also began to write regularly for the American Sunday School Union, an interdenominational organization in Philadelphia devoted to producing literature for the growing Sunday school movement. Sunday school classes were designed to teach basic literacy and biblical truth to children with no other opportunities for attaining a basic education. While Alexander viewed preaching as "the grand instrument" for bringing the truth of God to society, he believed that, after preaching, "the religious education of youth is the most hopeful means of benefiting society." He wrote numerous books for the Sunday School Union in its efforts of what he called "holy propagandism." While his *Princeton Review* articles were written for an educated audience, he believed that what those in his day most needed was not books of deep learning but books of widespread popular appeal.

Writing to Hall in 1841, Alexander stated: "I grow in my conviction, that in our day, when men have a thousand things to read, and won't read long at any thing, the books which reach the mass and colour its opinions, are not books of research, but books of feeling, of point, even of eccentricity; books written with a gush, *currente calamo* [with a flying pen]." While a pastor in Trenton, Alexander resolved himself to "devote much of my time to babes' books." Shortly after this, he wrote to Hall:

> My aim is to do something before I die to reach the millions of youth in our land. I have made up my mind to go for the nursery practice. Let others take the fathers and grandfathers, if I can only make an impression on the children. This I wish to do by writing; and I am not sure . . . that I will not do more in this way, as a pastor, than if I were to set about it *ex professo* [as a profession].

Alexander was able to follow through on this desire, publishing more than thirty small books with the American Sunday School Union over the course of his life.

Alexander thrived as a pastor in Trenton and found great joy in serving Christ in the church. He wrote to Hall in 1832 of his happiness in ministry in Trenton:

> If I am to be a pastor, and nothing but necessity could make me willing to be anything else, I believe I have more openings to serve Christ here, than in any more laborious charge. . . . Some of my most delightful hours have been spent in sick-rooms, by dying-beds, or among poor, unlettered believers, or especially in rejoicing with them that do rejoice for the first time in Christ.

His delight was increased in Trenton by his marriage in 1830 to Elizabeth Cabell, with whom he would have seven children. Eventually the demands of ministry wore Alexander down, and he was forced to seek a change of pace. He resigned his position in 1833 and relocated to Philadelphia to serve as the editor of the *Presbyterian*, an Old School Presbyterian periodical. Before the year was out, however, Alexander was appointed to serve as the professor of rhetoric and *belles lettres* at the College of New Jersey, and he accepted this position, believing (according to Hall) that "a less vexatious and more retired department would be better suited to his taste and circumstances."

Between Princeton and New York

During the eleven years that Alexander served as a professor at the College of New Jersey, he continued to pursue ministry oppor-

8.3 James Waddel Alexander (1804–59).

tunities outside the classroom. He preached regularly and continued to write books and articles as well. While laboring as a teacher in Princeton, he confided to Hall in 1839: "I sigh to be a pastor, instead of a professor." In keeping with his desire, in 1844 he accepted a call to become the pastor of Duane Street Church in New York City. In this busy metropolitan center, which he considered a virtual "Babel," Alexander worked tirelessly for those under his charge and for those outside his church. He took a special interest in the children in his weekly catechism classes and published *Thoughts on Family Worship* in 1847 to strengthen the spiritual work being done among families.

Alexander's writing career continued while he was a pastor in New York, as the overcrowding and poverty he encountered there further encouraged him to address the needs of the poor in writing. While in Trenton he had published two volumes addressed to the working classes, entitled *The American Mechanic and Workingman* (1838–39). During his New York City pastorate he published in 1844 a book entitled *Good, Better, Best*, which was a fictional narrative that advanced his vision of reforming society through the spread of the gospel. In 1847 he published *A Manual of Devotion for Soldiers and Sailors* and also *Frank Harper*, a moral tale he wrote "out of pity to town boys." These writings illustrate Alexander's concern for the poor and his desire to apply Christianity to the issue of social reform. This concern for reforming society by spreading the gospel and biblical truth would be one of the major themes of his life.

In 1849 the General Assembly of the Presbyterian Church appointed Alexander to be the professor of ecclesiastical history and church government at Princeton Seminary, thus filling the vacancy created by Samuel Miller's retirement. Upon initially hearing of this decision of the General Assembly, Alexander was filled with great sorrow:

> This thing gives me unspeakable pain. . . . Any little unction of flattery in the appointment is instantly more than absorbed by the greatness of the question, and the anguish of a separation from my charge, if I accept. . . . To *know* that I might remain here would be a joy unspeakable. No dream of mine respecting the social happiness of the pastoral relation have failed to be realized: in this I compare it to marriage. I have tried academic and Princeton life, and was less happy.

After reluctantly accepting the appointment, Alexander soon came to believe that the change was really for his own good: "I have seen as clearly that my powers were tasked to a tension [while in New York] which must soon be fatal; while, in the steadier routine of teaching, I might last a season, with ordinary favor of Providence." Alexander was inaugurated into this position on November 20, 1849, and his inaugural address was entitled "The Value of Church History to the Theologian of Our Day." In this new role at Princeton, the pace of Alexander's activity was just as ceaseless as it had been before: "I have preached as much as usual ever since I left New York, besides the tough work of getting ready for classes." After a short while at the seminary, Alexander bemoaned the loss of his pastoral charge: "I did not leave pastoral life willingly; I foresaw the very evils I begin to feel; but they distress me more than I reckoned for. I miss my old women; and especially my weekly catechumens, my sick-rooms, my rapid walks, and my nights of right-down fatigue."

Alexander would only serve as a professor at Princeton Seminary for two years, as his former church in New York unexpectedly sought to re-call him in 1850. Greatly missing "pulpit and pastoral work" and feeling that his real talent was in preaching rather than teaching, Alexander left Princeton in 1851 for his old church, which had relocated and now went by the name Fifth Avenue Church. The church prevailed upon Alexander to "first recruit his health by a voyage" before returning to ministry in New York City. This he did, taking a five-month tour of Europe.

He began his ministry at Fifth Street in November 1851, just a few weeks after his father passed away in Princeton. He immediately took up the task of writing a biographical memoir of his father, a book which appeared the following year as *The Life of the Rev. Archibald Alexander, D.D.* His tireless labors in New York brought on the need for another extended trip to Europe in 1857. Alexander had the bad habit of working himself into physical exhaustion, which made these frequent changes of scenery necessary for him. A natural tendency toward melancholy also afflicted him throughout the course of his life, and his emotional afflictions were increased by the early deaths of four out of his seven children.

FIG. 8.4

Selected Works of James W. Alexander

Letters to a Younger Brother, 1834

The Scripture Guide, 1838

The American Mechanic and Workingman, 1838–39

Memoir of the Rev. James Waddel, 1844

Good, Better, Best, 1844

Thoughts on Family Worship, 1847

Life of the Rev. Archibald Alexander, D.D., 1852

The American Sunday School and Its Adjuncts, 1857

Discourses on Common Topics of Christian Faith and Practices, 1858

The Revival and Its Lessons, 1858

Sacramental Discourses, 1860, posthumously

Forty Years' Familiar Letters, 1860, posthumously

Thoughts on Preaching, 1862, posthumously

When Alexander returned to New York in 1857, he soon found the city in a state of unexpected revival, known later as the New York City Prayer Revival. Writing to Hall in 1858, Alexander declared: "You may rest assured that there is a great awakening among us." The story of this revival was recorded in Samuel Prime's *The Power of Prayer* (1859). Alexander immediately set up special prayer meetings and sessions where he was available to counsel those with questions about spiritual matters. He also worked at publishing a series of tracts suited for those affected by the revival, which he published in 1858 as *The Revival and Its Lessons*. The round-the-clock schedule he kept during the 1858 Prayer Revival seems to have utterly broken his health. By the spring of 1859, Alexander was so weak that removal from the city of New York seemed necessary. On his way to a place of rest and recuperation, Alexander contracted dysentery and died on July 31, 1859, in Red Sweet Springs, Virginia.

James W. Alexander had labored for the cause of Christ between Princeton and the pastorate for more than thirty years. While he possessed a scholar's mind, he remained a pastor at heart and was deeply concerned with the plight of the poor. Although he served as a professor at both Princeton College and Princeton Seminary, his greatest love was for simple people with spiritual needs. He shied away from theological polemics and ecclesiastical disagreements and was strongly committed to a form of evangelical catholicity that made him willing to work with a variety of evangelicals, especially when it came to alleviating the needs of the poor. While committed to Presbyterianism and Reformed orthodoxy, Alexander was wary of what he called the "Fanaticism of the Symbol" within his own circles, and he showed appreciation for a wide variety of evangelical authors. In 1830 he stated: "I have read eight out of the ten volumes of Wesley's works, and esteem him one of the greatest and best men that ever lived." Alexander attached himself to evangelical agencies like the American Sunday School Union, driven by his concern for the great numbers of the poor and untaught who stood in need of both spiritual and material help. Expressing his evangelical catholicity, Alexander once stated: "I feel as if I could join with any who would humbly unite in direct and kind efforts to save sinners and relieve human misery."

James W. Alexander is remembered today as an accomplished preacher, a broad-ranging scholar, a social reformer, and a faithful pastor. His lifelong love of learning and patient labor in the world of books and ideas made him a kind of "walking encyclopedia." He labored to promote gospel piety and the experiential warmth of truly religious affections. He wrote books for children, immigrants, and the working classes, he translated hymns like "O Sacred Head Now Wounded" from German into English, and he labored hard at evangelism. In his zeal for doing good, he finally burned himself out, and he ceased his labor on earth at the age of fifty-five. His personal links to the Old Princeton faculty, as well as his extensive work for the *Princeton Review*, put him right at the center of Old Princeton thought and life, and his own life epitomized the kind of pastor that the seminary was trying to produce.

Joseph Addison Alexander: The Making of a Bible Scholar

Named after the famous British essayist, Joseph Addison Alexander was born in Philadelphia on April 24, 1809. Addison was the third son of Archibald and Janetta Alexander and was five years younger than his brother James. In between the two theologians was another brother, William Cowper Alexander, who would become a lawyer and a distinguished politician in the state of New Jersey. A physician, Archibald Alexander Jr.; a daughter, Janetta Alexander; a clergyman, Samuel Davis Alexander; and a second lawyer, Henry Martyn Alexander were also born into the Alexander family. While Samuel Davies Alexander and William Cowper Alexander would contribute a few articles to the *Princeton Review*, it was James and Addison who carried forward their father's devotion to theological study and service to Old Princeton in the most significant ways.

When Archibald Alexander moved his family to Princeton in 1812, Addison was just three years old, and Princeton would remain his home for essentially the rest of his life. As a young boy, Addison showed incredible mental discipline and intellectual interest. From the time he learned how to read, he read all that he could get his hands on. He also possessed the innate ability to master the vocabulary and inner workings of foreign languages with great ease. Under the direction of his father, Addison began studying Latin at around the age of five, with his father daily presenting him with lists of Latin words and their English meanings on little slips of paper. By the time he was six, Addison's father taught him the Hebrew alphabet and presented him with Hebrew words for memorization as well. When he turned ten, his father gave him a simplified Hebrew grammar that he had composed solely for his son's benefit. Arabic and Persian were soon added once Hebrew was mastered, and by the age of fourteen Addison had read through the Koran in Arabic. Greek, Spanish, French, Italian, German, Turkish, Danish, Portuguese, Coptic, Aramaic, Syriac, Polish, Malay, Chinese, and others would also follow! Added to his love of languages was a love of music, and one of Addison's favorite pastimes from boyhood on was playing the flute. In spite of his early shyness and attachment to books, Addison was by all accounts sociable, good-natured, and good-humored.

After short stints in a series of preparatory schools, Addison entered the College of New Jersey at the age of fifteen. He graduated at the head of his class in 1826 after only two years of study. He turned

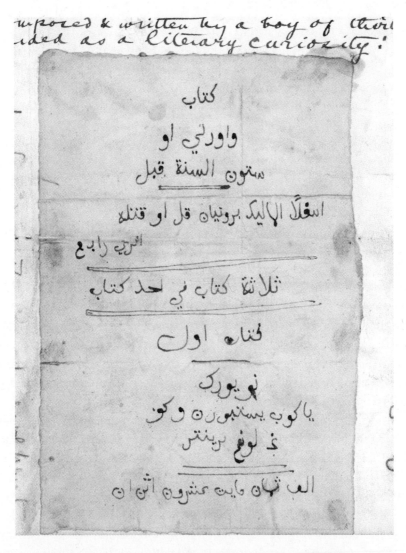

8.5 This 1822 manuscript is Joseph Addison Alexander's Arabic translation of the title page to Sir Walter Scott's 1814 novel *Waverly*. Addison was thirteen years old when he made this translation.

down an appointment as a tutor at the college in order to devote the next three years to a wide course of reading and independent study in a number of languages. One contemporary described this course of language self-study as follows:

> Through his familiarity with the Latin he, of course, easily acquired French, Italian, and Spanish, and he soon added German. It was his custom for many years to pursue his studies in all the languages that have been mentioned, daily. During his nineteenth year he read entire in the original languages the first eight books of the Bible, the Koran, Don Quixote, Gerusalemme Liberata, Luther's version of the Gospels, besides portions of other works. Among his English readings about this time were Coke upon Littleton, Vattel, Kent's and Blackstone's Commentaries, Chitty on Pleading, the Federalist, and Dugald Stewart's Philosophy. Not satisfied with his College Greek he recommenced the study of that language from the grammar, and read afresh the poets and historians critically. He [also] added the dialect of modern Athens to that of the classical Greek.

Of all his early studies, his primary areas were in "Oriental studies" and "Asiatic languages." Addison began writing articles at this time for what would become the *Princeton Review*, as well as for Robert Walsh's *American Quarterly Review* and the *National Gazette and Literary Register*. Addison's linguistic abilities and acquired knowledge of languages and literature made him much desired as a teacher. After his three years of self-study, Addison temporarily took a position as a teacher of Latin, history, geography, and composition and boarded at Edgehill High School, a college preparatory school that opened in 1829 just outside Princeton.

Addison experienced the converting grace of God while a teacher at Edgehill in the early months of 1830. It was the first time he had lived away from home, and although he had agreed intellectually with the truth of the gospel and lived a moral life while under his parents' oversight, he had not experienced the regenerating grace of God. According to his eulogist Robert Baird, Addison had long been "a punctual and serious attendant" upon religious services, Scripture reading, and prayer, but before his conversion in 1830 "there was no special manifestation of deep interest in religion as a personal matter."

Addison recorded in his journal in January1830 that he had been "deeply engaged in a study new to me, and far more important than all others—the study of the Bible and my own heart." From the same journal entry, Addison stated:

> I humbly trust that I am not what I was. I have still my old propensities to evil, but I have also a new will co-existing with the old, and counteracting and controlling it. My views respecting study are now

FIG. 8.6

Timeline of Joseph Addison Alexander's Life

April 24, 1809	Born in Philadelphia, Pennsylvania.
1824	Began studies at the College of New Jersey.
1826	Graduated from the College of New Jersey.
1829	Awarded master of arts degree by the College of New Jersey.
1830	Experienced conversion while a teacher at Edgehill High School.
1830	Became adjunct professor of ancient languages and literature at the College of New Jersey.
1833	Embarked on year-long study trip to Europe.
1834	Began instructing students in Semitic languages at Princeton Theological Seminary as Charles Hodge's assistant.
1835	Appointed professor of Oriental and biblical literature at Princeton Theological Seminary.
1839	Ordained by the New Brunswick Presbytery.
1845	Awarded doctor of divinity degree from Franklin and Marshall College.
1851	Became professor of biblical and ecclesiastical history at Princeton Theological Seminary.
1859	Became professor of Hellenistic and New Testament literature at Princeton Theological Seminary.
January 28, 1860	Died in Princeton, New Jersey.

changed. Intellectual enjoyment has been my idol heretofore; now my heart's desire is that I may live no longer to myself, but in Him in whom I have everlasting life. God grant that the acquisitions that I have been allowed to make under the influence of selfish motives may be turned to good account as instruments for the promotion of His glory.

Addison himself believed that God had used the "removal from my father's house" in the "directing of my attention to the subject of religion." The following month he recorded reading from Augustine's *Confessions*, Edwards's *Religious Affections*, John Owen's *Spiritual-Mindedness*, a biography of Henry Martyn, and the letters of John Newton as he continued to explore the depths of both his sin and the grace shown to him in his conversion. In the spring of that same year, on his twenty-ninth birthday, Addison wrote the following in his journal:

I desire with few words, but with a fixed heart, to consecrate myself, soul, and body, now and forever, to the God who made me. With this intent I now most solemnly renounce the service of the devil, my late master; abandoning not only certain sins, but *sin* itself; with all its pleasures, honours and emoluments; desiring and beseeching God never more to suffer me to taste the least enjoyment of a sinful nature. I also bind my conscience in the presence of the jealous God who searches the heart and cannot look upon iniquity without abhorrence, to watch against all temptation; and, if necessary, to resist unto blood striving against sin. At the same time I renounce all dependence upon any thing I may be, do or suffer, here or hereafter, as a ground of deliverance from hell—trusting for the mercy in the cross of Christ. And having thus discharged myself from all allegiance to the Prince of Darkness, I submit myself to God in Christ; desiring and consenting to be His forever, to do and suffer all his will, in the joyful hope of an eternal recompense. And now, having learned by sad experience, the deceitfulness of my own heart, the weakness of my resolution and the craft of Satan, I throw myself at thy feet, O Lord! And claim the promise of thy strengthening and illuminating grace to aid me in the performance of these vows. . . . For the sake of thy dear Son impart to me the gift of thy free Spirit to purify, enlighten and transform my heart! Through life may I be thine, and in death, O Lord, in death be thou my God! Again, and again, and again I solemnly devote myself to God the Father, God the Son, and God the Holy Ghost; desiring nothing, hoping nothing, fearing nothing if I may but be accepted in the name of Christ! Amen.

After half a year at the Edgehill school, Addison became in July 1830 a professor of ancient languages at the College of New Jersey in Princeton. Given his mastery of ancient languages and literature, teaching at the college was quite easy for him, and he altered only slightly the pace of his own personal studies and writing. He published that year his first book, *A Geography of the Bible*, for the American Sunday School Union and began to study subjects which he believed would help prepare him for pastoral ministry, including biblical criticism, systematic theology, philosophy, and church history. He also began a serious study of the Bible in its original languages and committed to memory the books of Psalms (in Hebrew and English) and Hebrews (in Greek and English), as well as other large portions of Scripture. In the midst of these studies, he also determined to make the hour between eight and nine each evening "sacred to devotion" and constrained himself to read only the Scriptures and "practical divinity" on Sundays. In this way, Addison progressed in both knowledge and godliness while laboring as a young college professor.

Addison's pursuit of godliness and knowledge of the Scriptures virtually consumed him at this point in his life. According to his nephew and biographer, his desire for piety and for understanding the Scriptures went hand in hand:

> The cultivation of personal piety, in the light of the inspired word, was now [in 1831] with him the main object that he had in life. The next most prominent goal that he set before himself was the interpretation of the original scriptures; for their own sake, and for the benefit of a rising ministry, as well as for the gratification he took in the work. The Bible was to him the most profoundly interesting book in the world. It was in his eyes not merely the only source of true and undefiled religion, but also the very paragon among all remains of human genius. . . . But more than this, the Bible was the chief object of his personal enthusiasm; he was fond of it; he loved it; he was proud of it; he exulted in it. It occupied his best thoughts by day and by night.

It was his meat and drink. . . . He succeeded perfectly in communicating this delightful zeal to others. His pupils all concur in saying that "he made the Bible glorious" to them.

Addison's spiritual experience was deepened at this point in his life by the fuller understanding of the grace of the gospel that he received from reading the autobiography of Thomas Halyburton. He noted in his journal:

Read a considerable part of Halyburton's life with avidity and astonishment. . . . On one head particularly I have been much edified. When my conscience has been wounded by relapses into sin, I have always been tempted to sink down into a sullen apathy, or else to wait a day or two before approaching God again. It seemed to me, on such occasions, that it would be presumptuous and insolent to ask God to forgive me *on the spot*. I never knew why I thought so until Halyburton told me. I had been trusting in my abstinence from sin, instead of Christ's atonement, so that when surprised and vanquished by temptation, I felt that my foundation was removed, my righteousness gone, and I had no righteousness wherewith to purchase favor. It pleased God this afternoon to use the memoir as an instrument in fixing on my mind a strong conviction that the only reasonable course is to come at once, and ask forgiveness in the name of Christ. . . . God's chief end in dealing with men's souls is not to discipline them nor save them; but to promote his glory. Now He chooses to glorify all his attributes together—His mercy as well as His justice. To distrust the extent of his forgiving mercy through Christ Jesus, therefore, is an insult. It is in vain that the sinner talks about his unworthiness and the greatness of his sins. Poor wretch;—if God thought of your unworthiness you might well despair; but it is to glorify Himself that He invites you! You may be sure, therefore, that He will receive you. This is an humbling and delightful doctrine.

As Addison carried out his work at the college, he also began his production of what would turn into a steady stream of articles. He had first begun writing journal articles while a teacher at Edgehill. Many of his earliest articles related to his study of Arabic and his analysis of the Koran. Since he had been reading Arabic and other Semitic languages from the time he was nine or ten, he had become a capable "Orientalist" by the time he was in his early twenties, possessing the ability not only of reading Hebrew and Arabic but also of writing it with ease.

In 1833 Addison decided to resign his position at Princeton College and follow in the footsteps of Charles Hodge to study abroad in Europe and become acquainted with European scholarship firsthand. Hodge had made his two-year journey to Europe less than seven years before, and he sent letters along with Addison to introduce him to the European scholars he had befriended. Setting off in April 1833, Addison followed largely in Hodge's footsteps, spending time in London, Paris, Geneva, Halle, and Berlin. While in Europe, he too developed a warm acquaintance with August Tholuck and heard E. W. Hengstenberg, Johann Neander, Friedrich Schleiermacher, and numerous others. While in London he heard Edward Irving preach and witnessed the exercise of "tongues" that had made Irving a sensation. Alexander wrote that his opinion of this experience was one of "unmingled contempt" and stated that "everything which fell from Irving's lips was purely flat and stupid. . . . I was confirmed in my former low opinion of him founded on his writings." He also had the opportunity to speak with General Lafayette in France and J. H. Merle d'Aubigne in Switzerland.

When Addison returned to America in May 1834, he found that he had been appointed as an assistant instructor at Princeton Seminary. Without hesitating, Alexander accepted the appointment and served as Charles Hodge's assistant, instructing seminary students in Semitic languages and literature. Addison took up his new post with great conscientiousness, and he wrote the following in his journal in the early days of his seminary professorship:

> Resolutions. 1. I will try to perform every act of my life with conscious regard to religious motives. I will eat, drink, talk, study, teach, write, suffer, not only as a Christian, but with Christian affections, with the love of Christ in my heart. 2. I will try to live for a death-bed, and for eternal life. I will try to remember what it is I am living for, and to form the habit of remembering it always—not at certain seasons only. 3. I will try to be tender-hearted and to love my fellow-creatures. I will deny myself, in order to cherish the affections. I will try to show that I am no misanthrope. 4. I will try to maintain an humble spirit; I will try to live as though it matters not whether I be known or unknown—honoured or despised. I will try to rejoice in the eminence of others. It is hard, but

I will try it in the strength of my Redeemer. But, O my Lord, Thou knowest I may try forever, yet in vain, without Thy grace! 5. I will try to hate sin. I will think and think about my Saviour's sufferings, till my heart is broken. I shall fail a hundred and a hundred times; but I will still persist till my proud heart yields, and I become a little child.

Addison's noted piety and accomplishments as a scholar had clearly fit him to be a member of the seminary faculty, and he would remain as a seminary professor in Princeton until his death some twenty-five years later.

The Unusually Gifted Professor

Addison Alexander's brilliance as a scholar made him an unusually gifted professor, but it did not make him the most patient or compassionate of teachers. Given the ease with which he was able to handle languages, he did not easily bear with the natural slowness with which other minds usually approach a new linguistic field of study. His early work in the classroom was noted for its severity, with "unforbearing reproofs and sarcasms" resulting from his impatience. He was especially intolerant of perceived laziness in his students. Alexander sought to resist his natural tendency toward harshness, and according to Charles Hodge: "If any manifestation of impatience escaped him in the recitation room, they [his students] were sure that the next prayer he made in their presence would show that he sought forgiveness of such lapses from his Father in Heaven." He gradually grew to be a more patient teacher, and his naturally affable and amiable disposition became more and more felt by his students as his years at the seminary progressed. In the words of his nephew and biographer, "gradually he became more and more tolerant and gentle, until toward the last, his steady meekness was more noticeable than the occasional flashes of his first or mistaken resentment." For the brightest and most diligent students, Alexander was a dearly loved teacher, and he often formed extra classes for the few students who wanted instruction in Arabic, Syriac, and Aramaic. Alexander's powerful command of the language and meaning of Scripture made his exegetical lectures especially instructive. One his students, Dr. James Ramsey, stated of him:

As an exegete, I hardly know how he could be excelled. His analyses, with which he introduced each exegetical lecture, so concise, so clear, so simple, were themselves far better than most commentaries. . . . To his lectures on the first ten chapters of Isaiah I owe more than to all the other instructions received in the Seminary, as to the method of analyzing and expounding Scripture. . . . I had not got through with the first chapter of Isaiah with Dr. Alexander's lectures till I felt as if I had become conscious almost of a new power. Every passage he touched seemed to be suddenly lighted up with a new beauty and glory, and often a single remark would be so suggestive that it seemed at once to pour light all over the Bible, to bring up into new and striking association other truths and passages, and to stimulate the mind to the highest activity, and fill it with wonder at the amazing fullness of God's word. . . . Another striking trait of his exegetical lectures was that his faith in the simple statements of the Bible was so childlike and so perfect. This reverence for the sacred text was one of his noblest qualifications for an instructor in these times.

Charles Hodge stated of his teaching that "the minds of his pupils were expanded under his influence, at the same time that they were elevated." In Hodge's words, "He made the Bible glorious to them." Alexander's abilities as a scholar and a teacher were almost immediately noted by the General Assembly. In 1835 they appointed him adjunct professor of Oriental and biblical literature at the seminary, but Alexander would not accept this promotion until 1838 after having taught for a few more years as an assistant to Hodge.

In addition to preparing young men for ministry in the classroom, Addison also sought to benefit the church at large through diligently writing on biblical and theological topics. For a period of time he served as a coeditor of the *Princeton Review*, and he would produce more than ninety articles for it altogether on topics as varied as "Arabic and Persian Lexicography" (1832), "Hengstenberg's Christology" (1836), "Melanchthon's Letters" (1838), "The Official Powers of the Primitive Presbyters" (1849), "Fairbairn's Typology" (1851), and "Prayer and Preaching" (1859). In 1836 he began to work on what would turn into a two-volume exegetical commentary on the book of Isaiah. In writing these commentaries, his youngest brother recounted how he caused to be made two standing desks reaching from one end to the other of his large study. . . . I should estimate that these stands held about fifty volumes, all of them open. He would first pass down the line where the commentaries were, then go to the lexicons, then to other books; and when he was through, he would hurry to the table at which he wrote, write rapidly for a few minutes, and then return again to the books: and this he would repeat again and again, for ten or twelve hours together. While this was in progress, nothing seemed to be an interruption. He would answer every question asked, or would stop and give some amusing description of what he had seen or heard on a trip to New York or Philadelphia, and then go on with his work.

When *The Earlier Prophecies of Isaiah* finally appeared in 1846 and *The Later Prophecies of Isaiah* the following year, Addison's international reputation as an evangelical Bible scholar and exegete became well established. He went on to publish three exegetical volumes on the Psalms in 1850, with commentaries on Acts and Mark also appearing during his lifetime.

Fig. 8.7

Selected Works of Joseph Addison Alexander

A Geography of the Bible, 1830

The Earlier Prophecies of Isaiah, 1846

The Later Prophecies of Isaiah, 1847

The Psalms Explained, 3 vols., 1850

Primitive Church Officers, 1851

The Acts of the Apostles Explained, 1857

The Gospel according to Mark Explained, 1858

Sermons, 1860, posthumously

The Gospel according to Matthew Explained, 1861, posthumously

Notes on New Testament Literature and Ecclesiastical History, 1861, posthumously

In 1838 Addison took steps to begin what would turn into a well-received preaching ministry, becoming a "probationer" under the

Presbytery of New Brunswick that April. His early efforts at preaching were eagerly anticipated, and his gift for preaching shone from the very beginning. After he was ordained the following year, he preached regularly and was frequently called away to preach in New York and Philadelphia. His sermons were noted for their eloquence and arresting originality. According to Charles Hodge, Addison's sermons "were sure to be original, evangelical, forcible, elegant, and tending to practical effect upon the conscience; sometimes transparently didactic, sometimes brilliant in imagination, but sometimes also too entirely devoted to instruction and careless of dress to meet the standard of popularity." His sermon style and format were quite varied, with some sermons being exegetical and others being more topical or devotional. Sometimes he would preach extemporaneously without any notes at all, but more often than not he would use a full manuscript in his preaching. At times he would earnestly read a full manuscript with scarcely a gesture or a look at the audience, and yet even in reading, he was eloquent and captivating. One of his students said of him:

> His preaching was to me exceedingly attractive and impressive. The style was so fine, and the order so lucid. The truth was so clearly and boldly stated, and the fervor so genuine and animating. . . . He was always logical and argumentative; always rhetorical and imaginative; always fervent and solemn. . . . No preacher ever impressed me so much with the sense of his *power*—a power both intellectual and spiritual—both in the man and in the message.

Ashbel Green similarly stated that Alexander's preaching "delighted while it instructed and impressed his hearers." Green also stated that:

> Dr. Alexander's discourses, even those which were most simple and least elaborate . . . always bore marks of his transcendent genius, which eschewed the commonplace paths trodden by ordinary men, and hewed out a fresh passage for itself. Though he dealt with old-fashioned truths, they were always presented in a new light, or approached by unexpected ways, or exhibited in novel forms. I knew no greater intellectual treat than to hear him pouring out his massive thoughts in

that vigorous English of his, which set forth his conceptions as sharply and clearly as if they were pictured on canvas, while he carried you up some mighty climax, or exposed the follies and inconsistencies of unbelief, or turned his withering sarcasm upon open opposers or false-hearted friends of true religion, or unfolded some of the grand themes of God's Word.

Two volumes of Addison's sermons (published posthumously in 1860) have left a record of his abilities in sermon-writing as well.

When his brother James left Princeton seminary in 1851 to return to his pastorate in New York, Addison took over James's lectures in Old and New Testament history. Seeing his versatility as a scholar, the General Assembly that year made Addison the professor of biblical and ecclesiastical history at Princeton Seminary. This appointment was not entirely favorable to Addison. In his words, he disliked "leaving the *terra firma* of inspired truth for the mud and sand of patristic learning." By the middle of 1852, however, he reported to his brother that "my mind is now at ease as to my professorship" and "I am quite willing to remain for the present as I am." As a professor of ecclesiastical history, he poured himself into his work and wrote up extensive lectures notes, even though the area of church history never fully suited him. He greatly admired the work of Philip Schaff, and Schaff sought to secure Addison's collaboration in writing a church history for English speakers. Addison turned Schaff down but encouraged him to produce what would later become Schaff's famous *History of the Christian Church* (1858–92).

Alexander remained in this post until 1859, when he successfully petitioned to be appointed professor of Hellenistic and New Testament literature. He was not to hold this position for long, however. After Addison's brother James passed away in July 1859, Addison suffered from severe depression and sharply declining health. In November of that year he developed a pulmonary hemorrhage after many months of visible decline. For the last month of his life, Alexander was confined to his home. Anticipating that death was near, he nurtured and comforted his soul with Adolphe Monod's *Les Audieux* [*Farewells*], John Flavel's writings, and hymns by Watts and Wesley. Leaving his study and his books for one last time, Addison Alexander fell asleep and died peacefully in his bed on January 28, 1860.

Although he possessed a massive intellect and was a scholar like few others, Addison Alexander lived and died as a man who walked with God. As such he impressed upon his students not only the intellectual riches that come from study but the incomparable riches for the soul that are found in knowing and experiencing the grace of God in one's heart. One seminary student stated that:

> The remark was often made that Dr. Addison was a man that walked with God, and was evidently growing in grace. His preaching, his lectures, and his prayers gave proof of this. And on all proper occasions he would converse on the subject of experimental religion with a zest and interest that showed how much he meditated upon it, and how he sought to have his own heart brought under its full power.

8.8 Joseph Addison Alexander (1809–60).

While Addison Alexander never attained the level of fame appropriate to his remarkable gifts, Charles Hodge once called him "incomparably the greatest man I ever knew." This greatness was derived not only from his linguistic abilities and scholarly attainments but also from his "fervent piety," which was evident to those who knew him.

Conclusion

James Waddel and Joseph Addison Alexander both embodied the Princeton ideal of learning and piety. Both of the brothers were highly educated scholars, committed churchmen, and accomplished preachers. While James focused on bringing biblical instruction to children and to the poor, Addison was more devoted to biblical studies and exegetical scholarship. While James served largely as a pastor, Addison served largely as a professor, and yet both brothers cared deeply about the experience of personal piety in their own hearts and in the hearts of those they sought to serve. Their numerous books and articles spread the Princeton theology far and wide, and they continue to testify today to the unique blend of deep piety and rich scholarship that was to be found among so many at Old Princeton.

9

OLD PRINCETON AND NINETEENTH-CENTURY AMERICAN CULTURE: JAMES W. ALEXANDER'S *FORTY YEARS' FAMILIAR LETTERS*

The letters of Dr. Alexander, of which we have spoken, are written in an unaffected, lively, sketchy manner, and present topics and opinions of permanent literary or social interest on every page. Their value to the young student is great; they exhibit the steps by which the scholar and divine ascended to an eminence in learning and piety; the facts of the day, as they are occasionally noted, show the observation of a sympathetic spectator, while the sentiment of the whole is animated by a kindly glow of humor.

—Cyclopaedia of American Literature (1881)

There is a gold mine of insights about the Princeton theologians' participation in American culture in J. W. Alexander's Forty Years' Familiar Letters.

—John W. Stewart

In 1879 John Frelinghuysen Hageman published his monumental *History of Princeton and Its Institutions*. In this work, Hageman lauded the published correspondence of James W. Alexander with these words:

The literary world may be challenged to produce any correspondence—any familiar letter-writing equal to this. That any gentleman could almost daily in every variety of circumstances . . . snatch his facile pen and dash off such classic gems as this correspondence discloses, is wonderful in the extreme. Time will add to the fame and worth of these letters. The wit and humor—the brilliant sallies of genius—the sound and sensible sentiments—the tender commendation, and the caustic reproof—which characterize nearly every page, will not allow this correspondence or its author to be laid aside and forgotten.

Sadly, Hageman's prediction has not proven true. The two large volumes that make up Alexander's *Forty Years' Familiar Letters* have all but been "laid aside and forgotten." In the same year that Hageman published his work, a memorial service was held for the Alexanders at Princeton Seminary, and at this gathering Theodore Cuyler lauded Alexander's "celebrated" and "auriferous" volumes of letters, stating:

James Hamilton, of London, once said to me that a perusal of them was the next best thing to a visit to America. The most brilliant Bishop in the Methodist Church also said to me that he regarded it as one of the dozen most remarkable works yet produced in this country! To the future historian it will be as valuable a picture of the times as Pepys' Diary and Burnet's Memoirs were to Lord Macaulay.

At the very outset of its publication in 1860, reviewers in a variety of periodicals noted the importance of Alexander's *Forty Years' Familiar Letters* for future historians. A reviewer in the *New Englander and Yale Review* stated that "the peculiarity of these letters is that they are flooded with the news of the day and the writer's comments upon them." Similarly, a reviewer in the *Mercersburg Review* stated that this published work will "grow more and more valuable as years elapse, because it gives a peculiarly life-like picture of the period it covers."

This assessment of Alexander's letters was shared by Charles Hodge as well. It was at Hodge's instigation that John Hall edited and compiled the more than eight hundred letters that Alexander had written to him over the course of their forty-year friendship. Two months after Alexander's death, Hodge wrote to Hall, urging him to publish this treasure trove of letters. Hodge believed that these letters were "of such peculiar interest and value" that they deserved to be published. He stated: "This would be a unique work. It would be a literary, a theological, a religious and a conversational history of the past forty years."

Alexander began writing letters to Hall in 1819 as a fifteen-year-old boy living in Princeton, and he continued writing until just a few weeks before his death in 1859 at the age of fifty-five. Hall was a few years younger than Alexander, and Alexander seemingly gave Hall his musings without a thought that they would someday be published. Regarding the style of Alexander's letters, a reviewer in the July 1860 *Methodist Quarterly Review* noted:

> The letters are the most perfectly unstudied effusions of the moment, aiming at no arrangement of topic, and running through a rapid change of disconnected subjects, without the formality of paragraphs. Their style is slightly above the conversational, and furnish opinions, feelings, and free remarks on surrounding events or living characters as they occur to the writer's thoughts.

Moving abruptly from topic to topic, Alexander wrote to Hall with a gushing pen on a wide variety of subjects, ranging from Dickens's novels to the local weather.

The letters are arranged chronologically, with chapter breaks inserted by Hall to mark the different phases of Alexander's life. The second volume contains an appendix with Alexander's ordination charge to Hall and an additional number of letters that Alexander wrote to Hall while journeying through Europe. Hall's explanatory footnotes are few, so at times the meaning of Alexander's comments remains unclear. While much personal material is contained in these letters, the collection opens up the whole cultural world of antebellum America. Alexander's letters not only give us a firsthand and candid account of this time period, but they also reveal to us how he, as a Princeton theologian, thought and interacted critically with various aspects of his contemporary world.

This chapter will examine statements made in Alexander's *Forty Year's Familiar Letters* that reveal his thinking on three major topics: politics, social reform, and slavery.

A Federalist in the Age of Jackson

As a young pastor in southern Virginia, Alexander expressed his support for president John Quincy Adams in numerous letters written to Hall between 1827 and 1828. Referring to himself as "an Adams man," Alexander mentioned to Hall how out of step his politi-

9.1 J. W. Alexander's more than eight hundred letters to John Hall were published at the instigation of Charles Hodge, who believed they would serve as "a literary, a theological, a religious and a conversational history" of the years between 1819 and 1859.

cal sentiments were with those around him: "I do not think it by any means incumbent upon me as an Adams man, or consistent as a preacher, to talk much about politics, but I am sorely vexed from day to day at the enormities of the opposition." In Virginia, it seemed to Alexander there was almost universal support for the candidate whom Adams narrowly defeated in the 1824 election, Andrew Jackson. Alexander confided to Hall in 1827 how opposed he was to these pro-Jacksonian sentiments:

> I take a lively interest in the improvements of our country, notwithstanding my being hemmed in with political heretics . . . I take no trouble to conceal my sentiments, although I enter into no disputes. Although I hear incessant eulogies of General Jackson, yet I am utterly at a loss to discover among the wagon-loads of chaff which they pour forth about him one grain of real qualification for the Presidency.

Andrew Jackson, for many in this time period, embodied the populist, democratic, and egalitarian idealism that was sweeping American social and political life in the 1820s–1840s. Called by some "the Age of Jackson," this period was one which elevated the common man to new positions of political power and influence in society. Resistant to these changes, Alexander and others at Princeton, like Charles Hodge, held to the older views of the Federalists, who preferred a certain level of social stratification and social hierarchy. Richard Carwardine has described the Federalists in these words: "Guided by a vision of a hierarchical society, and shivering at the tremors of emerging democracy, Federalists valued religion, education, and the law as the means of maintaining a harmonious and controllable social order." Alexander's Federalist (and later Whig) outlook made him critical of the populism and egalitarian ideals of what he called "this perverse and Jacksonian generation."

Instead of being swept up by the enthusiasm for Jackson around him, Alexander expressed to Hall his appreciation of the "simple dignity" of John Quincy Adams. In a deeper way, however, Alexander was drawn to the political thought of Adams's father, John Adams. In 1829, Alexander wrote to Hall of his growing appreciation for the second president of the United States:

I have been reading John Adams's Defence [sic] of the American Constitution, and have found it to be a very interesting work. I am especially pleased with his abstract of the history of the Italian republic, which I have never found so clearly given in any other book. It has almost set me upon studying Italian, and reading Machiavel, Guicciardini, Malavolti, etc., in the original. A general survey of all history, with reference to the principles of our constitution, would be a great and useful work. It seems to me that our Colleges ought to have lectures upon that very subject. The simple principles assumed as fundamental by Adams, have really cast a new light upon all the history I have read. The annals of all nations seem to be a commentary upon the doctrine that the three primary forms of government [monarchy, aristocracy, democracy] must be so tempered and balanced in every government, as to check the extravagance of each.

Although Adams had died in 1826 and Adams's Federalist Party had dissolved in 1820, Alexander continued to hold to the political ideas that were more popular in his father's generation than in his own. Charles Hodge was in hearty agreement with Alexander's political views, but many in his Princeton circle of family and friends were not. Writing to Hall in 1828, Alexander stated:

I suppose Archibald [Alexander's younger brother] in the plentitude of his Jacksonianism has informed you that Princeton is ornamented with a Hickory pole, in the most conspicuous part of the village. It is strange to see with what phrenetic zeal the Hickories are traversing all the country. Invasion or civil war could scarcely produce a greater fermentation among the populace. My fear is that New Jersey will give her vote for the Chieftain; and indeed, further, that he will be our President.

Even though New Jersey narrowly gave its vote to Adams in 1828, Jackson won in an electoral landslide, much to the disappointment of Hodge and Alexander.

In Alexander's mind, the spirit behind Jacksonian democracy was the same secular, godless, and discontented spirit that lay behind the French Revolution. Alexander's letters to Hall contain a number of references to the ongoing political and social upheavals that were yet taking place in France. In Alexander's mind the "ultra-democracy" of the Jacksonians in America would lead to the same sorts of destruction and violence if not kept in check. In 1829, Alexander would confess to Hall his conviction concerning the "abomination of absolute democracy." In 1836, he would write: "Democracy and I are less and less friends every day I live." And again, in 1843: "I am opposed to all ultra-democracy, of which the very extreme, I take it, is to make our tribute of respect dependent on mere popular like or dislike."

Out of step with the political currents in America, Alexander expressed appreciation for the older British conservative Edmund Burke. Writing to Hall in 1827, Alexander stated:

> I have been looking over Burke's works again and especially his Reflections on the French Revolution. Surely he is the prince of English writers. . . . The profundity of his reasoning, the political sagacity of his views, the rich contexture of his language, all render him the most fascinating and commanding of all writers on Government.

Alexander, like Burke and Adams, believed that the will of the common people in any given society should be balanced against the will of the educated and the wealthy. But since American society had no nobility, he was resigned to accept democracy in America as an unavoidable necessity. Writing to Hall in 1836, he stated: "Nothing else [but democracy] would do for a country like ours. It must be several ages yet before we have a noblesse, or a literary caste; and until we have, nominal aristocracy would be . . . ridiculous."

Alexander ultimately believed that all forms of government would eventually become oppressive unless God was duly recognized as Sovereign in society. Every political good in the American system— even the cherished good of American freedom—was insufficient to preserve a peaceful and free society. In a sermon called "Our Modern Unbelief," published toward the end of his life, Alexander stated:

> The great and invaluable gift of freedom furnishes no safeguard [for society] here, unless it be coupled with true religion. Freedom is only a condition, under which men's principles act. If those principles are destructive, freedom is but an open door to ruin. The absolute freedom of a thoroughly immoral people, "hateful

and hating one another," would be nothing short of hell. Indeed, the instinct of self-preservation does not allow men to remain long in any state approaching this; for, in dread of one another, they are fain to take refuge under the protective shadow of military domination or imperial tyranny.

It was this realization that kept Alexander's active political involvement at a minimum. He understood that political answers could not solve what are at heart moral and spiritual problems. And yet, this did not stop him from writing to Hall often about political and national affairs. He may not have thought it "consistent as a preacher to talk much about politics," yet his letters to Hall reveal that he thought a great deal about political affairs. His letters also show just how out of step Alexander and many of the leading Princetonians were with the prevailing winds of American political culture.

Socially Conservative Social Reform

Alexander and the Princeton theologians were deeply concerned with the condition of ordinary Americans, even though they disapproved of the populism of Jacksonian democracy. The industrial revolution, along with a massive influx of immigrants in the 1830s, had drastically altered the living conditions of many American cities, bringing poverty and physical distress to many. These things weighed heavily upon Alexander, and his letters to Hall reveal his concern for the practical and physical needs of those around him. As a pastor in Trenton in 1830, Alexander would write to Hall:

Christians are not touched as they should be with human suffering, bodily suffering, privation, etc., etc. Now, if a few men would concentrate their thoughts upon this, write upon it, paragraph upon it, influence the press, talk upon it, in a word Clarksonize, I believe great things must be done. In reading the N.T. I have recently been much struck with the fact that *all* the miracles of our Saviour were acts of benevolence, and usually in *relief of human bodily distresses*. Now, the thought has powerfully come over me, Am I, and are Christians, acting in any degree like their master?

The following year he would write:

> Do we not restrict our faith in prayer too much to *spiritual* blessings? I know these are infinitely the more important, and that our petitions for earthly good are to be under submission to the Divine will; but then how plain it is, that when Christ was on earth, he listened to the request of the sick and mourning, that he never chided any one who asked healing and deliverance, as asking amiss, and that he invariably heard the prayer of all such. How plain, but how much forgotten, that he is the same Saviour now, with just the same views of poor, suffering, and sinning men.

In 1835, Alexander wrote to Hall of his concern for the thousands of "factory children" in the United States. He wrote also of the "abnormal state" of the factory towns, where "thousands are herding . . . under influences ruinous to body and soul." While ministering in New York, Alexander wrote often of the "filth and putrescence" he encountered, especially in the wet and mucky streets of winter and early spring. From New York in 1851 he noted:

> My mind works incessantly on such themes as these:—the abounding misery; the unreached masses; the waste of church energy on the rich; its small operation on the poor; emigrant wretchedness; our boy-population; our hopeless prostitutes; our 4,000 grog-shops; the absence of poor from Presbyterian churches; the farces of our church-alms; confinement of our church-efforts to pew-holders; the do-nothing life of our Christian professors, in regard to the masses; our copying the Priest and Levite in the parable; our need of a Christian Lord Bacon, to produce a Novum Organon of Philanthropy; our dread of innovation; our luxury and pride.

While enjoying the comforts of education and status as Presbyterian clergymen, Alexander and the Princeton theologians were greatly concerned with the poor and impoverished that surrounded them.

Over the years, Alexander kept Hall abreast of the many works he personally enacted to better society, especially his efforts at bringing Christian truth and biblical instruction to the poor. Writing to Hall in 1839, Alexander stated: "Methinks no work of the age is more important than the getting the mob of our cities in contact with

Gospel-truth." To this end, Alexander gave himself to writing short books for popular audiences. He especially labored at writing children's books for the American Sunday School Union, stating "what we do for infants [i.e., children], we do for the best interest of man, in the most hopeful way."

While in New York, Alexander wrote to Hall also about his work in promoting Sunday schools and in setting up mission chapels for the poor. Many Protestant churches in Alexander's day, including his Fifth Avenue Presbyterian Church, were funded by a pew rental system. This had the effect of keeping many of the poor from coming to church, and Alexander expressed his frustration about this to Hall on many occasions. In 1851, Alexander wrote: "I wish I could turn out about twenty pews of rich folks and fill them with poor. But this is one of those dreams not to be realized. I never was stronger in my opinion, that all church-sittings ought to be free." In 1856, he would again write: "I utterly reject the entire pew-system— I speak in the cities—as against the spirit of Christianity." Although he didn't do away with the pew rental system in his church, Alexander led his New York congregation to set up a "mission chapel" alongside of his regular church, where the poor could come and sit freely to hear gospel preaching on a regular basis. He was encouraged in this mission work by the model he acquired from his father, namely, "the old Evangelical Society of our boyhood." He was also encouraged in his mission chapel work by David Nasmith of Glasgow, Scotland. Nasmith had been influenced in his work for the poor by Thomas Chalmers and was the founder of the widespread City Mission movement. Alexander met Nasmith in 1831, and he reported to Hall how he was "refreshed and awakened" by "some truly delightful hours" with Nasmith, stating: "I cannot but rank him among the best men of the age."

Alexander's involvement with social reform was not unusual for his time. In fact, the first half of the eighteenth century has been called by some "the Age of Reform." While Alexander's program for social reform consisted primarily in energetic efforts to more broadly spread the gospel and Christian truth, others took a more radical approach. One such group who did not do so was the utopian socialists, which included Robert Owen, Charles Fourier, Francis Wright.

The followers of the utopian socialists attempted to implement their vision of collectivist communalism in numerous locations in antebellum America. Built upon a secular and humanistic set of ideals, close to fifty Owenite and Fourierite communities were started, directly involving thousands of people. In 1844, Alexander wrote to Hall about this movement: "[Arthur] Brisbane, the Fourierist, and some aids, are looking out for a farm of a thousand acres in this neighbourhood [of Princeton], whereon to exemplify their socialism." Later that year, Alexander reported: "Parke Godwin, the leading Fourierite, is an alumnus of the College and Seminary. Cooke represents the scheme as becoming formidable, from the numbers taken in." While many were temporarily enamored with the utopian schemes of Owen and others, including even president John Quincy Adams, Alexander viewed them as a serious threat to the social order. By broadening the basic social unit to encompass a community of workers, Alexander felt that the utopian socialists were introducing ideas that would ultimately be destructive to the family. Writing to Hall, Alexander stated: "These Fourier-systems would make every one live in public, and obliterate little family circles, and all that we call Home." This, along with the radically secular philosophies they promoted, brought his strong disapproval, and he rejoiced to see most of them fail before the end of his life.

Another reform movement popular in Alexander's day was trade unionism. Like the utopian socialists, trade unionists promoted a form of economic collectivism as a means of reforming society. This too caused Alexander great concern. In 1830, he wrote Hall:

The movements of the Jacobin party calling themselves . . . the "Working Men," give me unfeigned alarm, more than any threats of disunion, or violence of mere party rage. If we love our country, something must be done. It will not do to despise so formidable an array. They are indeed, with us, not the *dregs*, but in the exercise of their elective franchise, the *primum mobile* of this nation. The Godwinism, Owenism, *sans culottism*, (*aut quocunque gaudent nomine*,) [or whatever name they delight in] which possesses them, may ruin us. Could not a series of "Letters to Working Men" be put in some popular journal commending honest labour, asserting the rights of mechanics, etc., but unveiling the naked deformity of this levelling system? Could not you serve your country, by doing something of the sort? It would be arduous, but by so doing, you would deserve well of posterity. No better work, I truly think, could just now engage any honest patriot.

In 1836, Alexander mused to Hall: "It occurs to me that a tract might be written in the dialogue form, after the model of [Hannah] More's *Village Politics*, against the trades unions; but how could it be circulated?" In answer to his own question, Alexander began writing a series of newspaper articles to the working classes under the pen name Charles Quill. A selection of these articles was republished in 1838 in book form as *The American Mechanic*. Continuing to write as Charles Quill, Alexander playfully informed Hall of his articles: "By recourse to the 'Newark Daily' you will see some able papers, by a great political economist [Charles Quill], on Trades Unions." The following year, Alexander wrote to Hall of his ongoing work along these lines:

> I should like to advise with you a little about the sequel to the American Mechanic, which I have been preparing. . . . The plan is just the same, but I have pitched the tone of it two or three degrees higher, as to style, allusion, etc. Still I wish it to be a book for the working classes. I feel encouraged to bestow such little labours as I may be able to put forth, more and more on the working classes, the rather because they are the great object of the infidels, socialists, agrarians, Owenites, Wrightites, and diabolians generally.

By writing as Charles Quill, Alexander encouraged "the working classes" to advance their position through noncommunal and noncoercive ways.

Alexander rejected social reform movements like utopian socialism and trade unionism ultimately because they did not deal with the root problem of human suffering and misery. Writing to Hall in 1839, Alexander stated: "The great work is to save souls. All our economical, political, and literary reformations are mere adjusting of the outer twig; religion changes the sap of root and trunk. This I never felt more than now. I see that when a people become godly, all the rest follows."

While Alexander busied himself to benefit society, he stood apart from those who were attempting to do so in a secular way. He approached social issues and social reform from a distinctly evangelical perspective, which prioritized the spreading of biblical truth. He wrote to Hall in 1834: "I am filled with enthusiasm about having the Bible more taught. Instead of as a mere *reading-book* in schools, it must be taught, after the Sunday School fashion; geography, archaeology and all. . . . The Bible— the Bible—it is this which must save America." This commitment to the

9.2 A copy of one of the more than eight hundred letters that James W. Alexander wrote to John Hall from 1819 to 1859. This letter, written only a few months before Alexander's death, gives an overview of his three-year pastorate in Trenton. Hall had solicited this particular information for his *History of the Presbyterian Church in Trenton*, which he published in 1859. (Courtesy of First Presbyterian Church, Trenton, New Jersey.)

Bible and to *Christian* social reform set Alexander and the Princeton theologians apart from many other social reformers in the nineteenth century.

The Question of Slavery

The question of slavery captivated Alexander and other prominent Princeton theologians as well. As a student at Princeton Seminary, Alexander wrote Hall in 1824 about his plans for relocation after graduation: "my feelings and prepossessions would lead me southward, but slavery appalls me." Although the United States had outlawed the importation of slaves in 1808, slavery enjoyed legal protection in parts of America until shortly after Alexander's death. Despite his feelings about slavery, Alexander was in fact settled in the South for his first pastoral charge, and there he was introduced to slave society firsthand. As he transitioned to life in slaveholding Virginia, Alexander wrote to Hall in 1826:

> The whole face of society exhibits an appearance very different from what one perceives in the North. Slavery of itself is enough to stamp a marked character upon the Southern population. The number of blacks which I met in the streets at first, struck me with surprise, but now every thing has become familiar. When I consider how much of the comfort, luxury, and style of Southern gentlemen would be retrenched by the removal of slave population, I can no longer wonder at the tenacity with which they adhere to their pretended rights.

Going on in this letter, Alexander described to Hall how he found slavery to impoverish the lives of slaves, even though many were treated kindly:

> The servants who wait upon genteel families, in consequence of having been bred among refined people all their lives, have often as great an air of gentility as their masters. The comfort of slaves in this country is greater, I am persuaded, than that of the free blacks, as a body, in any part of the United States. They are no doubt maltreated in many instances; so are children: but in general they are well clad, well fed, and kindly treated. Ignorance is their greatest curse, and this must ever follow in the train of slavery. The bad policy and destructive tendency of the system is increasingly felt.

Seeing firsthand how slavery left moral and intellectual degradation in its wake, Alexander desired the removal of the institution from American life. Writing to Hall in 1835, Alexander stated this as part of his considered position: "I abhor slavery, and think the public mind should be enlightened, and every lawful means immediately taken for an eventual and speedy abolition."

Even though he desired the abolition of slavery, Alexander refused to condemn slaveholders for their slaveholding *per se*. From his initial introduction to slave society, Alexander developed a sense of sympathy for many of the Southern slaveholders he had come to know personally. Writing to Hall in 1826, Alexander said:

> You hear daily complaints on the subject [of slavery] from those who have most servants. But what can they do? Slavery was not their choice. They cannot and ought not to turn them loose. They cannot afford to transport them; and generally the negroes would not consent to it. The probable result of this state of things is one which philanthropists scarcely dare contemplate.

This sense of sympathy for slaveholders was deepened over time by the close friendships he developed while serving as a pastor in Virginia. After leaving the South in 1828, Alexander continued to maintain his friendships with Southern slaveholders through occasional return visits. After he and his family were waited on by slaves at a Virginia plantation during a visit in 1842, Alexander reflected on his experience in a letter to Hall:

> I am more and more convinced of the injustice we do the slaveholders. Of their feelings towards their negroes I can form a better notion than formerly, by examining my own towards the slaves who wait on my wife and mind my children. It is a feeling most like that we have to near relations.

Personal experiences like this only deepened Alexander's sympathy for slaveholders. While disapproving of the system of slavery overall, Alexander recognized that many slaveholders took care of their slaves conscientiously and affectionately. He was sympathetic for the "Southern brethren" who were caught up in slaveholding, but at the same time he was thankful that he and Hall were not so entangled, as he wrote in 1835: "I rejoice that you and I are not laden with negro souls and bodies."

Alexander did not approve of the abolitionist movement of his day, even though he too desired the eventual end of slavery. He saw a sharp contrast between the militant abolitionism of William Lloyd Garrison and the patient efforts of earlier abolitionists like William Wilberforce, whom he respected. The abolitionism of his day was connected, in Alexander's mind, with the same humanistic, secular ideology he saw in utopian socialism, trade unionism, and the egalitarian "ultra-democracy" of the Jacksonians. David Calhoun has noted that the Princetonians' commitment to "a stable and hierarchical society" and their sense of alarm at the "terrors of the French Revolution and the disorders of Jacksonian democracy" kept them from supporting the abolitionist cause, and this is certainly true in the case of Alexander. He found the social radicalism and the "disorganizing Jacobinism" of contemporary abolitionism to be more humanistic in its origin than biblical. Believing that the Bible condoned a hierarchical relationship of authority and subservience, Alexander wrote to Hall in 1846:

> I can go a peg higher than you about slavery, and fail to see the scripturalness of much that is postulated now-a-days, respecting the popular idol, liberty. As existing, slavery is fraught with moral evil; the want of marriage, and of the Bible, and the separation of families, &c., &c., are crying sins; but I am totally unable to see the relation to be necessarily unjust. The moral questions are so various from the circumstances, that each must be decided apart.

Writing to Hall in 1847, Alexander stated his fundamental disagreement with the abolitionists: "I see no trace of the modern dogmas about absolute freedom in the Bible." Their ideology of social equality and their overestimation of individual liberty simply did not fit with Alexander's understanding of Scripture.

Another reason Alexander stood opposed to abolitionism was because he did not believe that immediate emancipation would be the best thing for many of the slaves, given the situation in antebellum America. He observed that, without education, without property, and faced with pervasive racism, freed blacks often ended up in a worse condition than slaves. When the famous politician John Randolph granted his large number of slaves their freedom in his will, Alexander wrote to Hall in 1838:

> They [Randolph's slaves] adored him [Randolph] as almost above the human standard, and preferred being his slaves to being free. It is perhaps (after all our abstractions) better for these negroes, as a set, that they are not freed. I say this seriously, founding my judgment on the following striking fact: Richard and John Randolph were brothers, and divided between them the estate of their father. Each took a moiety of the slaves. Richard set his free: John retained his on the estates. Col. Madison published the history of the former moiety and their offspring. They have almost become extinct; those who remain are wandering and drunken thieves, degraded below the level of humanity, and beyond the reach of Gospel means. The slaves of Roanoke are the descendants of the other moiety. They are nearly four hundred, and though not free, are sleek, fat, healthy, happy, and many of them to all appearance ripe for heaven. These I know to be facts, and they are worth more to me than a volume of dissertations on the right to freedom.

Because of the plight of many freed blacks in America, Alexander rejected the abolitionists' call for immediate emancipation as impractical and potentially harmful to those they sought to help. Alexander believed that simply freeing slaves would not necessarily give them a better life, as long as racist attitudes prevailed in the minds of the white majority. Alexander stated to Hall that "the prejudice of colour and caste" was the "real hindrance" to the elevation of blacks in antebellum America, and he viewed white prejudice against blacks as a serious evil to be addressed. Without removing racial prejudice and the widespread disapproval of cross-racial marriages, simply freeing the slaves would not alleviate their plight. He wrote to Hall in 1845:

> Amalgamation, say what they please, can go on, does go on, and will go on. . . . Leave [the emancipation question] out of view, and what becomes of our negroes, slave or free? Those called by mockery free people, are a race of Helots or Yahoos, in our estimation. We do not

give them our dinners, or our daughters; we debar them from pulpits, pews, and omnibuses; we deny them actual citizenship. We . . . hustle them off our streets more vehemently now that they are free, than when they were slaves. Educate them, and this prejudice makes them miserable.

In his views on slavery, Alexander was in overall agreement with Princeton's chief spokesman on the issue, Charles Hodge. Writing to Hall in 1856, Alexander stated: "Dr. Hodge has most admirably stated the slavery doctrine, in his [commentary on] Ephesians. . . . How nobly this clear enunciation of Scriptural principle towers above all the extravagancies of both sides!" Like Hodge, Alexander believed it wisest to take a gradual approach toward the removal of slavery. He wrote to Hall in 1847: "I am more and more convinced that our endeavours to do at a blow, what Providence does by degrees, is disastrous to those whom it would benefit." Alexander also believed that reforming slave laws would help slaves transition to freedom. He stated to Hall in 1846: "Our church, I am clear, ought to protest against the laws about reading, etc. As clear am I, that our States should regard slavery as a transition-state, to be terminated as soon as possible, and that they should enact laws about the *post-nati*."

The Princeton theologians supported other ideas intended to help blacks in antebellum America. Alexander reported to Hall in 1840 how his father, Archibald Alexander, was an enthusiastic proponent of African colonization—a scheme whereby slaves were purchased, given their freedom, and sent to Africa to form a Christian colony. Alexander once noted that his father "has this more at heart than any thing in the world." Alexander also supported African colonization, and he saw it as a powerful means of spreading Christianity. By sending Christians to form a Christian society in the midst of paganism, the gospel might be spread powerfully to unevangelized lands.

My mind expands when I look at the mighty conquests of our language. If we could only pour in the gospel with this tide of conquest and colonization! Since, in our day, God so signally blesses colonies for the spread of civilization, ought we not to follow the lead of

Providence, and strike in as much as possible with the divine plan? The hope of great effects is more reasonable from such efforts than from insulated assaults on the mass of heathenism. It is the difference between firing a ball against a walled town, and entering a breach with a victorious army.

As an advocate of Christian colonization, Alexander rejoiced to hear in 1849 that large numbers of Christians were relocating to California to set up Christian communities. Writing to Hall about this, he said: "Having long believed colonies to be the best missions, I see in this a most hopeful means for spreading the gospel. California churches can send missions with ease to China, Japan, and Polynesia." Viewing Christian colonization as "God's means of civilizing and Christianizing the world," Alexander enthusiastically supported colonizing freed slaves to places in Africa like Liberia.

Overall, Alexander was more concerned with the spiritual condition of blacks in America than with freeing blacks who were still in a state of slavery. While many were consumed with the slavery question, Alexander believed that Christians should be more concerned with the souls and eternal well-being of slaves than with their temporal circumstances. Writing to Hall in 1847, Alexander said: "To give the gospel to the slaves, is a duty pressing above all others." Earlier, from Virginia in 1838, he had written:

> The law (thanks to the meddling of anti-slavery societies) forbids schools, and public teaching to read; it was not so when I lived here: but I hold it to be our business to *save their souls*; and however criminal slavery might be, I see with my eyes that God has so overruled it, as that the slaves are more open to Gospel truth than any human beings on the globe.

Instead of condemning slaveholders, Alexander pressed believing slaveholders to labor at evangelizing their slaves. He commended to Hall slaveholders he knew of who were faithful in evangelizing and giving biblical instruction to their slaves. One such was Paulina Le Grand. When Alexander was a pastor in Virginia, he resided on Le Grand's estate, and she became a close friend. Writing to Hall in 1827, Alexander told of her spiritual concern for her slaves:

Mrs. Le Grand lodges and boards a good Episcopalian . . . for this business [of evangelism] among her slaves. . . . Now it is my deliberate belief, that more of these slaves are likely to go to heaven, than of an equal number of servants of pious people in our Middle States; and such being the hopefulness of the work, how earnestly ought Christians to engage in it! Thousands might be got to attend public preaching, as hundreds now do.

Upon Le Grand's death in 1845, Alexander recounted to Hall the experience of this Christian slaveholder:

She was distressingly exercised about slavery. But what could she do? She often asked me, but I was dumb. She had as many as possible taught to read, and this up to the present time. A large number of her slaves are real Christians, not to speak of perhaps a hundred who have gone to heaven. I fully believe that more of them have secured eternal life, than would have been the case in any freedom conceivable. And surely, if eternity is more than time, this is a consideration to be pondered. But she saw no escape; individual opinion was inert.

Another individual whom Alexander commended in his letters to Hall was Charles Colcock Jones. Jones was a graduate of Princeton Seminary, and Alexander was very enthusiastic about his work among slaves. Writing to Hall in 1841, Alexander stated: "C. C. Jones, of S.C., preaches to the slaves three times on Sunday, and every evening in the week. Yet this is the man whom the young Andoverians would not let preach in their chapel. *Sit anima mea cum Jonesio* [My spirit is with Jones]!" Alexander knew of others like Jones, and in 1840 he similarly commended to Hall their work in slave evangelism: "I know of five or six men who are silently wearing out life in most devoted labour among the slaves. Slavery must and will end; I hope peaceably; but, anyhow, we ought to save the souls of this generation."

Alexander personally labored in slave evangelism and was so enthusiastic about it that he worked to recruit others to the task. He frequently commended such work to Hall and in 1843 posed this question to him:

Quere: whether all missionary enterprises among us ought not to yield precedence to the work of evangelizing the Southern slaves? Ministers ought to be among them, in sufficient numbers, even if they were to be emancipated to-morrow; so that the question has no limitation from that of Abolition. Next in order, I think, come the Indians, whose condition is now more favourable than that of any heathen tribes on earth, for receiving the gospel. The prestige, however, of this mission = 0.

After Alexander moved from Virginia, he continued to inform Hall of his personal labor at slave evangelism whenever his travels took him to the Southern states. His work among the slaves was exceeded, however, by his many labors among freed blacks in the North. His letters to Hall tell of his regular preaching to freed blacks and his attempts to set up Bible classes for blacks in Trenton and in New York as well. While serving as professor of rhetoric and *belles lettres* at the College of New Jersey, he preached weekly to a black congregation and was the founding pastor of a black church in Princeton, Witherspoon Street Presbyterian Church. Alexander noted to Hall that he was scorned by "some of the lowest of the white canaille" in Princeton as "the preacher to the blacks," but also noted his great joy in this ministry nevertheless. In 1835 he wrote to Hall that "I believe my happiest hours are spent on Sunday afternoons in labouring among my little charge [the congregation of blacks]."

Alexander's approach to black slavery in America grew out of his socially conservative perspective in general. It also reflected his strong evangelical convictions, which were not shared by many of the prominent abolitionists in his day. Summarizing his overall views on the plight of slaves in antebellum America, Alexander wrote to Hall while visiting the estate of Mrs. Le Grand in 1842:

My mind has been, and is, filled with the negroes. What I say on this point I say with, I do believe, as much love for the race as any man feels; and with an extent of observation perhaps as large as I can pretend to on any subject, having seen the worst as well as the best of their condition. And the result of all, increasingly, is, what you I am sure would agree to if you were on the spot, that the *average physical evils* of their case are not greater than of sailors, soldiers, shoeblacks, or low operatives; while their *moral evils* are unspeakably great. My point is this, then: The soul of the negro is precious and must be saved. Aim at this, at this first, at this directly, at this independently of their bondage, and the other desirable ends will be promoted even more surely than if the latter were made the great object. A gradual emancipation is that to which the interior economy of the North-Southern States was tending, is tending, and will reach; it is desirable; in my view it is inevitable; it is craved by thousands here; but an emancipation even gradual may arrive in such sort as to leave a host of blacks to be damned, who, by the other means, may be Christianized, while their eventual freedom is not less certain. It is the salvation of the slave, which is infinitely the most important, which moreover Southern Christians *can* be led to seek, and of which the very seeking directly tends to emancipation. I say this, on the obvious principle, that when the owner by seeking the salvation of his slave, gets (as he must) to love him, he will not rest (I speak of the mass) without trying to make him a free-man. I cannot describe the pleasure I have had in preaching and talking to the slaves: if I have ever done any good, this is the way.

Through the spread of Christian truth to slaves and slaveholders, "the other desirable ends" of social reform would be promoted and gradually attained.

Given his personal encounters with evangelical slaveholders and unorthodox abolitionists, Alexander's letters to Hall reveal thoughts on slavery that are quite different from ours in the twenty-first century. Alexander's father, Archibald Alexander, once stated: "It is a sound maxim, that men living at one time must not be judged by the opinions of an age in which all the circumstances are greatly changed." We should keep this in mind when reading Alexander's personal musings to Hall on slavery. Alexander and the Princetonians did desire the abolition of slavery, but they thought that it should be sought gradually and by Scriptural means. Alexander prioritized doing good to the souls of slaves, and he believed that this was where the focus of Christian philanthropy toward slaves should be. His "moderate" position caused him and others like him at Princeton to differ both from the abolitionists and the pro-slavery faction within his own denomination. On this issue, the Princeton theologians stood apart from both of these groups as they sought to work out a scriptural position they thought best suited to meet the needs of the day.

Conclusion

James W. Alexander's *Forty Year's Familiar Letters* contains a unique account of the historical circumstances that shaped the broader world of Old Princeton. Compiled and edited by his friend John Hall, Alexander's letters give us a Princeton theologian's firsthand account of these historically significant times. Among other things, they give us an indication of how the Princeton theologians engaged the social and political issues of their day. While the Princetonians shared in many ways the values of the culture of which they were a part, the letters of James W. Alexander show us many other ways in which they may be considered *countercultural*. While social egalitarianism and secular visions of social reform produced powerful trends in the broader American culture, the socially conservative Princeton theologians resisted these trends. Though they may not have engaged their culture in ways that would be universally applauded today, they did in fact attempt to think biblically and critically regarding the culture and times in which they lived.

10

ARCHIBALD ALEXANDER HODGE

*We have had, of later years, no abler theologians than the Hodges,
and we fear it will be many a day before we see their like. . . . We value
every morsel about the Princeton worthies; may their influence long
endure. Even apart from his theological excellence, the sayings of the
younger Hodge are full of Scripture and wit. The modern school thinks
us fools, but certainly we were taught by wise men. . . . Finer minds
than those of the Princeton tutors have seldom dwelt among the sons
of men. We count it a precious memory that we once spent a day with
the younger Hodge. No better textbook of theology for colleges and
private use is now extant than the old edition of "Hodge's Outlines."*

—Charles Spurgeon

We commend the Outlines of Theology *to all who would be well
instructed in the faith. It is the standard text-book of our college. We
differ from its teachings upon baptism, but in almost everything else
we endorse Hodge to the letter.*

—Charles Spurgeon

*I was struck with his [Archibald Alexander Hodge's] directness and
sincerity, intellectually as well as morally. His mind, like his heart,
worked without ambiguity or drawback. Hence his energy in the
perception and statement of truth—a quality that showed itself in his
uncommon ability to popularize scientific theology.*

—W. G. T. Shedd

Just as Archibald Alexander's sons carried on the Old Princeton tradition, so too did Charles Hodge's sons. His third son, Caspar Wister Hodge (1830–91), was tutored as a boy by Addison Alexander and went on to become a New Testament professor at the seminary from 1860 to 1891. His grandson Caspar Wister Hodge Jr. (1870–1937) also went on to became a professor of theology, serving from 1901 to 1937. Yet it was his firstborn son, Archibald Alexander Hodge (1823–86), who did the most to carry forward the Old Princeton tradition after Charles Hodge's death in 1878. A. A. Hodge only taught at the seminary for nine years, but he was an important theologian in his own right and an unusually gifted teacher, possessing an "uncommon ability to popularize" the theology of Old Princeton. He was also among the many connected with Old Princeton to personally advance the gospel to the ends of the earth as a foreign missionary.

Growing Up as the Son of Charles Hodge

Archibald Alexander Hodge was born on July 18, 1823, in Princeton to Charles and Sarah Bache Hodge. "Archie" was named after his father's teacher and mentor in the faith and was the first of eight children, all of whom lived to adulthood. At the time of Hodge's birth, his father had just become a professor at the seminary, and young Archibald was privileged to grow up in a climate of spiritual and theological stimulation. His parents' home was located just a few hundred feet from the main seminary building, and his father's study was an important place on campus for theological conversation and spiritual counsel. Archibald later recounted how he was drawn to the conversations that his father would have with his colleagues in his study:

> Here almost every night, for long years, came Professors Dod and Maclean, and frequently Professors J. W. Alexander, Joseph Henry, and the older professors, A. Alexander, and Samuel Miller, President Carnahan, and frequently, when visiting the town, Professors Vethake and Torrey, and Dr. John W. Yeomans. Thus, at least in the eyes of the young sons gleaming out from the corners, from the shadows of which they looked on with breathless interest, this

FIG. 10.1

Timeline of A. A. Hodge's Life

July 18, 1823	Born in Princeton, New Jersey.
1841	Graduated from the College of New Jersey.
1843	Began studies at Princeton Theological Seminary.
1847	Ordained as an evangelist by the Presbytery of New Brunswick.
1847	Married Elizabeth Holliday.
1847	Began mission work in Allahabad, India.
1851	Became a pastor in Lower West Nottingham, Maryland.
1855	Became a pastor in Fredericksburg, Virginia.
1860	Published *Outlines of Theology*.
1861	Became a pastor in Wilkes-Barre, Pennsylvania.
1862	Awarded a doctor of divinity degree from the College of New Jersey.
1864	Became a professor of didactic and polemic theology at Western Theological Seminary.
1866	Became a pastor in Allegheny City, Pennsylvania.
1867	Published *The Atonement*.
1868	First wife Elizabeth died.
1869	Published *A Commentary on the Confession of Faith*.
1876	Awarded an LL.D. degree from Wooster College
1877	Became associate professor of exegesis, didactic, and polemical theology at Princeton Theological Seminary.
1878	Father Charles Hodge died.
1879	Became professor of didactic and polemical theology at Princeton.
1880	Published *The Life of Charles Hodge, D.D.*
November 12, 1886	Died in Princeton, New Jersey

study became the scene of the most wonderful debates and discourses on the highest themes of philosophy, science, literature, theology, morals, and politics.

Archibald and the other Hodge children were allowed free access to their father's study, and under the care of his parents, Archibald was converted at an early age. While he possessed both faith and piety from the time he was young, he did not formally join his family's church until 1842.

Young Archibald was not a particularly "bookish" or zealous student as a child. His desire for study did not awaken until after he entered Princeton College, where he excelled as a student, particularly in mathematics and the natural sciences. Hodge developed a particularly close relationship with one of his professors, the renowned scientist Joseph Henry, who went on to become the founding president of the Smithsonian Institution in Washington, DC. Next to Archibald's father, Henry exerted a greater influence on his mind and mental development than any other teacher. After graduating in 1841, Hodge became a tutor at the college alongside of Joseph Henry and Albert Dod in mathematics. In the words of Charles Salmond, "Among his [A. A. Hodge's] treasured recollections to the end, was his early association with Professor Henry in the laboratory, and his lasting friendship with that distinguished man."

In 1843 Hodge decided to leave the field of natural science to study the Bible and theology at Princeton Seminary. As a seminary student, he was especially devoted to the study of systematic theology and the doctrines of the Christian faith. His father's lectures, along with his assigned studies in Turretin's *Institutes of Elenctic Theology*, formed the backbone of his theological education at the seminary. He found his father's lectures on theology so helpful that he and a small group of friends collectively worked at transcribing and compiling a manuscript of them. While Hodge may have been among the first of his father's students to produce a "bootleg" of his father's lectures, he wasn't the last. After graduating from seminary in 1846, he was licensed and ordained by the Presbytery of New Brunswick the following year.

A Missionary to India

After leaving the seminary in 1846, Archibald Hodge acted upon a long-held desire to communicate the gospel to the unreached peoples of the world and offered himself as a candidate for mission work with the Presbyterian Board of Foreign Missions. He had taken a keen interest in foreign missions from the time he was a child. At the age of ten, he had written a letter with his younger sister Mary to "the heathen" that he intended to be delivered by a missionary couple departing for Sri Lanka. In it he and his sister wrote:

Dear Heathen: The Lord Jesus Christ hath promised that the time shall come when all the ends of the earth shall be his kingdom, and God is not a man that he should lie neither is he the son of man that he should repent. And if this was promised by a being that cannot lie, why do you not help it to come sooner by reading the Bible and, attending to the words of your teachers and loving God and renouncing your idols, take Christianity into your temples? And soon there will be not a nation, no, not a space of ground as large as a footstep that will want a missionary. My sister and myself have by small self-denials procured 2 dollars which are enclosed in this letter to buy tracts and Bibles to teach you. Archibald Alexander Hodge, Mary Elisabeth Hodge, Friends of the Heathen.

Fourteen years later Hodge was accepted by the mission board, and in August 1847 he left with his young wife, Elizabeth, for India. This event was momentous for the Hodge family, for with Archibald's departure the Hodges were releasing their firstborn son out into the world for the first time. In his own words: "Such an experience makes an epoch in any family, leaving it changed forever. Our family was never completely regathered on earth again, for before [I] returned from India [my] mother was making the beginnings of the home in heaven. The parting was the occasion of the utter pouring forth of the treasures of love of both [my] parents' hearts." Hodge's mother Sarah died late in 1849 before he had returned.

While in India he worked in Allahabad, in the northern part of the country. During his short time there, he helped establish and strengthen the work that had been started by others. His service as a missionary came to an abrupt end after less than three years due to a severe illness that affected both him and his wife. To the disappointment of his fellow missionaries in Allahabad, he was forced to leave India in 1850, bringing his wife and two children with him. Hodge's experience as a missionary, though brief, marked his life to the end and increased his zeal for the cause of foreign missions. According to Francis Patton:

> His experience in the mission-field enhanced his zeal for the mission-cause, gave him a grasp of the missionary problem, and an interest in missionaries that made him always the trusted counselor of all those among his pupils who contemplated a missionary career. If the students wished advice, they went to him: if the Sunday evening missionary meeting was to be addressed, he was called upon: if, at the Monthly Concert, the expected speaker failed to arrive, he was called upon: if the son of a converted Brahmin was sent here to be educated, he was his guardian: if a penniless Oriental, bent on knowledge, and seeking it, that he might carry the gospel back to his countrymen, sought premature admission to the Seminary, he found an eager advocate in Dr. Hodge, if anything could be said in his behalf.

Similarly, Charles Salmond, a student of his, stated:

> Long after his return from India,—aye, even to his last breath—he was a missionary at heart; and he would on occasion speak to his students on the subject of the evangelization of the world, not only with the authority of personal experience, but with the glow of an enthusiasm which had manifestly felt it a greater sacrifice to leave the mission-field than to give up home to enter it. In his prayers, too, the same spirit of wide-embracing love for the perishing souls of heathendom most touchingly appeared. At a Missionary Convention in Princeton, not long before his death, when he was asked to lead devotions, "the fountains of his heart seemed broken up . . . and a gush of tender moving petition melted the whole assembly to tears [quoting from William Paxton]."

Although he left the mission field in 1850, it could well be said that the mission field never really left him.

10.2 Many Princetonians were involved in missionary work in Hawaii, then called the Sandwich Islands. Above is a whalebone walking stick made in 1824 by a Hawaiian chieftain for Archibald Alexander. On his deathbed in 1851, Alexander handed it down to Charles Hodge as "a kind of symbol of orthodoxy."

Archibald Hodge was one of many to go from Old Princeton to a foreign country as a missionary. Students at the seminary from its very beginning received strong encouragement to consider the work of foreign missions. The "Plan of the Seminary" adopted in 1811 stated that the seminary was to establish "a nursery for missionaries to the heathen, and to such as are destitute of the stated preaching of the gospel; in which youth may receive that appropriate training which may lay a foundation for their ultimately becoming eminently qualified for missionary work." Missionaries were frequently invited to speak at the seminary, and a monthly concert of prayer for foreign missions was held as a regular part of seminary life. Students at Old Princeton formed missionary societies to promote prayer for missions, to raise money for missions, to spread information about the work of God around the world, and to engage in correspondence with missionaries, including, among others, William Carey. David Calhoun has written that "between 1844 and 1859, about eighty percent of all Princeton Seminary students became members" of a student-led missionary society and "one out of every three students leaving the seminary during its first fifty years went out to preach the gospel 'on missionary ground.'" Calhoun continues:

Almost six hundred served for at least some time in "destitute places" in America. Thirty-seven went to the American Indians. Seventeen became missionaries to the slaves. One hundred and twenty-seven men went to foreign mission fields—from Turkey to the Sandwich

Islands [Hawaii], from Brazil to Afghanistan, from West Africa to Northern China. In the words of Henry Boardman at the Seminary Centennial Jubilee service, "many a Pagan land has reason to bless God that [Princeton Seminary] has been established."

Some of the seminary's more famous missionaries in the mid-1800s included William Thomson (Beirut), Walter Lowrie (China), John Nevius (China), Stephen Mattoon (Siam), Ashbel Green Simonton (Brazil), and Henry Kellogg (India).

Archibald Hodge's missionary work in India highlights the emphasis that Old Princeton put on missions and how common missionary involvement would have been for its graduates. Far from being an "ivory tower," Old Princeton was a place where theological studies were undertaken alongside the cultivated awareness of the great need for God's Word to be taken to all the peoples of the world.

The Making of a Theological Teacher

Upon returning from India in May 1850, Archibald Hodge took a position as a pastor in Lower West Nottingham, Maryland. He remained in this rural charge of northeast Maryland for four years, even though his salary was barely able to sustain his family. In September 1855 he was called to become a pastor in Fredericksburg, Virginia, where he was to remain until July 1861. While in Fredericksburg he became aware of his gifts for extemporaneous speaking and theological exposition. He made this discovery by embarking on an extended preaching series that surveyed the whole scope of Christian doctrine. These theological expositions were published in 1860 as *Outlines of Theology*. Hodge stated in the preface of this book that:

> The conception and execution of this work originated in the experience of the need for some such manual of theological definitions and argumentation, in the immediate work of instructing the members of my own pastoral charge. The several chapters were in the first instance prepared and used in the same form in which they are now printed, as the basis of a lecture delivered otherwise extemporaneously to my congregation every Sabbath night. In this use of them, I found these preparations successful beyond my hopes. . . . Having put this work

thus to this practical test, I now offer it to my brethren in the ministry, that they may use it, if they will, as a repertory of digested material for the doctrinal instruction of their people.

Given its origin in local church ministry, Hodge's *Outlines* are easy to read and clearly organized, even while possessing rich theological depth and precision.

Published more than ten years before the first volume of his father's *Systematic Theology*, Hodge's *Outlines of Theology* won him widespread acclaim as an accomplished theologian. One contemporary stated that "It would be difficult to find a work of the same size where so much theology is so clearly presented, and at once so briefly and so interestingly discussed." Charles Spurgeon enthusiastically used it as a textbook in his Pastors' College, and his praise of it is well known. Hodge organized his *Outlines* under distinct headings (e.g., "Attributes of God," "Providence," "Regeneration," "Baptism," etc.) and presented the material as answers to a series of questions. In this way it resembled his own seminary textbook, Turretin's *Elenctic Theology*. He stated that he found this form of organization "the most convenient and perspicuous method of presenting an 'outline of theology' so condensed." Hodge's questions began with God and the nature of theology, and then moved on to creation, providence, and the fall. After addressing the person and work of Christ, he tackled the various components in the application of redemption, with eschatology and the sacraments bringing the book to its conclusion. Hodge acknowledged in the preface how dependent he was on his father's lectures for the material in the *Outlines*. In his words:

> I have, with his permission, used the list of questions given by my father to his classes of forty-five and six [i.e., 1845 and 1846]. I have added two or three chapters which his course did not embrace, and have in general adapted his questions to my new purpose, by omissions, additions, or a different distribution. To such a degree, however, have they directed and assisted me, that I feel a confidence in offering the result to the public which otherwise would have been unwarrantable.

In 1879, having taught theology in seminaries for more than a decade, Hodge produced an expanded edition of the *Outlines*. This new edition contained approximately 50 percent more material than the first. In it, Hodge summed up his theological position as follows:

> The point of view adopted in this book is the evangelical and specifically the Calvinistic or Augustinian one, assuming the following fundamental principles: 1st. The inspired Scriptures are the sole, and an infallible standard of all religious knowledge. 2d. Christ and his work is the centre around which all Christian theology is brought into order. 3d. The salvation brought to light in the gospel is supernatural and of FREE GRACE. 4th. All religious knowledge has a *practical end*. The theological sciences, instead of being absolute ends in themselves, find their noblest purpose and effect in the advancement of personal holiness, the more efficient service of our fellow-men, and THE GREATER GLORY OF GOD.

By the time of his death in 1886, *Outlines of Theology* had been reprinted in England and translated into Welsh, modern Greek, and Hindustani.

With the outbreak of war in 1861, Hodge left Virginia and accepted a pastorate in Wilkes-Barre, Pennsylvania. By this time, his gifts as a preacher had come into full bloom, and he continued his plan of systematic doctrinal instruction and preaching that he had begun while in Virginia. His ministry in Wilkes-Barre was blessed by a "revival of religion" that lasted for several months, and numerous individuals were received into church membership. Even though his ministry in Pennsylvania was a fruitful one, he would only stay for three years. In July 1864 he was elected unanimously as the chair of didactic, polemic, and historical theology at Allegheny Theological Seminary in Allegheny City, Pennsylvania (now a part of Pittsburgh). While serving as a seminary professor, he also served as a pastor, first as a supply pastor in Pittsburgh and, starting in 1866, as the settled pastor of the North Church in Allegheny City. He would serve in both roles until his move to Princeton.

Archibald Hodge's dual service as a pastor and a professor contributed to the pastoral spirit which pervades his theological works. Such simultaneous service helped give his preaching solid and precise theological substance, while his seminary teaching was characterized by vivid illustration and practical application. In this dual capacity,

Hodge also published two additional doctrinal works: *The Atonement* (1867) and *A Commentary on the Confession of Faith* (1869). Both of these doctrinal expositions were intended to defend confessional orthodoxy and benefit laymen as well as pastors.

Career at Princeton

In 1877 Archibald Hodge was appointed to succeed his father as the professor of systematic theology at Princeton Seminary. Charles Hodge was now approaching eighty, and he had been teaching theology at the seminary for more than fifty years. For the first sixty-five years of its existence, the seminary had had only two professors of theology. The seminary directors had considered hiring Archibald Hodge to assist his father four years earlier in 1873, but Charles Hodge was not in favor of this, as he was yet experiencing good health and unabated energy. In the later months of 1876, it became clear to the elder Hodge that he needed an assistant, and he made this known to the directors of the seminary. On November 18, 1877, Archibald Alexander Hodge took his place as the seminary's third professor of theology. His inaugural address was entitled "Dogmatic Christianity, the Essential Ground of Practical Christianity." In this address he declared his belief that right theology or "knowledge of the truth" is "an essential prerequisite to right character and action." In his words, "The truth revealed in the Scriptures, and embraced in what evangelical Christians style Christian dogma, is the great God-appointed means of producing in men a holy character and life. . . . [W]e affirm that the truths set forth in the Word of God in their mutual relations are necessary means of promoting holiness of heart and life." Realizing that some were tempted to separate theology from life, Hodge stated:

> the great end of dogma is not the gratification of the taste for speculation, but the formation of the character and the determination of the activities of our inward and outward life in relation to God and our fellow men. There is a patent distinction between the logical and the moral aspects of truth, between the manner of conceiving and stating it which satisfies the understanding and that which affects the moral nature and determines experience. Neither can be neglected without

injury to the other. For if the laws of the understanding are essentially outraged, the moral nature cannot be either healthfully or permanently affected; that which is apprehended as logically incongruous by the understanding, cannot be rested in as certainly true and trustworthy by the heart and conscience and will. . . . Any theological method which sacrifices the moral and experiential aspects of the truth to a metaphysical and speculative interest will soon lose its hold upon the consciences of men, and itself experience that law of change which determines the fluctuations of all mere speculative systems.

In keeping with the path laid out for him by both Archibald Alexander and his father, Archibald Alexander Hodge sought from the beginning to carry forward the intermingling of theology and piety he had inherited from his father and namesake.

Charles Hodge died the following June, leaving the younger Hodge as the leading theologian of the seminary. As his father had done before him, Hodge poured his energies into preaching, teaching, and presiding over the Sunday afternoon "conference" of seminary students, which met each week for prayer and an exposition related to "the life of God in the soul, and to the practical duties having their root therein." As a seasoned preacher, Hodge excelled in extemporaneous speaking, and few of his sermons were ever written down. Hodge's method of preaching was to first "brood" upon a subject for a while and then to preach upon it. If the subject he preached seemed to open up with power and clarity, he would continue brooding upon it and preach it again elsewhere. In this way, his sermons were always growing and taking on new shape, being the fruit of cultivations that had taken place previously. He took his preaching seriously and restrained his natural wit and humor, leaving jokes and witticisms out of the pulpit. He instead sought to leave his hearers with a sense of solemnity, and at times his preaching left a deep impression. According to Francis Patton:

> To hear him when he was at his best was something never to be forgotten. All in all—in thought, expression, and delivery, each of these great sermons was a wonderful combination: it was a union of theology, philosophy, Christian experience, knowledge of human nature . . . facile utterance, a disdain of elocution, few gestures, the face lighted

up, the eye opened wide as though the speaker saw a vision of glory, the voice trembling when the Savior's name is mentioned, the sensitive frame responding to the pressure of emotion, and emotion finding vent at last in involuntary tears.

William Paxton referred to Hodge's preaching as an amazing blend of emotion and intellect:

> His chief and most remarkable mental characteristic was his power to mingle the intellectual and emotional—to interpenetrate and transfuse the most abstruse thinking with the warm glow of devotional emotion. . . . The doctrines he taught were the life and comfort of his own soul, and they came from the depths of his experience, warm and glowing, and entered as living forces into the souls of others. . . . [His preaching] was theology popularized, illustrated, and enforced, sometimes with burning power.

Undoubtedly, Hodge's years as a settled pastor helped him understand the power of emotion and earnestness in communicating theological truths to the hearts of men.

Unlike his father, Archibald Hodge was more of a teacher than a scholar or a writer. While fond of reading, he read and studied more as a generalist than as a disciplined specialist. He did, however, possess a natural gift for explanation and illustration that exceeded his father's. William Paxton referred to Hodge's "faculty for original illustration" as "astonishing and unrivalled." As such, he was able to popularize successfully the theology of Old Princeton, and his gifts in doing this shone most brightly in the classroom.

A. A. Hodge approached the role and work of a theological professor with a clear purpose in mind. According to Francis Patton, he did not merely seek to recite the results of his "special investigation" as a professor, thus presupposing his students' self-motivation and interest, nor did he seek merely to stimulate the students' interest, leaving them to investigate independently and reach a conclusion on their own. As a professor of systematic theology, Hodge saw it as his duty "to see that a certain definite body of instruction is safely and surely transferred from his mind to the minds of those who hear him." His primary concern was not only to present theological truth so that his students might receive it if they chose; he also labored "to see that they receive it." With his focus not so much on his lectures as on his students, Hodge sought to instill "the body of truth . . . into their mental life" and give them something that "can never be forgotten . . . something that is their very own, something that is indeed a part of their very selfhood." Hodge accomplished this by presenting theological truths with the utmost precision and clarity, presenting alternative positions with the same clarity, inviting questions and objections, and illustrating his position with conviction. In Patton's words:

> The students saw every doctrine, as it presented itself to his vision. They benefited from his power of concise statement and clear definition. He held up the representative systems of theology with such

10.3 Archibald Alexander Hodge (1823–86).

sharpness of outline and such accuracy of articulation, that they knew them as one knows the face of a familiar friend. They questioned him, and he answered their questions. They raised objections, and so woke in him the hot fires of his polemic. They failed sometimes to comprehend a dogma, and he swept the universe for illustrations, and poured them out so copiously and with such manifest spontaneity, that they overwhelmed him with their applause.

While at Allegheny Seminary, his practice was to first lecture upon a subject and then devote an hour to discussing it with his students, encouraging them to ask questions and pose objections. According to one writer: "His capacity upon such occasions to pour out a stream of instruction beyond the lecture, his readiness in answering objections, and his singular power of curious and original illustrations excited the wonder of the students, and aroused a great enthusiasm for the study of theology." One of his former students stated regarding his teaching that:

> His patience and intellectual charity were both large, and he allowed the greatest freedom of debate to his scholars. In these contests, he was always chivalrous, and dismounted to meet his adversary on equal terms. . . . His many peculiarities of speech and manner never impaired his courtesy as a gentleman or his dignity as a professor. He had a powerful brain, a large heart, and the simple faith of a little child. He taught the knowledge of God with the learning of a scholar, the sympathy of a loving man, and the enthusiasm of a loving Christian.

While at Princeton he would regularly have students "recite" or summarize and explain from memory the assigned section of his father's *Systematic Theology* and then submit their recitations to the rigors of Hodge's Socratic questioning. In this way, according to Salmond, "the young men left the class-room not only possessing the truth taught, but with it possessing them." Depending on the responses of the students to his questioning, new avenues of instruction would open up into which Hodge would instinctively lead his students, drawing from the wealth of biblical, theological, and historical material of which he had mastery. By actively interacting with his students and engaging their questions and recitations, Hodge adapted the form of his theological instruction on the spot to fit the particular needs his varied students possessed. In this way, he was able to shed light on the dark areas peculiar to each class and lead their minds and hearts further into the light of theological truth.

In 1885 Hodge published *Questions on the Text of the Systematic Theology of Dr. Charles Hodge*, a short book of questions linked to the text of his father's *Systematic Theology*. This book was published to help students at the seminary analyze and retain the material in his father's text and prepare for their classroom recitations. In the first forty pages of this book, Hodge also examined and categorized the "various methods and schemes according to which the material of Christian theology has been arranged." Under the headings of "The Topical Method," "The Federal Method," "Theology Exhibited as the Doctrine of the Kingdom of God," "The Anthropological Method," "The Trinitarian Method," "The Theological Method," and "The Christo-centric Method," Hodge presented the outlines of numerous theological works that organized their material along these various lines. He did so in the belief that there was great value in considering the different ways in which doctrines could be arranged and "viewed from differing points of observation." In this way, Hodge again demonstrated his abilities as a theologian and his interest in theological organization and pedagogy.

Shorter Writings

Archibald Alexander Hodge was not by nature a writer, and he was averse to what he called "the drudgery of writing." Even so, in 1880 Hodge was asked to coedit the *Presbyterian Review* alongside of Charles A. Briggs. The *Review* was recast in 1880 to represent and serve "all the varied interests and sections" of the entire denomination of Northern Presbyterians, which in 1869 had reunited following its 1837 division. Unlike his father, Archibald Hodge had supported the reunification of the Old School and New School Presbyterians. He believed that reunion was justified because, in his words, "Both branches were now completely and equally (with slight and transient exceptions) Presbyterian in their organization, and the graver departures from the old Calvinistic system had ceased to prevail." At the same time, he realized that some Old School Presbyterians desired reunification in order to "make up for the loss of the Southern Church" and because some possessed "an intense sympathy with that branch of the Church which was largely leavened with New England ideas." The reunification was also advanced because the "interest in original [theological] speculation" that had prevailed in the preceding generation had been substituted with "an interest in the history and comparison of theological doctrines and systems." Reunification was also furthered, Hodge admitted, by "the general spirit of the age which deprecates the value of doctrinal distinction and emphasizes the value of character, and practical energy and work."

Hodge wrote a handful of journal articles for the *Presbyterian Review* and other similar journals that reflected his solidly conservative positions. One of his articles entitled "The *Ordo Salutis*" (1878) was singled out by Francis Patton as perhaps one of his few "original contributions to the science of theology" and "the best piece of theological work he ever did." In this article Hodge expressed his concern with the "tendency observable among many modern preachers and writers to ignore, if not positively to deny, the absolute necessity of a gratuitous justification as an essential precondition of the very beginnings of all moral reformation." In this short article, Hodge addressed the relationship between justification and God's bestowal of regeneration and faith to a sinner: "What is the true order of causation? Is the righteousness of Christ imputed to us that we may believe, or is it imputed to us because we believe?" While Hodge understood that both justification and God's transforming work (regeneration/sanctification) flow out of union with Christ, he argued that a theological and logical priority must be given to justification:

> The change of relation to the law signalized by the term justification, involving remission of penalty and restoration to favor, necessarily precedes and renders possible the real moral change of character signalized by the terms regeneration and sanctification. . . . We are pardoned in order that we may be good, never made good in order that we may be pardoned. We are freely made co-heirs with Christ in order that we may become willing co-workers with him, but we are never made co-workers in order that we might become co-heirs. These principles are of the very essence of Protestant soteriology. To modify,

and much more, of course, to ignore or to deny them, destroys absolutely the thing known as Protestantism, and ought to incur the forfeiture of all recognized right to wear the name.

To establish this point, Hodge went so far as to argue that a kind of provisional imputation of righteousness was granted to the elect from birth, providing the foundation for all of God's gracious acts toward them before their conversion and culminating in regeneration and the implanting of faith. According to Hodge: "The satisfaction and merit of Christ are imputed to the elect man from birth, so far as they form the basis of the gracious dealing provided for him in preparation for his full possession." Hodge quoted from William Ames and Herman Witsius to show that he was not alone in this idea of a kind of conceptual imputation that occurs prior to both regeneration and the imputation that brings about the "actual possession" of it. According to Hodge, "It is only when *justificatio forensis* [legal justification] maintains its Reformation position at the head of the process of salvation that it has any firm or secure standing at all."

FIG. 10.4

Selected Works of Archibald Alexander Hodge

Outlines of Theology, 1860

The Atonement, 1867

A Commentary on the Confession of Faith, 1869

Outlines of Theology (expanded edition), 1879

The Life of Charles Hodge, D.D., 1880

Manual of Forms, 1883

Popular Lectures on Theological Themes, 1887, posthumously

Another of Hodge's more significant articles was published in 1881 and was entitled "Inspiration," which he wrote along with Benjamin B. Warfield. In this article Hodge and Warfield reasserted Charles Hodge's conservative position regarding the authority and inspiration of Scripture, and also sharpened it in response to newer challenges from critical scholarship. According to Hodge and Warfield, the doctrine of the inspiration of Scripture means that God "presided over the sacred writers in their entire work of writing, with the design and effect of rendering that writing an errorless record of the matters He designed them to communicate, and hence constituting the entire volume in all its parts the Word of God to us." Hodge and Warfield asserted that this inspiration can be properly called "plenary" (or "full") and "verbal," even while they denied a "dictation" theory and other "mechanical conceptions" of inspiration. God's inspiration of Scripture "extended to the verbal expression of the thoughts of the sacred writers, as well as to the thoughts themselves," and therefore "the divine superintendence and guarantee extends to the one as much as the other." Since the Scriptures "not only contain, but are the Word of God, . . . all their elements and all their affirmations are absolutely errorless." Hodge and Warfield further asserted that this is "the historical faith of the Church," namely, that "all the affirmations of Scripture of all kinds, whether of spiritual doctrine or duty, or of physical or historical fact, or of psychological or philosophical principle, are without error, when the *ipsissima verba* [very words] of the original autographs are ascertained and interpreted in their natural and intended sense." Hodge and Warfield went on to defend this position from Scripture itself and responded to a number of objections raised by critics regarding the internal consistency or factual accuracy of portions of Scripture. In the decades that followed, Warfield would continue to argue along the lines developed in this article, making the theology of Old Princeton synonymous with the defense of Scripture's inspiration, infallibility, and inerrancy. In 1892, the Northern Presbyterians formally adopted the position of Hodge and Warfield over against the critical views of Charles A. Briggs, who was suspended the following year from ministering within the Presbyterian Church. In 1927, however, this position was ruled to be no longer binding on the church by the General Assembly.

The last article Hodge wrote before his death was entitled "Religion in the Public Schools." It was published posthumously in 1887. In this article Hodge voiced the same social concern his father had expressed about the secularization of America's political and public life, and he protested the growing secularization of literature used for public education. In his words, "the entire literature provided [by the government for the schools] has been laboriously purged from every theistic or Christian reference." This was taking place, stated Hodge, under the mistaken assumption that religious elements can be harmlessly separated from other areas of learning such as history, ethics, and science. According to Hodge, "it is absolutely impossible to separate religious ideas from the great mass of human knowledge":

> Education involves the training of the whole man and of all the facul-
> ties, of the conscience and of the affections, as well as of the intellect.
> The English language is the product of the thought, character, and
> life of an intensely Christian people for many centuries. A purely
> nontheistic treatment of that vocabulary would not merely falsify the
> truth of the subject, but would necessarily make it an instrument of
> conveying positively antitheistic and antichristian ideas. All history
> is a product of divine Providence, and is instinct with the divine ends
> and order. This is especially true of the history of the Anglo-Saxon
> race, which is a record of the conflict of religious ideas and forces
> from the first. It is self-evident that a nontheistic or a non-Christian
> treatment of that history would be utterly superficial and misrepre-
> senting. It cannot be questioned that morals rest upon a religious
> basis, and that a nontheistic ethics is equivalent to a positively anti-
> theistic one. The same is no less true of science in all its departments.
> It ultimately rests upon the ground that the universe is a manifestation
> of reason. If God is not therein recognized he is denied, and a non-
> theistic science has always been and will always be a positively atheistic
> and materialistic one.

Hodge held that it does not follow from "the American principle of the absolute divorce of church and state" that the state is to function on the basis of a secular or agnostic framework. On the contrary, the American state and its lawmakers, Hodge argued, are to operate according to the revelation of God given both in Scripture and "through the natural law written upon the heart," since "the state and the Church are both divine institutions, having different ends, spheres, laws, methods, and agents." They are "both equally divine institutions, and the members and officers of each are alike subject to God, and bound to obey every word He directs to either one of them in their appropriate sphere." What is further, Hodge went to great lengths to argue that America is a "Christian country, in the sense that Christianity is an original and essential element of the law of the land." Because it is a "Christian country" in its legal character, schools should be legislated to teach in accordance with a kind of "general Christianity." In this line of argument, Hodge carried forward the same general views that were promoted by his father regarding the role of Christianity in American life.

Hodge also published a number of other shorter articles and addresses, including an article on the "Vedantists [i.e., Hindus] of Young Bengal" (1851), "The Consensus of the Reformed Confessions" (1884), and "The Relation of God to the World" (1887). This last article was published posthumously and reflects Hodge's lifelong fascination with the topic of God's relationship and interaction with his creation. Shortly before his death he presented a series of popular lectures on theological topics in Philadelphia, including topics such as providence, miracles, prayer, the Trinity, predestination, God's covenants with man, and sanctification. These lectures drew large crowds and were immensely popular. After his death the lectures were published as *Popular Lectures on Theological Themes*. In these shorter pieces, Hodge's gift as a communicator and popularizer of Old Princeton's conservative positions is evident.

After a brief period of sickness, A. A. Hodge died suddenly on November 12, 1886, at the age of sixty-three. In eulogizing Hodge, William Paxton memorialized one of the traits that had made him such an effective teacher of theology. In Paxton's words,

> Many have the idea that the chair of Theology is a frigid, icy throne, from which are dispensed cold distractions and rigid dogmas. But it was not so with him; the doctrines which he taught were the life and comfort of his own soul, and they came from the depths of his experience, warm and glowing, and entered as living forces into the souls of others.

Paxton also noted how Hodge's effectiveness as a teacher grew out of his warmhearted experience of Christ, which infused all his varied talents and intellectual gifts:

> The centre of all [Archibald Alexander Hodge's] religious experience was Christ. . . . [H]e had a religious experience which found all its sources of life in the Bible. . . . He had a faculty for definition which

seemed to be intuitive. He had a power of statement that appeared to be sufficient without argument. He had a capacity for analysis by which every subject seemed to fall to pieces in his hands in the clearest and most definite forms. He had a force of logic which made his conclusions inexorable. He had a faculty for putting things which forced them upon the attention and fastened them upon the memory. He had a balance of mind that gave to everything its due proportion. He had a faculty for original illustration that was astonishing and unrivalled. He had an imagination to originate novel conceptions and to throw a glow and splendor around everything that he did. But his chief and most remarkable mental characteristic was his power to mingle the intellectual and the emotional—to interpenetrate and transfuse the most abstruse thinking with the warm glow of devotional emotion.

With his unique ability in blending religious and emotional experience into the presentation of his subject, Hodge was an effective popularizer of theology. In this way he greatly advanced the Old Princeton agenda to conserve evangelical truth and promote evangelical piety and warmhearted spirituality.

Conclusion

According to Archibald Alexander Hodge, systematic theology requires both piety and mental clarity. In his words, "Let it be remembered that systematic theology has its essence simply in clear thinking and clear speaking on the subject of that religion which is revealed in the Scriptures. A man can outgrow systematic theology, therefore, either by ceasing to be clear-headed, or by ceasing to be religious, and in no other way. I suppose some escape in their haste by both ways at once." While A. A. Hodge was not as significant a theologian or exegete as his father, his abilities as a teacher and communicator of theology were unmatched. In this particular area he was, in the words of Francis Patton, "marked by genius." Whether communicating in the pulpit, the classroom, or the far reaches of India, his concern for the faithful transmission of biblical truth, for clarity of expression, and for effective teaching were unequalled.

11

OLD PRINCETON AND THEOLOGY: ARCHIBALD ALEXANDER HODGE'S *THE ATONEMENT*

His [Archibald Alexander Hodge's] published works show both logical and theological power. While founding upon the massive and luminous system of his venerated father, he methodizes, condenses, and fortifies with an originality that evinces his competence to have made a system of his own.

—W. G. T. Shedd

Dr. Hodge's book on the atonement was written during the agitation of the reunion question and is still one of the best treatises we have upon the subject.

—Francis L. Patton

Agreeing so nearly with Professor Hodge, we always welcome his most weighty and judicious works, and to the present volume [The Atonement] *we give our warmest commendation. No one can read it without owning that the hand of a master theologian is visible on every page. No minister can well afford to leave it unread.*

—Charles Spurgeon

By the end of the Civil War, New School and Old School Presbyterians in the North were seeking to formally end the division that had separated the two groups since 1837. Some of those at Princeton had misgivings about reunification, especially Charles Hodge. These misgivings were due to the New School's more relaxed views of confessional subscription and their willingness to tolerate deviations from the Westminster Confession of Faith. One of the main areas of doctrinal deviation and dispute at this time was on the nature of the atonement. The New School had tolerated a wide range of views on this subject, including a "governmental view" of the atonement adopted from New England theology (also referred to as "New Divinity"). Horace Bushnell's "moral view" of the atonement also called the traditional view into question and was advanced in his *The Vicarious Sacrifice* (1866).

That same year, Archibald Alexander Hodge was asked to write a series of articles for a Presbyterian periodical on the doctrine of the atonement. He was asked to do so to clear away misrepresentations of the traditional, penal-substitutionary view of Christ's atoning work and to offer "a restatement of the venerable faith of the Reformed Churches . . . specifically adapted to the circumstances of the present generation." These articles grew into a book of more than four hundred pages, appearing the following year as *The Atonement*. Hodge called this work "the best contribution within my power to the vindication of the ancient faith of the Presbyterian Church and of the unquestionable and only legitimate interpretation of her standards." With New School tendencies in mind, Hodge stated that he offered his work

> to repel with all my might alike all those positive heresies which attack [the confessional view of the atonement] openly, and with even greater solicitude that latitudinarian indifference to exact conceptions and careful statements of doctrine which tends secretly, yet not less certainly, to destroy the truth, and which in the present age is our chief source of danger.

With reunification almost certainly on the horizon, Hodge went on to state, "I would pray and labor that in gaining breadth we may not lose height, and in gaining peace and love we may not lose purity and truth."

True to Hodge's gifts as a teacher and popularizer of theology, Hodge's *Atonement* is a well-organized and clearly presented work of theology. He wrote it first to clearly define and state the doctrine of Christ's atoning work on the cross, "defining all the points involved," showing the "scriptural evidence" for such doctrine, and illustrating that "the true Church has always, from the days of the apostles to the present, in all its branches, been in essential agreement as to the essential elements of the doctrine as taught at large in the confessions of the Reformed and Lutheran Churches." Large amounts of the book were written to answer common objections made against the confessional doctrine of the atonement, as well as other "erroneous views held in opposition to the truth." Finally, Hodge also attempted to "state and prove the common doctrine of the Reformed Churches as to the design of the Atonement with respect to its objects [i.e., its extent]."

The Confessional Doctrine of Christ's Atoning Work

Hodge began his *Atonement* by stating the doctrine of the atonement as it is found in Scripture, giving his understanding of the doctrines connected to it as well. Some of these doctrines include the holiness and justice of God, the immutability of God's moral law, the federal headship of Adam, the propitiatory and typical nature of sacrifices in the Old Testament, the priesthood of Christ, union with Christ, and justification by faith through the active and passive obedience of Christ. By covering this ground, Hodge's *Atonement* contains a full articulation of the entire doctrine of redemption. His elaboration is set against the backdrop of "two absurdly inconsistent attacks, originating in rationalistic sources," namely, the subjugation of scriptural revelation to human reason on the one hand, and the rejection of "definite views of doctrine" in exchange for "vague, undetermined, and loosely-held views" on the other. His doctrinal exposition was intended to answer these attacks by fully setting forth the scriptural doctrine of the work of Christ.

As far as terminology is concerned, Hodge preferred to use the word "satisfaction" over the word "atonement" to speak of Christ's redeeming work. This word more clearly indicates *how* Christ atoned for his people's sins, namely, by satisfying "all the demands of law upon which the favor and fellowship of God were suspended." While the word "atonement" represents "only the satisfaction which Christ rendered to the justice of God in vicariously bearing the penalty due to our sins," the word "satisfaction" includes "that satisfaction which Christ rendered in his vicarious obedience to the law as a covenant of everlasting well-being." Yet even the concept of satisfaction was not broad enough, according to Hodge, to contain what Christ accomplished on the cross. Hodge asserted that there are three primary "forms of conception under which the work wrought by Christ for the salvation of men is set forth" in Scripture, namely: "that of an expiatory offering for sin," "that of the redemption of the life and liberty of a captive by the payment of a ransom in his stead," and "the satisfaction of the law by the vicarious fulfillment of its demands." These three conceptions "are designed both to limit and to supplement each other," so that there is a varied richness in Scripture's presentation of the atonement. In Hodge's words, "The Holy Ghost has ideally represented the work of Christ as marked by the precise point of convergence of the bleeding sacrifice, of redemption by the substitution of a personal ransom, and of the vicarious bearing of the curse of the law by a substitute in the stead of the criminal." Beyond the teaching of these three conceptions individually, "The teaching of Scripture is not that Christ is a sacrifice, *and* a ransom, *and* a bearer of the curse of the law," but that redemption, ransom, satisfaction, expiation, propitiation, representation, and substitution all must be understood in light of each other and are all part of Scripture's integrated presentation of Christ's atoning work.

The nature of Christ's atoning work on the cross is most fundamentally presented in Scripture as penal and substitutionary in nature. In other words, Christ "vicariously suffer[ed] the penalty of the broken law as the substitute of his people." Hodge elaborated on this summary statement by saying, "Christ was in a strict and exact sense the substitute of his people; i.e., by divine appointment, and of his own free will, he assumed all our legal responsibilities and thus assumed our law-place, binding himself to do in our stead all that the law demanded of him when he suffered the penalty due us." Christ suffered "the very penalty of the law" on the cross, that is, he received the just punishment that our sins deserved. He "assumed the guilt" of our sins, and the "penal obligation" of our guilt was "willingly assumed by, and imputed to him—i.e., charged to his account." Because of the "legal oneness which the divine will had constituted between [Christ] and us," the guilt of our sin was justly "charged to his account." As such, "the Lord hath laid on him the iniquity of us all," Christ was "offered to bear the sins of many," and he "bore our sins in his own body on the tree" (Isa. 53:6; Heb. 9:28; 1 Peter 2:24).

Hodge grounded the substitutionary nature of Christ's atoning work on the representative relationship or "federal headship" that Christ has with his people. Christ bore our sins because he was constituted by God as a representative head and legal substitute for his people. Hodge understood this relationship as parallel with the federal headship that Adam originally possessed over the human race. Hodge went to great lengths to explain and defend the federal headship of Adam, arguing from Romans 5:18 that "there is a precise parallelism between the way in which our 'condemnation' follows from the disobedience of Adam, and in which our 'justification' or 'being made righteous' follows from the obedience of Christ." As Adam was a federal or representative head of the human race, so too is Christ the federal head of his people. Hodge argued at length against rival conceptions of the imputation of Adam's sin and Adam's headship, including the notion of "mediate imputation" found in New England theology and the "realist" notion of Adam's headship advanced by Reformed theologian W. G. T. Shedd. While admitting that the union between Christ and his people is "both federal and vital" and that it "transcends all natural analogies," Hodge defended the concept and primacy of Christ's "federal union" with his people. He did so to protect the substitutionary nature of the atonement, as well as the doctrine of justification through the imputation of Christ's righteousness.

Hodge found further support for the vicarious and substitutionary nature of the sufferings of Christ in the Old Testament sacrifices. According to Hodge, the sacrifices "were universally regarded by those offering them as vicarious sufferings, expiating sin and propitiating God. . . . They were, moreover, certainly typical of [i.e., a foreshadowing of] the sacrifice of Christ." Citing detailed and "abundant proof" from the Old Testament, Hodge argued for the "traditional and orthodox view" of the sacrifices, namely, that "The death of the bleeding sacrifice was a *paena vicaria*, a vicarious punishment, the life of the victim being substituted in the stead of the life of the offerer." Christ came in fulfillment of the prophetic foreshadowing contained in the sacrificial system, in spite of the contrary assertions of "the Socinians and rationalists" and writers like Horace Bushnell.

Hodge explained that the motive Christ had in going to the cross was "the amazing love of God to his own people." By going to the cross Christ "expiated the guilt of sin," "fulfilled the demands of law," and "propitiated justice," thus reconciling us to God and securing our salvation. The work of Christ "produced no change in God, any more than do [other] acts of creation and providence," since "the infinite justice and the infinite love exercised in the sacrifice of Christ were in the divine mind from the beginning." What Christ did was "to render possible the concurrent exercise of the justice and the love [sic] in the treatment of the same sinful persons." He expands on this point by saying:

> Our doctrine is not in the least inconsistent with the glorious truth that the love of God for his own people is eternal and self-originated—the cause and not the effect of the Atonement. The fact is, that his love for their persons, and his holy displeasure for their sins, were co-existent states of mind from eternity. And yet the apostle takes upon himself to say that the very elect themselves, so beloved, were, because of God's righteousness, "by nature the children of wrath, even as others" (Eph. 2:3). . . . Such a change in our relations to God was wrought by the work of Christ, that his infinite righteousness coincides with his infinite love in all their blessed manifestations and operations towards his own people for ever.

Christ's work brings a real change in our relationship to God when accomplished in history and applied to our hearts, and yet all three persons of the Trinity were united in their eternal love for us, even while we were sinners and under his wrath.

When the penal and substitutionary nature of the atonement is kept at the forefront, Hodge believed it was possible to acknowledge other secondary effects of the atonement as well. While Christ's "direct intention was to satisfy justice on [his people's] behalf, and thus secure, on legal terms, their salvation," he also

> necessarily satisfied the natural demand of the sinner's conscience for expiation, and subdued his sullen alienation, and removed his distrust of God, by the supreme exhibition of divine love made on the cross. At the same time, and by the same means, he gave to the whole moral universe the highest conceivable demonstration of God's inexorable determination to punish all sin, just because he did so punish it even in the person of his Son.

While Christ's atonement does uphold the honor of God's moral government, does work a powerful effect on us ("it melts the hearts, subdues the rebellion, and dissipates the fears of sinful men"), and does give us a wonderful example of sacrificial love for us to emulate, these effects are secondary and by themselves fail to adequately describe what Christ accomplished. It was Hodge's assertion that many of the "heterodox" views being proposed as alternatives to the penal substitutionary view were not so much "false" as they were "essentially defective." By making secondary effects of the atonement primary, the heterodox views had taken the heart out of it.

Turning to the testimony of history, Hodge asserted that the penal substitutionary view of the atonement "has in its essential principles been the faith of the great body of God's people from the beginning." In his assessment, the penal substitutionary view had been held by the church "in every particular age and section of the Church precisely in proportion to its general orthodoxy and spiritual vitality." According to Hodge:

> The doctrine that Christ has redeemed men from the claims of divine justice by his vicarious sufferings has always been more clearly conceived and more frequently and emphatically insisted upon in the exact proportion as the Church has been faithful in the profession of other fundamental truths and abundant in the fruit of the Spirit. . . . Those who were most eminent in the defense of the truth as to the supreme divinity of our blessed Lord, as Athanasius the Great; those

who stood to the last faithful in resisting the inroads of Popery, as Claude, bishop of Turin (821–39); the best of the schoolmen, as Anselm, Hugh St. Victor, Bernard, Bonaventura and Thomas Aquinas; both of the two great sections (Greek and Roman) into which the Church divided; the great evangelical teachers . . . and finally, *all* of the great evangelical denominations into which the Churches of the Reformation have been developed, who now embrace the sum total of Christ's kingdom on the face of the earth; all these . . . in whatever else they have differed have agreed in maintaining that the virtue of the redemption of Christ resides in its power to expiate sin and thus to propitiate God.

Hodge provided a survey of each period of church history with numerous quotations to back up his claim. He fully acknowledged that the penal substitutionary view of the atonement was not "conceived of in all its elements or stated with scientific accuracy in the early ages of the Church," and yet this could also be said of most major orthodox doctrines, which were "at first conceived obscurely, stated vaguely, and mixed with incongruous and even inconsistent elements," only reaching their "mature form . . . through a process of growth." Hodge acknowledged that "the mind of the Church advanced more slowly in the development of the doctrine of the atonement than in the case of any other of the great fundamental doctrines of Revelation." He admitted "the prevalence of the eccentric idea that Christ was delivered up as a ransom-price to Satan," which had "so long confused and dis-figured the ideas of ecclesiastical writers upon the subject of redemption." While this "eccentric" view was in serious error, it correctly went so far as to assert that "the sufferings of Christ were necessary to remove obstacles to our salvation existing exterior to ourselves." Hodge also acknowledged the presence of the moral influence and governmental views in the church's history, but he linked these views to "such heretics as Scotus Erigena and Abelard," "the Socinians of the sixteenth century," "the semi-Socinian Dutch Remonstrants," and "the heretical French Professors of Saumur." In his judgment, "true spiritual religion has never flourished among those who have explicitly denied" the expiatory nature of Christ's atoning work.

Objections Answered

Having laid out the penal substitutionary view of the atonement and its place in Scripture and church history, Hodge went on to respond to five objections raised against the penal substitutionary view of the atonement. The first is the assertion that the penal substitutionary view ascribes a kind of "vindictiveness" to God that "revolts the moral sense" in its insistence upon God's punitive justice. Hodge found those who made this claim at fault for attempting to "resolve justice into benevolence," thus denying justice to God "in our strict and absolute sense of the word." Hodge responded further by asserting that "the idea of oughtness [i.e., justice] is more elemental than the idea of benevolence. It is an independent and ultimate idea which stands by itself. . . . It is intrinsically supreme and absolute." God's justice is one of his most fundamental attributes. To deny God his fundamental justice is "an obvious contradiction to all the sacred and profane history of God's providential dealings with men from the beginning until now, to all the moral judgments of men, to the principles of all human law and religions, and to all the revealed principles of the Scriptures." Justice cannot be subsumed into a notion of benevolence because God clearly at times exercises judgment in a way that does not serve a benevolent end (e.g., for those who receive the eternal punishment of hell). God's justice is a basic and supremely wonderful attribute of God, and not to be equated with vindictiveness, which is a "miserable vice festering in the heart of a sinful creature." According to Hodge, God's "inexorable determination to treat all sin according to its intrinsic ill-desert is a peerless excellence crowning all the other moral attributes of a wise, righteous and benevolent Ruler."

The second objection Hodge addressed is the assertion that the penal substitutionary view of the atonement excludes grace from the way God saves sinners. According to Hodge, there were some who believed that the traditional view made the atonement "a mere commercial transaction," whereby the Son makes a payment to the unwilling Father, forcing him to grant forgiveness that he was not graciously willing to grant. Hodge replied by asserting the dual love that both the Father and the Son had in planning the salvation of sinners:

Christ is not of a different nature from the Father, but is of one essence, nature, feeling, mind and purpose with him from all eternity. He did not die to make the Father cease to hate us, but was given because God SO LOVED THE WORLD, in order to reconcile that infinite love with infinite justice in their concurrent exercises with regard to their common objects. . . . Christ is the one satisfied as well as the one satisfying, the one punishing as well as the one punished; but he loves us enough to punish himself in our place. This is THE wonder of eternity. This is the inexhaustible theme of the heavenly song of adoration and gratitude for ever.

Hodge also asserted that a technical distinction must be made between the forgiveness of a sinner and the forgiveness of sins, so that while "sin is never that which is forgiven [strictly considered] . . . *the sinner* is forgiven and the penalty due his sin not executed upon him." The sins of a believing sinner receive their just due, while the sinner himself receives God's forgiving grace.

The third objection Hodge addressed is the assertion that it is not just for God to punish Jesus on the cross for the sins of another. Hodge responded to this objection by first stating that "it must be conceded by all that justice cannot demand and execute the *punishment* of a sin upon any party that is not truly and really responsible for it, and that the sin of one person cannot be really expiated by means of the sufferings of another, unless they be in such a sense legally one that in the judgment of the law the suffering of the one is the suffering of the other." It is in fact the case, according to Hodge, that "Christ *does* sustain this unique relation to his people," for "the eternal Logos, in council with the Father and Holy Ghost, assumed the responsibility of the federal relations of his elect to the law from all eternity." Christ sustains such a unique union with his people that "his suffering the penalty due to [his people's] sins is in full legal effect equivalent to the execution of the penalty on them."

The fourth objection Hodge answered was one raised by Socinus and others, namely, that the temporal sufferings of one man are not equivalent to the eternal sufferings due to several men. In other words, how is divine justice satisfied by the temporal sufferings of one man in place of "the eternal death of an incalculable multitude"? Hodge responded by pointing out that this objection flows naturally from the low view of Christ's person held by Socinus and his followers. The answer to it is found in "the supreme divinity of our Lord." While "Christ suffered solely in his human nature," it was "the eternal, august, supreme, second Person of the Godhead [who] obeyed and suffered in the stead of sinners." Instead of the law's demands being "relaxed" to receive the temporal sufferings of Christ in place of the eternal sufferings of many, "the law is 'magnified' by such an obedience and by such a penal suffering, as it could not be by the several eternal sufferings of all creatures actual or possible; and justice is not only satisfied, but glorified, borne aloft and set ablaze in the crown of God."

The fifth and final objection Hodge addressed in this section is the objection that the penal substitutionary view of the atonement dishonors Christ by implying that he was made on the cross to be personally sinful in his character. Hodge responded by asserting that the traditional doctrine "always has been simply that the legal responsibilities (penal and federal) of his people were by covenant transferred to Christ." While "the sinful act and the sinful nature are inalienable [i.e., not able to be taken away or transferred from sinners], the guilt or just liability to punishment is alienable [able to be taken away and transferred], or [else] no sinner can be saved." Our own "evil nature" is not transferred to Christ but "remains inalienably our own until we are changed by the Holy Ghost in regeneration and sanctification." All that is transferred to Christ is the guilt of our sins, not the corruption of them.

The Moral Influence and Governmental Views of the Atonement Refuted

After responding to these objections, Hodge discussed the moral influence and governmental views of the atonement, which alike denied that Christ's sufferings were "designed to produce a justice-propitiating effect terminating upon God." Both of these approaches limited the purpose of the atonement to something which rested in the minds and hearts of men: the moral influence view understood the purpose of Christ's sufferings and death to "produce an effect terminating as a moral impression in the subjective condition of the individual sinner," while the governmental view saw it as designed "to produce an effect terminating as a moral impression in the public mind of the subjects of the moral government of God." Both the moral influence and the governmental view saw the need of the atonement as rooted in the moral sentiments of man instead of in the holy and just character of God.

Though often associated with Horace Bushnell and his contemporaries, the moral influence view of the atonement, or the general view that "the great end of the death of Christ was to produce a moral impression upon the hearts of sinners, and thus lead to their moral and spiritual reformation," was actually expressed much earlier by Abelard (1079–1142) and Socinus (1539–1604). Such writers asserted that Christ died for the central purpose of showing us the love and faithfulness of God and to provide us with a moral example that we might imitate. In this way, reconciliation and salvation are opened up for us through our own personal change and response to what God has demonstrated to us through Christ. Hodge replied to this view by asserting that "the precious truth which [this view] undeniably contains has always been held by the Church as an integral part of the orthodox doctrine," and that "the infinite love of God" is upheld "with far greater consistency and illustrated with far greater force" by the penal substitutionary view than by the moral influence view. In fact, the moral influence view reduces the "tragic suffering voluntarily incurred in fidelity to high principle and out of unquenchable love for us" to a contrived display "intentionally gotten up with the design of producing a pathetic effect upon us." If the moral influence view is correct, then "the glorious transactions of Gethsemane and Calvary, which the Church has always regarded as infinitely real, intense with divine attributes in action, are reduced to the poor level of scenes deliberately contrived for effect, finding their sole end in their effect as scenes."

The governmental view of the atonement, or the view that Christ died in order to uphold the honor of God's moral government in the eyes of his creatures, was first expressed by Hugo Grotius (1583–1645) before becoming popular among the advocates of the New England theology. The New England theologians, such as Samuel Hopkins, Nathanael Emmons, and Jonathan Edwards Jr., asserted that Christ died not to take the punishment of sinners and appease the justice of God directly but to perform something similar that would have the same effect and vindicate the honor of God's law in the eyes of his creatures. His death was "a substitute for a penalty," and it allowed God to grant pardon and favor to whomever he desires without suffering the indignity of allowing his broken law to go unanswered. Rather than paying the penalty for specific sins, Christ died so that his creatures might take his law and benevolent moral government seriously. As with the moral influence view, Hodge asserted that this view contained "truths of the very highest importance" and yet failed to uphold these truths with consistency. By making the sufferings of Christ only indirectly related to the sins of his people, the governmental view makes both the act of atonement and the subsequent "relaxation" of God's law arbitrary acts of God:

> How in the name of reason is it possible that the undeserved sufferings of Christ, which were not the penalty which the law demanded, should make it consistent with God's rectoral justice to relax the law, and omit the penalty altogether in the case of repentant sinners? . . . And how could he truly and really express his abhorrence of our sins by means of the sufferings of Christ, unless the real legal responsibility for our sins were first laid upon Christ, and they were then strictly punished in him?

By making the death of Christ a mere "contrivance to take the place of the penalty of the law," the advocates of the governmental theory were guilty of representing "the sacred tragedy of Gethsemane and Calvary as an illusive example of punishment where there was no real punishment—an 'expression' of divine attributes which were not really exercised in the case." Hodge noted the internal contradiction inherent in the governmental view by stating:

> It is very grievous that the sacred death of our Lord should be thus characterized as an attempt upon God's part . . . to impose upon the moral universe an "expression" of attributes not actually in *exercise*, an "exhibition of punishment" where there is no punishment, and to make an example in which sin is *dealt* with without punishment an emphatic demonstration of his purpose always to punish it.

If the death of Christ was not an act of actual punishment, it cannot rightly serve as an example of punishment. The governmental theory thus fails for denying the key components of penalty and substitution. Hodge also criticized the governmental view for denying the absolute necessity of the atonement and the immutability of God's perfect standard of justice, as well as for fundamentally altering the related doctrine of justification by the imputed righteousness of Christ.

The Extent of the Atonement's Intended Application

Hodge closed *The Atonement* with a separate section that addresses the question: "Did Christ die with the design of making satisfaction to divine justice in behalf of all men, indiscriminately, or in behalf of his elect seed personally and definitely?" Hodge affirmed the second of these two views. He did not believe, though, that his previous assertions regarding the substitutionary nature of the atonement always led individuals to adopt a limited and definite understanding of the atonement. As evidence of this, he referred to "an honorable company of scholars and saints," namely orthodox Lutherans, "who hold at once the strictest views as to the sin-expiating, justice-satisfying nature of the atonement and the broadest views as to its indefinite and universal character." In his opinion, the question of the extent of the atonement is "less essential and intrinsic" than those principles "fundamental to the system of faith known as evangelical." At the same time, Hodge strongly held and defended the Reformed understanding of a limited and definite atonement.

Hodge recognized that different groups had different theological reasons for asserting that the atonement was unlimited or indefinite in its design. Some held this position as a central tenet of a fundamentally Arminian scheme of salvation. Others, like the New England theologians, maintained certain Reformed convictions and yet held to an unlimited atonement because of their understanding of the governmental nature of the atonement. Still others, like Amyraldus of Saumur (1596–1664), held to an otherwise Reformed understanding of salvation except on this point. Hodge attributed this third position to an "absence of clearness of thought and consequent inaccuracy in the use of terms."

Hodge believed that the debate over the design and extent of the atonement was often confused by an imprecise statement of the issue. He said that the dispute was not a disagreement about the "actual application of the saving benefits of Christ's work," since none but universalists denied that the atonement was limited in this respect. Neither was the dispute over the "sufficiency," "applicability," or "universal offer" of Christ's work. Hodge affirmed the universal sufficiency of the atonement, stating that

> the Reformed Churches have uniformly taught that no man has ever yet perished, or ever will perish, for want of an atonement. . . . Christ's obedience and sufferings were of infinite intrinsic value in the eye of the law, and . . . there was no need for him to obey or to suffer an iota more nor a moment longer in order to secure, if God so willed, the salvation of every man, woman, and child that ever lived.

This universal sufficiency flows from "the supreme divinity of the glorious victim," and was asserted by such Reformed theologians as Francis Turretin, Herman Witsius, and John Owen. The atonement should not be conceived strictly as a commercial transaction, since the death of the divine Son of God is of infinite value. According to Hodge, it is "altogether a false representation" to regard the Reformed position "strictly as a commercial transaction," since the Reformed theologians "unite with other Christians in glorying in the infinite sufficiency of the satisfaction of Christ to reach and to save all men who have been or who will be created." In addition to the infinite value and sufficiency of Christ's death, Hodge affirmed that the atonement also has a universal "applicability" to it, such that "Christ did and suffered precisely what the law demanded of each man personally and of every man indiscriminately, and it may be at any time applied to the redemption of one man as well as to another, as far as the satisfaction itself is concerned." The atoning work of Christ is thus "offered to all men indiscriminately" and is "most certainly and freely available to each and every sinner to whom it is offered, upon condition that he believes." Hodge also affirmed that Christ "died with the design as well as effect of securing many benefits, short of salvation, for the non-elect as well as for the elect."

After giving these areas of agreement, Hodge went on to state that the debate on the extent of the atonement revolves solely around the "intended application" of the atonement. Regarding this point Hodge asserted the traditional Reformed position, namely, that it was the design of the redemptive work of Christ "to carry into effect [God's] purpose of election . . . in pursuance of an eternal covenant between the Father and [Christ] for the purpose as well as with the result of effecting the salvation of his own people." It was no "general and impersonal philanthropy or love of mankind in general" which prompted Christ to die on the cross, but "the highest conceivable love which God can have for a creature," namely, "a personal love of certain definite individuals foreknown from eternity." The death of Christ not only removed all legal impediments to salvation but also meritoriously procured "its gracious application" and "the gracious influences of the Holy Ghost" to produce faith and repentance in the hearts of the elect. Christ's atoning work was not limited because of any consideration regarding "the degree, duration or kind of sufferings or acts of vicarious obedience which Christ rendered," but only on account of "the purpose he had in rendering them," namely, "to accomplish the purpose of election." In this way, the atonement is limited and definite in its design and extent.

Hodge asserted next that "all true Augustinians and Calvinists have necessarily held that Christ died definitely and personally for the elect," while "all Arians, Pelagians, semi-Pelagians, Socinians, and Arminians, have in perfect consistency with their several systems, maintained the general and indefinite reference of the atonement." The definite view of the atonement's extent, Hodge argued, could be clearly seen in Augustine and his followers, even though "the Schoolmen who followed Augustine" muddled the church's common position with their assertion that Christ's death was "sufficient for all, efficient for the elect." Hodge believed this statement was close to the truth and yet "inaccurate in terms" and "more likely to confuse than to clear the question." Hodge also asserted that Calvin held to the sufficient/efficient formula of the Scholastics and at times used "general terms with respect to the design of Christ's death in a more unguarded manner than would *now* be done by one of his consistent disciples." Even so, Hodge argued that Calvin explicitly denied the notion of "an indiscriminate atonement." Calvin also clearly subordinated "the purpose of redemption to the purpose of election" and "denies utterly" in his 1 John commentary "that the apostle, in saying that Christ is 'the propitiation for the sins of the whole world' (*totius mundi*) could have meant to include the reprobate." After Calvin, the doctrine became formally established by the Reformed creeds and confessions of the seventeenth century as "the common consensus," notwithstanding the departures of Amyraldus and the so-called "Marrow Men" of the eighteenth century.

Hodge believed that the personal and definite design of the atonement to save the elect "certainly follows" from the substitutionary nature of the atonement, and that "the very conception of substitution necessarily involves definite, personal relations." The concept of satisfaction also entails a definite and limited extent to the atonement, since "all of those for whom Christ has . . . made perfect satisfaction must be saved." Hodge also pointed to numerous passages of Scripture that represent the atonement as effective in its accomplishment and that describe the atonement as that which procures the faith and repentance of the elect. Hodge also pointed to numerous passages which speak of "the eternal Covenant of Redemption" between the Father and the Son, that speak of Christ's "peculiar and personal love" as a motive for his sufferings, and that explicitly limit the design of Christ's death to the elect. Hodge closed his discussion by briefly responding to a number of objections to the limited atonement view, including objections derived from the "large class of Scripture passages" such as 1 Timothy 2:3–6; 1 John 2:1–2; and John 3:16, which say that "Christ 'suffered for all,' and gave his life for the 'world.'" Hodge agreed with Moses Stuart that these passages indicate that Christ died for "all men without distinction, that is, both Jew and Gentile" and were written to oppose "the Jewish idea that the Messiah was connected appropriately and exclusively with the Jews." Hodge asserted on this point that:

> The phrase that Christ died for the whole world may be taken in three senses: (a.) That he died for Jews as well as Gentiles, for a people elect out of all nations and generations. (b.) That he died to secure many advantages for all men from Adam to the last generation, especially for all citizens in Christian lands. (c.) That he died to secure the

salvation of each and every man that ever lived; that is, that he died in the same sense for the non-elect as for the elect. The first two we affirm; the latter we deny.

Hodge also pointed out that those who hold to a universal atonement must themselves qualify many of the "all" passages, such as Colossians 1:20; 1 Corinthians 15:22; and Ephesians 1:10, in order to avoid falling into universalism.

In sum, Hodge followed the Reformed tradition in asserting both the limited and unlimited aspects of the atonement's extent. In his words:

All the legal obstacles in God's way of saving any are removed, and hence the salvation of all is now legally possible, *a parte Dei* [from the part of God]. . . . In a strictly objective sense the atonement is as freely available, on the condition of faith, to the gospel-hearing non-elect as it is to the elect. . . . Hence it follows that if we look down the line of purpose and causation from God toward mankind, it is plain that Christ could have had no other purpose in dying than to save those whom he actually does save. But if we look upwards from the position of the sinner, to whom the universal offer of a personal interest in the atonement of Christ is brought, it is evident that Christ did *so* die for the sins of the whole world that if *any man* hears the offer and is willing to accept it, a free and perfect atonement is his for the taking. Hence it follows, that in all ages many of the most rigid predestinarians have said, in the words of Calvin himself, "*Passus est Christus pro peccatis totius mundi* [Christ suffered for the sins of the whole world]," while it has been only very superficial critics who have inferred therefrom that these men intended to decide against the doctrine of the Reformed Churches, which is that Christ designed in his death to secure the salvation of his elect, and of none others.

Even while asserting that God designed the atonement with the intention of applying it to the limited and specific group of God's elect, Hodge was also clear that Christ's atonement is "sufficient for all" and "exactly adapted to the needs of each." He also believed it is to be "offered indiscriminately to all," given the clear command of Christ in Matthew 28:19–20. In Hodge's words:

As far as God's *preceptive will* is concerned, the atonement is universal. It is to be preached to all, and to be accepted by all. It is for all as far as determining the duty of all and laying obligations upon all. And practically it makes salvation objectively available to all upon the condition of faith. God's *decretive will* or design in making the atonement is a very different matter.

Conclusion

Regarding the atonement, A. A. Hodge asserted the orthodox position that Christ died as a penal substitute for his people, paying the penalty demanded by God's law and offering full satisfaction for their salvation. The atonement not only removed every legal impediment to their salvation but also purchased every spiritual grace (including faith and repentance) for God's elect, as well as the common grace shown to mankind in general. God designed and intended the atonement of Christ to be applied to those who actually have it applied to them, and while there are significant universal aspects to the atonement, its extent is limited and definite in its intention and design.

A. A. Hodge's *The Atonement* demonstrates the clarity, depth, and insightfulness that are found in many of the great theological works that came out of Old Princeton. In keeping with views of the Old School Presbyterians, Hodge and the Princeton theologians maintained the evangelical doctrinal positions found in the Reformed tradition of confessional Protestantism. Hodge's exposition of the atonement demonstrates how the Princeton theologians held firmly to the doctrinal positions of the Westminster Confession and reapplied them to the challenges that arose in the nineteenth century with little substantive alteration. Instead of modifying their theology, if anything, they only sharpened and clarified their doctrinal positions and reasserted them with a new voice and vigor.

12

OLD PRINCETON: PAST, PRESENT, AND FUTURE

It seemed to me that the old Princeton—a great institution it was—died when Dr. Warfield was carried out.

—J. Gresham Machen (February 20, 1921)

The death of Warfield and of Old Princeton . . . meant a new beginning, with a new leader. Though he would be the first to see himself as well below Warfield's stature, the mantle fell on Machen.

—Stephen J. Nichols

Old Princeton ceased to exist in 1929, but through its history and literature it still inspires, instructs, and encourages.

—David B. Calhoun

Old Princeton came to an end when Princeton seminary was reorganized in 1929. Its reorganization disestablished the Old School theological convictions which had held firm under the theological leadership of Archibald Alexander, Charles Hodge, and Archibald Alexander Hodge. In 1887 the mantle of leadership fell on Benjamin B. Warfield, who robustly and faithfully carried forward the Old Princeton convictions as a "lion of orthodoxy," and with Warfield's death in 1921 the mantle was unofficially passed to J. Gresham Machen. When the Presbyterian General Assembly reorganized the seminary in 1929, Machen self-consciously sought to preserve Old Princeton's theological commitments by leaving Princeton and forming Westminster Theological Seminary in nearby Philadelphia.

Since its reorganization in 1929, Old Princeton has been interpreted in different ways, with scholars today differing over the role that Enlightenment philosophy played in the formulation of its theology. Even in the midst of this debate, Old Princeton's historical and theological legacy continues to provide a model for theological education, evangelical spirituality, and theological understanding. Through its defense of scriptural orthodoxy and its commitment to genuine spiritual experience Old Princeton still, in the words of David Calhoun, "inspires, instructs, and encourages."

Old Princeton's Last Days

After A. A. Hodge's death in 1886, the theological leadership of Princeton Seminary fell upon the shoulders of Benjamin B. Warfield (1851–1921) of Kentucky. A host of other professors like William Henry Green (1825–1900), Francis Landey Patton (1843–1932), Robert Dick Wilson (1856–1930), and Geerhardus Vos (1862–1949) also helped defend and carry forward the Old Princeton tradition, but it was B. B. Warfield who became its preeminent theological champion in the late nineteenth century. Warfield had graduated from Princeton Seminary in 1876 and was called from Western Theological Seminary in 1887 to become Princeton's professor of didactic and polemic theology. At Western Seminary he had been a professor of New Testament exegesis and literature, and like Charles Hodge before him, he made a mid-career jump from the field of biblical studies to that of theology. This was only one way in which Warfield followed after Charles Hodge. In his 1887 inaugural address entitled "The Idea of Systematic Theology Considered as a Science," Warfield stated, "I rejoice to testify to you today that though the power of Charles Hodge may not be upon me, the theology of Charles Hodge is within me, and that this is the theology which, according to my ability, I have it in my heart to teach to the students of the coming years." Warfield would in fact use Hodge's *Systematic Theology* as his theology textbook and as the basis for his students' recitations in theology.

FIG. 12.1

Timeline of Benjamin B. Warfield's Life

November 5, 1851	Born in Lexington, Kentucky.
1868	Began studies at the College of New Jersey.
1873	Began studies at Princeton Theological Seminary.
1876	Married and traveled to Europe, studying at the University of Leipzig.
1877	Became supply pastor in Baltimore, Maryland.
1878	Began teaching New Testament literature and exegesis at Western Theological Seminary in Allegheny, Pennsylvania.
1879	Ordained as an evangelist by the Ebenezer Presbytery.
1880	Awarded a doctor of divinity degree by the College of New Jersey.
1881	Wrote "Inspiration" article for the *Presbyterian Review* with A. A. Hodge.
1887	Became professor of didactic and polemic theology at Princeton Seminary.
February 16, 1921	Died in Princeton, New Jersey.

Warfield spent more than thirty years at Princeton battling the confessional laxity that was on the rise in the "broadening" Presbyterian church in the North. Most of the major doctrines of the faith came under attack in these years as Darwinism and theological liberalism became more accepted, even in American Presbyterian circles. The evangelical doctrine of Scripture came under assault as critical theories promoted by Julius Wellhausen and David Friedrich Strauss came to America from Europe. Charles Augustus Briggs championed these critical and naturalistic views of Scripture within the American Presbyterian church, while clergymen like Henry Sloane Coffin and David Swing promoted views of theological evolution and development that challenged the Old School Presbyterians' adherence to confessional doctrine. Increasing ecumenical desires for visible church unity, as well as the growing "practical" and societal concerns pro-

FIG. 12.2

Selected Works of Benjamin B. Warfield

The Right of Systematic Theology, 1897

The Power of God Unto Salvation, 1903

The Lord of Glory, 1907

The Plan of Salvation, 1915

The Saviour of the World, 1916

Faith and Life: Conferences in the Oratory of Princeton Seminary, 1916

Counterfeit Miracles, 1918

The Works of Benjamin B. Warfield (10 vols.), 1932, posthumously

   Vol. 1: *Revelation and Inspiration*

   Vol. 2: *Biblical Doctrines*

   Vol. 3: *Christology and Criticism*

   Vol. 4: *Studies in Tertullian and Augustine*

   Vol. 5: *Calvin and Calvinism*

   Vol. 6: *The Westminster Assembly and Its Work*

   Vol. 7: *Perfectionism, Part One*

   Vol. 8: *Perfectionism, Part Two*

   Vol. 9: *Studies in Theology*

   Vol. 10: *Critical Reviews*

Selected Shorter Works (2 vols.), 1970, 1973, posthumously

moted by those enamored with the social gospel, made Old Princeton's attention to doctrinal orthodoxy appear even more passé.

Warfield championed traditional orthodoxy in this theological climate through his masterful scholarship and tireless writing. He wrote a number of articles for the *Presbyterian Review* and later became its editor. Many of Warfield's writings were devoted to the defense of the inspiration and inerrancy of Scripture. He also defended a whole range of biblical doctrines in numerous articles that were later compiled and published in 1932 as a ten-volume set entitled *The Works of Benjamin B. Warfield*. Additional articles by Warfield were compiled by John E. Meeter in the 1970s and republished in two volumes as Warfield's *Selected Shorter Writings*. Many of the articles in this collection, such as "The Religious Life of Theological Students," in addition to his sermons, addresses, and longer works, reveal Warfield's concern for the spiritual and religious life of believers, as well as for doctrinal orthodoxy.

Warfield continued his teaching and tireless writing until his death in 1921. To his students he was known as a devoted husband and a gentleman of seriousness and amiability. He lived a quiet life and took regular walks with his close friend and colleague, Geerhardus Vos. While going on a short walk across campus to Vos's house in the winter of 1920, Warfield collapsed and never fully recovered. He died on February 16, 1921, at the age of sixty-nine.

After Warfield's death, the mantle of Old Princeton fell in 1921 to one of Warfield's most gifted students, J. Gresham Machen. Though officially Charles Hodge's grandson, Caspar Wistar Hodge Jr., succeeded Warfield as professor of theology at the seminary, and while Caspar Hodge and Machen were agreed in their commitment to the Old School theology of Old Princeton, it was Machen who took the lead in championing the conservative orthodoxy that had been handed down to them by Warfield. Machen had been born in 1881 into the home of a prominent Baltimore lawyer and had come to faith at the age of fifteen. After studying classics at Johns Hopkins University, Machen enrolled at Princeton Seminary in 1902. After graduating in 1905 and studying for a few months in Europe, Machen joined the faculty of Princeton Seminary in 1906 as an instructor in New Testament. In response to the growing challenges posed to a traditional understanding of the New Testament, Machen published *The Origin of Paul's Religion* in 1921, winning the respect of even his critics and establishing his reputation as a formidable New Testament scholar. As the Fundamentalist-Modernist controversy was heating up with the publication of *The Fundamentals* in 1915 and Harry Emerson Fosdick's "Shall the Fundamentalists Win?" sermon in 1922, Machen published his famous *Christianity and Liberalism* in 1923 to address theological liberalism head-on. In this book Machen boldly declared:

> What the liberal theologian has retained after abandoning to the enemy one Christian doctrine after another is not Christianity at all,

FIG. 12.3

Timeline of J. Gresham Machen's Life

July 28, 1881	Born in Baltimore, Maryland.
1898	Began studies at Johns Hopkins University.
1902	Began studies at Princeton Theological Seminary.
1906	Became instructor of New Testament at Princeton Theological Seminary.
1918	Served for a year with the YMCA in France during World War I.
1921	Published *The Origin of Paul's Religion*.
1921	Awarded doctor of divinity degree by Hampden-Sydney College.
1923	Published *Christianity and Liberalism* and *New Testament Greek for Beginners*.
1929	Left Princeton Seminary to start Westminster Theological Seminary.
1930	Published *The Virgin Birth of Christ*.
1936	Ministerial credentials rescinded by the Presbyterian Church (USA).
1936	Chosen as first moderator of the Orthodox Presbyterian Church (OPC).
January 1, 1937	Died in North Dakota.

but a religion which is so entirely different from Christianity as to belong in a distinct category. . . . Despite the liberal use of traditional phraseology modern liberalism not only is a different religion from Christianity but belongs in a totally different class of religions. . . . The liberal attempt at reconciling Christianity with modern science has really relinquished everything distinctive of Christianity, so that what remains is in essentials only that same indefinite type of religious aspiration which was in the world before Christianity came upon the scene. In trying to remove from Christianity everything that could possibly be objected to in the name of science, in trying to bribe off the enemy by those concessions which the enemy most desires, the [liberal] apologist has really abandoned what he started out to defend.

Christianity and Liberalism established Machen as a champion of conservative orthodoxy and remains an important book to this day. He followed this in 1925 with *What Is Faith?* and in 1930 with *The Virgin Birth of Christ*, both of which also challenged the assertions of theological liberalism.

FIG. 12.4

Selected Works of J. Gresham Machen

The Origin of Paul's Religion, 1921

A Brief Bible History: A Survey of the Old and New Testaments, 1922

Christianity and Liberalism, 1923

New Testament Greek for Beginners, 1923

What Is Faith?, 1925

The Virgin Birth of Christ, 1930

Christian Faith in the Modern World, 1936

The Christian View of Man, 1937, posthumously

God Transcendent, 1949, posthumously

What Is Christianity?, 1951, posthumously

Education, Christianity, and the State, 1987, posthumously

Selected Shorter Writings, 2004, posthumously

After many years of battling to retain their Old School distinctiveness in an ever-broadening denomination, the Old Princeton stalwarts finally lost in 1929 when the General Assembly voted to reorganize the seminary's governing boards, giving liberals and moderates control of the institution. This decision, according to Machen, "destroyed" Old Princeton and replaced it with "a new institution of an entirely different type." In response to the restructuring, Machen left Princeton that same year and established Westminster Theological Seminary in Philadelphia with the intention of carrying forward the Old Princeton commitment to conservative orthodoxy. As he stated at the opening convocation of the new seminary,

> Though Princeton Seminary is dead, the noble tradition of Princeton Seminary is alive. Westminster Seminary will endeavor by God's grace to continue that tradition unimpaired; it will endeavor, not on a foun-

12.5 Pictured here are the graves of Archibald Alexander (left), James W. Alexander (middle), and Joseph Addison Alexander (right) in Princeton Cemetery. The Hodges, Samuel Miller, and B. B. Warfield are buried close by, as are Aaron Burr Sr., Aaron Burr Jr., Jonathan and Sarah Edwards, Samuel Davies, Samuel Finley, John Witherspoon, Samuel Stanhope Smith, and Ashbel Green. Grover Cleveland is buried in this cemetery as well.

dation of equivocation and compromise but on an honest foundation of devotion to God's Word, to maintain the same principles that the old Princeton maintained.

Machen took with him from Princeton Oswald T. Allis, Robert Dick Wilson, and Cornelius Van Til, while a number of conservatives sympathetic to his cause, like William Park Armstrong, Caspar Wistar Hodge Jr., and Geerhardus Vos, opted to stay at Princeton Seminary.

The institution that was built up by the Alexanders, the Hodges, Samuel Miller, Benjamin B. Warfield, and a host of others abandoned its commitment to conservative confessional theology under the pressure of theological liberals and moderates who did not hold to the theological positions or priorities that had defined Old Princeton for more than a hundred years. The intellectual and cultural forces that took hold of the Presbyterian church in the North were eventually too much for that denomination's Old School seminary to withstand. The broadened denomination no longer had room for a seminary committed to a "narrow" orthodoxy.

Interpreting Old Princeton

The Princeton theologians self-consciously sought to uphold the seventeenth-century confessional theology of the Reformed tradition. Their theology was that of the Westminster Confession, and they aspired to do very little in the way of constructive originality. Charles Hodge went so far at his sesquicentennial observance to celebrate his belief that "no new idea has ever come out of Old Princeton," and he positively asserted that "I have never advanced a new idea." While the Princeton theologians constructed and adapted their polemical and apologetic arguments to fit the intellectual and theological climate of their day, they self-consciously sought to uphold the theology of their tradition while all sorts of modifications and deviations were occurring around them.

Some scholars throughout the years have charged the theologians of Old Princeton, in spite of their claims to the contrary, with deviating from their own Reformed tradition in substantial ways and embracing significant elements of thought that were foreign to earlier

Reformed thinkers. These scholars see Old Princeton's theology, therefore, as an illegitimate offshoot of the Reformed tradition. This charge was made early on by the liberal Charles Briggs, who argued in 1889 that the Princeton theologians were "betrayers" of the eighteenth-century American Presbyterianism espoused by the Tennents and Jonathan Dickinson. Briggs claimed that the Princeton theologians' close adherence to the Westminster Confession had produced a kind of "orthodoxism" that should itself be rejected as heterodox. In his words, "It is the theology of the elder and younger Hodge that has in fact usurped the place of the Westminster theology in the minds of a large portion of the ministry of the Presbyterian Churches, and now stands in the way of progress in theology and of true Christian orthodoxy; and there is no other way of advancing in truth except by removing the errors that obstruct our path." Briggs's rejection of the Princeton theology, however, was only a part of his broader rejection of orthodox doctrine. In 1893 Briggs was suspended from ministry in the Presbyterian church for his rejection of the verbal inspiration and inerrancy of Scripture.

Sydney Ahlstrom argued in a 1955 article that Princeton theology was seriously compromised by a philosophical commitment to Scottish Common Sense Realism and that this significantly affected the Princetonians' theological formulations regarding their understanding of anthropology, apologetics, and ethics. According to Ahlstrom, Archibald Alexander's *Outlines of Moral Science* reads like it was written "by some mild English Latitudinarian bent on mediating the views of Butler, Reid, and Price," and Charles Hodge was himself "caught up in the anthropocentrism [man-centeredness] of Scottish philosophy." Ahlstrom further asserted, "The foundation of his [Hodge's] ethic and his conception of natural theology . . . are Scottish rather than Calvinistic. . . . The optimism of the Scottish Renaissance interposes itself and separates his theology from that of John Knox and John Calvin." Other historians, like Mark Noll, have carried forward Ahlstrom's assertions, stating that "Old Princeton was heavily, even uniquely, indebted to [Scottish Common Sense] philosophy." Even Cornelius Van Til criticized Hodge and Warfield's apologetic for inconsistently granting to natural human reason powers that it does not possess.

Certain statements in the introductory sections of Hodge's *Systematic Theology* have gathered widespread criticism for promoting a "scientific" approach to theology that seemingly minimizes the effects of the fall upon the human mind and makes true theological knowledge readily and naturally available to men through unaided rational processes. The most controversial statement is Hodge's description of the theologian's task: "The Bible is to the theologian what nature is to the man of science. It is his store-house of facts; and his method of ascertaining what the Bible teaches, is the same as that which the natural philosopher adopts to ascertain what nature teaches. . . . The theologian is to be guided by the same rules as the man of science" (*Systematic Theology*, 1:10–11). Such a statement seems to minimize the subjective element of spiritual reception and the necessity of spiritual illumination in order for a proper understanding of spiritual truths.

Those who have used this passage to criticize Hodge for a supposedly rationalistic approach to theology are perhaps guilty of minimizing other statements and neglecting the full context of Hodge's discussion of theology. Hodge's emphasis on external and objective theological facts was meant to counter the subjective approaches to theology that were then being advanced by the disciples of Friedrich Schleiermacher and others. Further, Hodge placed a premium on the importance of revelation and spiritual illumination, and he provided this statement just a few sections after that quoted above:

> Although the inward teaching of the Spirit, or religious experience, is no substitute for an external revelation, and is no part of the rule of faith, it is, nevertheless, an invaluable guide in determining what the rule of faith teaches. The distinguishing feature of Augustinianism as taught by Augustine himself, and by the purer theologians of the Latin Church throughout the Middle Ages, which was set forth by the Reformers, and especially by Calvin and the Geneva divines, is that the inward teaching of the Spirit is allowed its proper place in determining our theology. The question is not first and mainly, What is true to the understanding, but what is true to the renewed heart? *The effort is not to make the assertions of the Bible harmonize with the speculative reason, but to subject our feeble reason to the mind of God as*

revealed in his Word, and by his Spirit in our inner life (*Systematic Theology*, 1:16; emphasis added).

Commenting on Ephesians 4:17–18, Hodge wrote further about the moral nature of truth and the integrated faculties of the human soul:

> There is an element of feeling in our cognitions and an element of intelligence in our feelings. The idea that the heart may be depraved and the intellect unaffected is, according to the anthropology of the Bible, as incongruous, as that one part of the soul should be happy and another miserable, one faculty saved and another lost. . . . Truth is not merely speculative, the object of cognition; it has moral beauty. In scriptural language, therefore, knowledge includes love; wisdom includes goodness; folly includes sin; the wise are holy, fools are wicked. Truth and holiness are united as light and heat in the same ray. There cannot be the one without the other. To know God is eternal life; to be without the knowledge of God is to be utterly depraved. Saints are the children of light; the wicked are the children of darkness. To be enlightened is to be renewed; to be blinded is to be reprobated.

Both Hodge and Archibald Alexander affirmed the effects of the fall upon the human mind, and yet they believed that arguments for the truth from nature, experience, and reason are valid and have their place. Knowing that his father's position might likewise be misunderstood, James W. Alexander explained his father's view on "natural religion" as follows:

> In regard to this the only safe way of defining his [Archibald Alexander's] theological position would be to publish his treatises, and anything short of this might be misapprehended. While he was far from being a rationalist, he was never satisfied with the tactics of those reasoners who under the pretext of exalting revelation dismiss with contempt all arguments derived from the light of nature. Here he freely declared his judgment that many sound able and pious men had greatly erred. He rendered due homage therefore to the labours of such writers as [Bernard] Nieuwentyt, the younger Turrettine, and [William] Paley and spent much time in considering and unfolding with nice discrimination the various schemes of argument for the

Being and Perfections of God and the necessity and antecedent probability of a revelation.

While granting reason and "the light of nature" its place, the older Alexander was critical of those who, in his words, gave "more confidence to common sense and human reason than to the declarations of God."

Much recent scholarship is now questioning the assertions of Ahlstrom regarding the Princeton theologians' supposed accommodation to Scottish philosophy and Enlightenment rationalism. A number of scholars are now concluding that the Princeton theologians did not value "common sense" in such a way that undercut their Reformed understanding of human corruption, blindness, and inability due to sin. Instead, the Princeton theologians merely affirmed reason and "common sense" in a way that recognized the commonality that all men possess by being created in God's image and as the recipients of God's natural revelation and common grace. Paul Helseth, for one, has researched these questions at length and has concluded that "in the main, the Princeton theologians remained more or less consistently Reformed as they labored to combat the rising tide of religious subjectivism in their day." Helseth says this even while acknowledging that certain assertions in the Princetonians' writings "lend plausibility to the charge of accommodation." The debate as to whether the theological and apologetic method of the Old Princeton men is consistent with their theological convictions is likely to continue, even while more and more are no longer assuming the "Ahlstrom thesis" and are going back to read the Princeton theologians with new eyes.

Profiting from Old Princeton Today

The debate over Old Princeton's theological and apologetic method, while significant, has often been a distraction and has no doubt turned some away from reading and profiting from the wealth of spiritual, biblical, and theological insight the Princeton theologians have to offer. This is a great misfortune, because the Princetonians and their writings are a neglected treasure.

The Princeton theologians promoted and modeled a learned piety that elevated the value of both theological truth and spiritual experience. In this way, they resembled the English Puritans of the sixteenth and seventeenth centuries. Indeed, Puritans like Owen, Flavel, and Bunyan were very important to the Princeton theologians, especially to Archibald Alexander and his oldest son. According to the seminary's original plan, all seminary students were to have read during the course of their studies "the best practical writers on the subject of religion," and certainly many of the Puritans would have been recommended to meet this requirement. Echoing the Puritans' emphasis on the heart, the Princeton faculty emphasized "experimental" (or "experiential") Christianity and "vital piety" as a necessary part of the Christian life. Piety in the heart, for the Princeton theologians, was something to be carefully guarded and daily cultivated. They believed that worldliness, materialism, and sensuality were a major threat to piety and spirituality, and for this reason they warned against the spiritually deleterious effects of a number of things in their culture, including the entertainment industry of their day. Samuel Miller published against "the nature and effects of the stage" on account of the theater's "direct and unavoidable tendency to dissipate the mind and to lessen, if not destroy, all taste for serious and spiritual employments." Archibald Alexander also stated: "I find it to be incumbent on me . . . to give my public testimony against [theatrical exhibitions] as being, notwithstanding the partial good which may result from them, unfriendly to piety—unfriendly to morality—unfriendly to health—unfriendly to domestic happiness—and unfriendly to true delicacy and genuine refinement." With these remarks the Puritans would have been in wholehearted agreement. More directly than the Puritans, the Old Princeton emphasis on piety was drawn from Whitefield, Edwards, the Tennents, and other New Side Presbyterian leaders who had a direct impact on the seminary's antecedent institutions. Given their historical connection with the Great Awakening, the Princeton theologians placed a premium on genuine conversions, and they looked favorably upon "revivals of religion," even as they were critical of the abuses and innovations that became prominent under Charles Finney.

Along with their emphasis on piety, the Princeton theologians placed a premium on education for the development of the mind and the cultivation of spiritual life, moral discernment, and aesthetic taste. Education in both the content and the theology of the Scriptures was what they valued the most. Their "Old School" understanding of Christianity was that it is fundamentally a doctrinal religion, and the doctrines they embraced as scriptural were the doctrines of Protestant and Reformed orthodoxy as they came to be distilled in the Westminster Confession of Faith and were presented by post-Reformation writers such as Francis Turretin. The Princeton theologians' explanations and defenses of Christian doctrine, as well as their biblical expositions, are clear, rich, insightful, and, in many places, eloquent. Their engagement with alternative theologies remains directly relevant for the theological issues facing the church

12.6 This famous sketch of Princeton Theological Seminary (c. 1843) from Mercer Street is only partly historical. In the middle is the main seminary building. Machen lived on the fourth floor throughout his Princeton career. On the far left was Archibald Alexander's home (built in 1819), and on the far right was Charles Hodge's home (built 1825). A. A. Hodge and B. B. Warfield later lived in Hodge's house as well. Miller Chapel, just to the left of Alexander Hall (built in 1834), was moved in 1933 toward the middle of campus. The proposed library (just to the right of Alexander Hall) was never built in that location, but was built on the other side of Mercer Street. Perhaps the library was drawn in here to represent the balance and dual emphasis given to both piety and scholarship.

today. Even when disagreeing with their theological opponents, the Princeton theologians were more often than not models of moderation in tone and in spirit.

The Old Princeton theologians are perhaps best known for their strong defense of scriptural inspiration and inerrancy, and most would agree that Warfield's articles on this subject are some of the most thoroughgoing and helpful. Some have asserted that the concept of scriptural inerrancy was created by Archibald Alexander Hodge and Benjamin B. Warfield in the early 1880s and that it was not previously found at Old Princeton. This is most certainly mistaken, for although the word "inerrancy" was not commonly used by previous Princeton theologians, certainly the concept of scriptural inerrancy was held by them. Archibald Alexander wrote of the scriptural authors being "so assisted and strengthened . . . as to be preserved from all error and mistake" and "preserved from inaccuracy and error." Charles Hodge wrote in his 1857 "Inspiration" article for the *Princeton Review* that "Infallibility, or absolute freedom from error, is claimed for a book containing sixty-six distinct productions, on all subjects of history, of law, of religion, of morals; embracing poetry, prophecy, doctrinal and practical discourses, covering the whole of man's present necessities and future destiny." In his *Systematic Theology* text, Hodge stated that the inspiration of Scripture is "not confined to moral or religious truths," but also includes "statements of facts, whether scientific, historical, or geographical." Warfield's understanding of inerrancy was certainly not original with him, and it should not be viewed as a Princetonian innovation of the late nineteenth century.

The Princeton theologians also provide a helpful example for engaging the world with missionary zeal and cultural reflection. Missions, both foreign and domestic, was a priority of the Princeton professors, and they saw biblical truth and the working of God's Spirit as the great need of every culture and nation. Countless Old Princeton graduates enrolled in mission work and did not despise the call to leave family and comfort behind for ministry in distant lands. Engagement with political and societal issues are also a part of the Old Princeton legacy, and yet the priority in social engagement until Machen's generation was for the spread of the gospel and of biblical truth to all parts of society. Samuel Miller, Charles Hodge, and James W. Alexander engaged in cultural analysis the most, and yet they each believed that the priority for God's people should also be upon Christian proclamation and instruction in biblical truth. Their answer to societal problems was found in Sunday schools, mission chapels, tract writing, and evangelism. The Princeton theologians resisted the call to place national and societal concerns above the commitment to eternal concerns and to the truth. Old Princeton fell when temporal and societal concerns began to take priority within its parent denomination.

In many ways, Old Princeton yet provides a model for theological education. At Old Princeton the study of theology was not disconnected from local church and denominational life. The seminary's original plan mandated that each professor be "an ordained minister of the gospel," and most of the faculty members were devoted churchmen engaged in the denominational discussions of their day. The Princeton faculty lived, ate, raised their families, and worshipped in the midst of their students. They engaged their students individually through the common "recitation" method of instruction and provided individual counsel to them in their homes. The faculty did not believe in the impartation of knowledge for the sake of knowledge and were mindful of their charge to produce godly and equipped ministers of the gospel. As Samuel Miller heralded at Archibald Alexander's inaugural service: "O my fathers and brethren, let it never be said of us on whom this task has fallen, that we take more pains to make polite scholars, eloquent orators or men of mere learning than to form able and faithful ministers of the New Testament."

In their robust articulation and powerful defense of Reformed orthodoxy, the Princeton theologians have few equals. To read their works is to be challenged, instructed, and often inspired. In seeking to articulate, defend, and live out the truth of God in their day, the Princeton theologians have left behind a legacy which yet testifies to that truth and gives much-needed guidance for God's people today.

SUGGESTIONS FOR FURTHER READING

For a fuller introduction to Old Princeton, one can do no better than to pick up David B. Calhoun's two-volume *Princeton Seminary* (Banner of Truth, 1994–96). These volumes are deeply stirring and a valuable gold mine of insight and information. James Garretson has recently compiled two major anthologies of source material that are extremely valuable as well. His *Pastor-Teachers of Old Princeton* (Banner of Truth, 2012) contains memorial addresses delivered for the faculty of Old Princeton that are both biographical and instructive. Garretson's two-volume *Princeton and the Work of the Christian Ministry* (Banner of Truth, 2012) contains more than thirteen hundred pages of various lectures, sermons, and addresses delivered by the faculty of Old Princeton. Mark Noll's *The Princeton Theology, 1812–1921* (Baker, 1983) is an anthology of articles mostly related to Old Princeton on Scripture, science, and theology, and also contains a helpful introductory essay.

For understanding Old Princeton's identification with the Great Awakening and New Side Presbyterianism, Archibald Alexander's *The Log College* (1851; repr. Banner of Truth, 1968) is a good place to start. Along with this, read the relevant sections of Hodge's *The Constitutional History of the Presbyterian Church in the United States of America* (1839–40) for Hodge's perspective. Thomas Murphy's *The Presbytery of the Log College* (Presbyterian Board of Publication, 1889) also contains a great deal of relevant and helpful information, as do the essays contained in *Colonial Presbyterianism: Old Faith in a New Land* (Pickwick, 2007), edited by S. Donald Fortson III.

The story of Princeton Seminary's beginning has been told in James Garretson's "Archibald Alexander and the Founding of Princeton Theological Seminary" (*The Confessional Presbyterian* 8, 2012) and in Mark Noll's "The Founding of Princeton Seminary" (*Westminster Theological Journal* 42, fall 1979). Though he is often neglected, Ashbel Green played a very significant role in the founding of the seminary. Joseph Huntington Jones compiled and edited Green's mostly autobiographical account in *The Life of Ashbel Green, V.D.M.* (Robert Carter & Brothers, 1849).

James W. Alexander's appreciative and detailed account in *The Life of Archibald Alexander, D.D.* (1854; repr. Sprinkle, 1991) is still outstanding and is the best place to start to read more about Princeton Seminary's first professor. Lefferts A. Loetscher has written a critical biography of Archibald Alexander entitled *Facing the Enlightenment and Pietism: Archibald Alexander and the Founding of Princeton Theological Seminary* (Praeger, 1983). James Garretson has published a fine study of Archibald Alexander's understanding of the Christian ministry in *Princeton and Preaching: Archibald Alexander and the Christian Ministry* (Banner of Truth, 2005), but those wanting to understand Alexander's approach to the Christian life in general can do no better than to read his own *Thoughts on Religious Experience* (1844; repr., Banner of Truth, 1989).

A recent biography of Samuel Miller by James Garretson is entitled *An Able and Faithful Ministry: Samuel Miller and the Pastoral Office* (Reformation Heritage, 2014). Miller's son Samuel compiled a large two-volume biography full of detailed information entitled *The Life of Samuel Miller, D.D.* (1869; repr., Tentmaker, 2002). For a complete list of Miller's works, see the very helpful article by Wayne Sparkman entitled "Samuel Miller, D.D. (1769–1850): An Annotated Bibliography" (*Confessional Presbyterian Journal* 1, 2005).

The only biography of Charles Hodge for many years was that by his son A. A. Hodge, *The Life of Charles Hodge* (1880; repr., Banner of Truth, 2010). This detailed volume contains Hodge's autobiography of his early years as well as a number of his letters. Two large and very helpful biographies have appeared recently, W. Andrew Hoffecker's *Charles Hodge: The Pride of Princeton* (P&R Publishing, 2011) and Paul C. Gutjahr's *Charles Hodge: Guardian of American Orthodoxy* (Oxford, 2011).

No full-length biographies of James Waddel Alexander and Joseph Addison Alexander have yet appeared. J. W. Alexander's two-volume *Forty Years' Familiar Letters* (1860; repr. as *The Life of J. W. Alexander: Forty Years of Familiar Letters*, Audubon Press, 2008) gives rich insight into his life and times, even though densely presented. His *Thoughts on Preaching* (1864; repr., Banner of Truth, 1988) is still very helpful, and a published collection of his sermons now is in print under the title *A Shepherd's Heart: Sermons from the Pastoral Ministry of J. W. Alexander* (1860; repr., Solid Ground, 2004). Joseph Addison Alexander's nephew Henry Carrington Alexander produced a large and detailed two-volume biography of his life entitled *The Life of J. A. Alexander* (1870; repr., Audubon Press, 2008). Two volumes of J. A. Alexander's sermons are now in print under the title *Theology on Fire* (1862; repr., Solid Ground, 2004).

No full-length biography of A. A. Hodge has been written, though the Garretson anthology of memorial addresses contains two short biographical sketches, one by Francis L. Patton and one by William M. Paxton. Most of Hodge's major works (*Outlines of Theology, Commentary on the Confession of Faith* [sometimes as *The Confession of Faith*], *Popular Lectures on Theological Themes* [sometimes as *Evangelical Theology*], and *The Atonement*) continue to be accessible.

B. B. Warfield still awaits a biographer, though many works have appeared recently that analyze his life and thought. Gary L. W. Johnson's *B. B. Warfield: Essays on His Life and Thought* (P&R Publishing, 2007) is a good place to start. Warfield's two-volume set of *Shorter Writings* (P&R Publishing, 2001) is also an accessible entry point to reading Warfield himself. Fred Zaspel has recently provided a large summary of Warfield's theology in *The Theology of Warfield: A Systematic Summary* (Crossway, 2010), as well as a shorter work entitled *Warfield on the Christian Life* (Crossway, 2012).

For more on J. Gresham Machen, one should consult the *Guided Tour* book in this series and the suggestions given there by Stephen J. Nichols. Machen's *Christianity and Liberalism* (1923; repr., Eerdmans, 1997) and his *Shorter Writings* (P&R Publishing, 2004) are also great places to start for reading Machen's writings.

For understanding the long-standing claim that Old Princeton's theology was compromised by Enlightenment Rationalism (specifically Scottish Common Sense Realism), one should read Sydney Ahlstrom's "The Scottish Philosophy and American Theology"

(*Church History* 24, 1955). While many articles have been written challenging this assertion, one should start with Paul K. Helseth's *"Right Reason" and the Princeton Mind: An Unorthodox Proposal* (P&R Publishing, 2010). Helseth has recently built upon the argument of his book in his article " 'Right Reason' and the Science of Theology at Old Princeton" (*Confessional Presbyterian Journal* 8, 2012).

The end of Old Princeton has been described very helpfully in Bradley J. Longfield's *The Presbyterian Controversy* (Oxford, 1991). Ned Stonehouse's biography of Machen, *J. Gresham Machen: A Biographical Memoir* (Eerdmans, 1954), has much useful information about this, and Machen's perspective on the conflict has been well-preserved in Edwin H. Rian's *The Presbyterian Conflict* (1940; repr., Committee for the Historian of the OPC, 1992). D. G. Hart's *Defending the Faith: J. Gresham Machen and the Crisis of Conservative Protestantism in Modern America* (P&R Publishing, 2003) and his recent article entitled "The Reorganization of Princeton Theological Seminary and the Exhaustion of American Presbyterianism" (*Confessional Presbyterian Journal* 8, 2012) are helpful as well.

All of the articles contained in the original *Princeton Review* have been digitized and made freely available on the Princeton Theological Seminary library's website (www.ptsem.edu/library). This is an outstanding resource, containing hundreds of articles produced by the Old Princeton circle. The seminary has made available for free many items related to Old Princeton on the Internet Archive (www.archive.org) as well. The *Index Volume* to *The Biblical Repertory and Princeton Review* (Peter Walker, 1871) is an invaluable resource covering the authors and articles that appeared from 1825 to 1868. This volume contains short biographies and article lists for the authors who wrote for the *Review*, Charles Hodge's history of the *Review*, and a helpful topical index to the *Review*'s articles. The *Index Volume*, like many other sources related to Princeton, can be found for free on Google Books (books.google.com).

Selected Bibliography

Ahlstrom, Sydney E. "The Scottish Philosophy and American Theology." *Church History* 24, no. 3 (Sep. 1955): 257–72.

Alexander, Archibald. *The Log College*. 1851. Reprint, Edinburgh: Banner of Truth, 1968.

———. *Thoughts on Religious Experience*. 1844. Reprint, Edinburgh: Banner of Truth, 1989.

Alexander, Henry Carrington. *The Life of Joseph Addison Alexander, D.D.* 2 vols. New York: Charles Scribner, 1870.

Alexander, James W. *Forty Years' Familiar Letters of James W. Alexander, D.D.* 2 vols. Edited by John Hall. New York: Charles Scribner, 1860.

———. *The Life of Archibald Alexander, D.D.* 1854. Reprint, Harrisonburg, VA: Sprinkle Publications, 1991.

———. *A Shepherd's Heart: Sermons from the Pastoral Ministry of J. W. Alexander*. 1860. Reprint, Birmingham, AL: Solid Ground Christian Books, 2004.

———. *Thoughts on Preaching*. 1864. Reprint, Edinburgh: Banner of Truth, 1988.

Barker, William S. "The Social Views of Charles Hodge (1797–1878): A Study in Nineteenth-Century Calvinism and Conservatism." *Presbyterion: Covenant Seminary Review* 1 (spring 1975): 1–22.

The Biblical Repertory and Princeton Review, Index Volume from 1825 to 1868. Philadelphia: Peter Walker, 1871.

Calhoun, David B. *The Last Command: Princeton Theological Seminary and Missions (1812–1862)*. Ph.D. dissertation, Princeton Theological Seminary, 1983.

———. *Princeton Seminary*. 2 vols. Edinburgh, Banner of Truth, 1994–96.

The Centennial Celebration of the Theological Seminary of the Presbyterian Church in the United States of America at Princeton, New Jersey. Princeton: Theological Seminary of the Presbyterian Church at Princeton, 1912.

Coalter, Milton J., Jr. *Gilbert Tennent, Son of Thunder: A Case Study of Continental Pietism's Impact on the First Great Awakening in the Middle Colonies*. Westport, CT: Greenwood Press, 1986.

DeWitt, John. "Archibald Alexander's Preparation for His Professorship." *Princeton Theological Review* 3 (1905): 573–94.

Duyckinck, Evert A., and George L. Duyckinck. *Cyclopaedia of American Literature*. Edited by M. Laird Simons. 2 vols. Philadelphia: Baxter Publishing, 1881.

Forston, S. Donald III, ed. *Colonial Presbyterianism: Old Faith in a New Land*. Eugene, OR: Pickwick Publications, 2007.

Garretson, James M. *Pastor-Teachers of Old Princeton*. Edinburgh: Banner of Truth, 2012.

———, ed. *A Scribe Well-Trained: Archibald Alexander and the Life of Piety*. Grand Rapids: Reformation Heritage, 2011.

Green, Ashbel. *The Life of Ashbel Green, V.D.M.* Edited by Joseph H. Jones. New York: Robert Carter, 1849.

———. *The Life of the Rev. John Witherspoon, D.D., LL.D.* 1802. Reprint, Harrisonburg, VA: Sprinkle Publications, 2007.

———. *A Plan of the Theological Seminary*. 1811.

Gutjahr, Paul C. *Charles Hodge: Guardian of American Orthodoxy*. New York: Oxford University Press, 2011.

Hall, John. "A Sermon on the Death of Dr. Alexander." In *Home, the School, and the Church, or, The Presbyterian Education Repository*, 93–105. Philadelphia: C. Sherman, 1853.

Hart, D. G. *Defending the Faith: J. Gresham Machen and the Crisis of Conservative Protestantism in Modern America*. Phillipsburg, NJ: P&R Publishing, 2003.

Hart, D. G., and John R. Muether. *Seeking a Better Country: 300 Years of American Presbyterianism*. Phillipsburg, NJ: Presbyterian & Reformed, 2007.

Hart, D. G., and Mark A. Noll, eds. *Dictionary of the Presbyterian and Reformed Tradition in America*. Philipsburg, NJ: P&R Publishing, 2005.

Helseth, Paul Kjoss. *"Right Reason" and the Princeton Mind: An Unorthodox Proposal*. Phillipsburg, NJ: P&R Publishing, 2010.

———. " 'Right Reason' and the Science of Theology at Old Princeton Seminary: A New Perspective." *Confessional Presbyterian Journal* 8 (2012): 74–90.

Hodge, A. A. *The Atonement*. Philadelphia: Presbyterian Board of Publication, 1867.

———. *The Confession of Faith*. 1869. Reprint, Edinburgh: Banner of Truth, 1998.

———. *Evangelical Theology: A Course of Popular Lectures*. 1890. Reprint, Edinburgh: Banner of Truth, 1976.

————. *The Life of Charles Hodge.* 1880. Reprint, Edinburgh: Banner of Truth, 2010.

————. *Outlines of Theology.* 1860. Reprint, Edinburgh: Banner of Truth, 1991.

Hodge, Charles. *The Constitutional History of the Presbyterian Church in the United States of America.* 2 vols. Philadelphia: William S. Martien, 1839–40.

————. *Discussions in Church Polity.* Edited by William Durant. New York: Charles Scribner's Sons, 1878. Reprint, Seoul: Westminster Publishing House, 2001.

————. "Memoir of Dr. Alexander." *Biblical Repertory and Princeton Review* 27 (1855): 133–59.

————. *Systematic Theology.* 3 vols. 1871–72. Reprint, Grand Rapids: Eerdmans, 1997.

Hoffecker, W. Andrew. *Charles Hodge: The Pride of Princeton.* Philipsburg, NJ: P&R Publishing, 2011.

————. *Piety and the Princeton Theologians.* Phillipsburg, NJ: P&R Publishing, 1981.

Huggins, Ronald. "A Note on Archibald Alexander's Apologetic Motive in Positing 'Errors' in the Autographs." *Westminster Theological Journal* 57 (1995):463–70.

Johnson, Gary L. W. *B. B. Warfield: Essays on His Life and Thought.* Phillipsburg, NJ: P&R Publishing, 2007.

Le Beau, Bryan F. *Jonathan Dickinson and the Formative Years of American Presbyterianism.* Lexington, KY: University Press of Kentucky, 1997.

Leitch, Alexander. *A Princeton Companion.* Princeton: Princeton University Press, 1978.

Loetscher, Lefferts A. *Facing the Enlightenment and Pietism: Archibald Alexander and the Founding of Princeton Theological Seminary.* Westport, CT: Greenwood Press, 1983.

Longfield, Bradley J. *The Presbyterian Controversy: Fundamentalists, Modernists, and Moderates.* New York: Oxford University Press, 1991.

Machen, J. Gresham. *Christianity and Liberalism.* 1923. Reprint, Grand Rapids: Eerdmans, 1997.

————. *Selected Shorter Writings.* Edited by D. G. Hart. Phillipsburg, NJ: P&R Publishing, 2004.

Kerr, Hugh T., ed. *Sons of the Prophets: Leaders in Protestantism from Princeton Seminary.* Princeton: Princeton University Press, 1963.

Miller, Samuel. *A Brief Retrospect of the Eighteenth Century.* 2 vols. New York: T. & J. Swords, 1803.

———. *An Essay on the Warrant, Nature, and Duties of the Office of the Ruling Elder*. Philadelphia: Presbyterian Board of Publication, 1832.

———. *Letters on Clerical Manners and Habits*. New York: G. & C. Carvill, 1827.

———. *Thoughts on Public Prayer*. Philadelphia: Presbyterian Board of Publication, 1849. Reprint, Harrisonburg, VA: Sprinkle Publications, 1985.

Miller, Samuel, Jr. *The Life of Samuel Miller, D.D., LL.D.* 2 vols. Philadelphia: Claxton, Remsen, and Haffelfinger, 1869. Reprint, Stoke-on-Trent, UK: Tentmaker Publications, 2002.

Nichols, Stephen J. *J. Gresham Machen: A Guided Tour of His Life and Thought*. Phillipsburg, NJ: P&R Publishing, 2004.

Noll, Mark A. "The Founding of Princeton Seminary." *Westminster Theological Journal* 42 (Fall 1979): 72–110.

———. *Princeton and the Republic, 1768–1822*. Vancouver: Regent College, 2004.

———. "The *Princeton Review*." *Westminster Theological Journal* 50 (1988): 283–304.

———. *The Princeton Theology, 1812–1921*. Grand Rapids: Baker, 1983.

Reid, Daniel G., Robert D. Linder, Bruce L. Shelley, and Harry Stout, eds. *Dictionary of Christianity in America*. Downers Grove, IL: InterVarsity, 1990.

Salmond, C. A. *Princetoniana. Charles and A. A. Hodge: With Class and Table Talk of Hodge the Younger*. Edinburgh: Oliphant, Anderson, & Ferrier, 1888.

Smith, David P. *B. B. Warfield's Scientifically Constructive Theological Scholarship*. Eugene, OR: Pickwick Publications, 2011.

Sprague, William B. *Annals of the American Pulpit*. 9 vols. New York: Robert Carter and Brothers, 1857–59.

Stewart, John W., and James H. Moorehead. *Charles Hodge Revisited: A Critical Appraisal of His Life and Work*. Grand Rapids: Eerdmans, 2002.

Stonehouse, Ned B. *J. Gresham Machen: A Biographical Memoir*. Grand Rapids: Eerdmans, 1954.

van Rensselaer, Cortlandt. *The Theological Seminary of the Presbyterian Church at Princeton, New Jersey*. N.p., 1844.

Whitefield, George. *George Whitefield's Journals*. 1905. Reprint, Edinburgh: Banner of Truth, 1986.

Zaspel, Fred G. *The Theology of Warfield: A Systematic Summary*. Wheaton: Crossway, 2010.

———. *Warfield on the Christian Life: Living in Light of the Gospel*. Wheaton: Crossway, 2012.

ABOUT THE ILLUSTRATIONS

1.1 Events Leading Up to the Founding of Princeton Seminary.

1.2 Sketch of Nassau Hall, built in 1756 as the first building in Princeton for the College of New Jersey. From *Memorial Book of the Sesquicentennial Celebration of the Founding of the College of New Jersey and of the Ceremonies Inaugurating Princeton University*. New York: Charles Scribner's Sons, 1898.

1.3 Early Presidents (and Interim Presidents) of the College of New Jersey (Princeton University).

1.4 Portrait of Jonathan Dickinson (1688–1747). From *Memorial Book of the Sesquicentennial Celebration of the Founding of the College of New Jersey and of the Ceremonies Inaugurating Princeton University* (New York: Charles Scribner's Sons, 1898).

1.5 Portrait of Aaron Burr (1716–57). From *Memorial Book of the Sesquicentennial Celebration of the Founding of the College of New Jersey and of the Ceremonies Inaugurating Princeton University* (New York: Charles Scribner's Sons, 1898).

1.6 Portrait of Jonathan Edwards (1703–58). From *Memorial Book of the Sesquicentennial Celebration of the Founding of the College of New Jersey and of the Ceremonies Inaugurating Princeton University* (New York: Charles Scribner's Sons, 1898).

1.7 Portrait of Samuel Davies (1723–61). From *Memorial Book of the Sesquicentennial Celebration of the Founding of the College of New*

Jersey and of the Ceremonies Inaugurating Princeton University (New York: Charles Scribner's Sons, 1898).

1.8 Portrait of Samuel Finley (1715–66). From *Memorial Book of the Sesquicentennial Celebration of the Founding of the College of New Jersey and of the Ceremonies Inaugurating Princeton University* (New York: Charles Scribner's Sons, 1898).

1.9 Portrait of John Witherspoon (1723–94). From *Memorial Book of the Sesquicentennial Celebration of the Founding of the College of New Jersey and of the Ceremonies Inaugurating Princeton University* (New York: Charles Scribner's Sons, 1898).

1.10 Portrait of Samuel Stanhope Smith (1751–1819). From *Memorial Book of the Sesquicentennial Celebration of the Founding of the College of New Jersey and of the Ceremonies Inaugurating Princeton University* (New York: Charles Scribner's Sons, 1898).

1.11 Portrait of Ashbel Green (1762–1848). From *Memorial Book of the Sesquicentennial Celebration of the Founding of the College of New Jersey and of the Ceremonies Inaugurating Princeton University* (New York: Charles Scribner's Sons, 1898).

1.12 Excerpt from From Ashbel Green's *Plan of the Theological Seminary* (1811).

2.1 Timeline of Archibald Alexander's Life.

2.2 Portrait of Archibald Alexander (1772–1851). Special Collections, Princeton Theological Seminary Library.

2.3 Manuscript of Archibald Alexander's lecture on the moral qualifications for ministry. From the Archibald Alexander Manuscript Collection. Special Collections, Princeton Theological Seminary Library.

2.4 Selected Works of Archibald Alexander.

3.1 Title page of Alexander's *Thoughts on Religious Experience* (Philadelphia: Presbyterian Board of Publication, 1841).

4.1 Timeline of Samuel Miller's Life.

4.2 Selected Works of Samuel Miller.

4.3 Manuscript of Samuel Miller's lecture on Arminianism and the Synod of Dort. Miller gave this lecture almost once a year from 1823 to 1841, and it was eventually published in 1841 by the Presbyterian Board of Publication as an "Introductory Essay" to a reprint of the *Articles of the Synod of Dort*. From the Samuel Miller Manuscript Collection. Special Collections, Princeton Theological Seminary Library.

4.4 Portrait of Samuel Miller (1769–1850). Special Collections, Princeton Theological Seminary Library.

5.1 Title page of Samuel Miller's *An Essay on the Warrant, Nature, and Duties of the Office of the Ruling Elder in the Presbyterian Church*, 2nd ed. (New York and Boston: Jonathan Leavitt and Crocker & Brewster, 1832).

5.2 Title page of Samuel Miller's *Letters on Clerical Manners and Habits*, 2nd. ed. (New York: G. & C. Carvill, 1827).

6.1 Timeline of Charles Hodge's Life.

6.2 Selected Works of Charles Hodge.

6.3 Portrait of Charles Hodge (1797–1878). Special Collections, Princeton Theological Seminary Library.

7.1 Article on "The Relation of the Church and the State" by Charles Hodge. From *The Biblical Repertory and Princeton Review* 35, 4 (1862): 679–93.

8.1 Timeline of James W. Alexander's Life.

8.2 Letter from James Alexander to Addison Alexander, written in 1829. The first part of the letter is written in Italian and shows the brothers' shared love for words and languages. From the Joseph Addison Alexander Manuscript Collection. Special Collections, Princeton Theological Seminary Library.

8.3 Portrait of James Waddel Alexander (1804–59). From *Forty Years' Familiar Letters of James W. Alexander, D.D.*, edited by John Hall, vol. 2 (New York: Charles Scribner, 1870).

8.4 Selected Works of James W. Alexander.

8.5 Manuscript of Joseph Addison Alexander's 1822 Arabic translation of the title page to Sir Walter Scott's novel *Waverly*. From the Joseph Addison Alexander Manuscript Collection. Special Collections, Princeton Theological Seminary Library.

8.6 Timeline of Joseph Addison Alexander's Life.

8.7 Selected Works of Joseph Addison Alexander.

8.8 Portrait of Joseph Addison Alexander (1809–60). From *The Life of Joseph Addison Alexander*, by Henry Carrington Alexander, vol. 1 (New York: Charles Scribner, 1870).

9.1 Portrait of James Waddel Alexander (1804–59). His more than eight hundred letters to John Hall were published at the instigation of Charles Hodge, who believed they would serve as "a literary, a theological, a religious and a conversational history" of the years between 1819 and 1859. From the author's personal collection.

9.2 Letter from James W. Alexander to John Hall, written only a few months before Alexander's death in 1859. This letter is perhaps the only surviving copy of those that made it into Hall's *Forty Years' Familiar Letters*. Courtesy of First Presbyterian Church, Trenton, New Jersey.

10.1 Timeline of A. A. Hodge's Life.

10.2 Photograph of Archibald Alexander's whalebone walking stick, made in 1824 by a Hawaiian chieftain for Archibald Alexander. On his deathbed in 1851, Alexander handed it down to Charles Hodge as "a kind of symbol of orthodoxy." Special Collections, Princeton Theological Seminary Library.

10.3 Portrait of Archibald Alexander Hodge (1823–86). Special Collections, Princeton Theological Seminary Library.

10.4 Selected Works of Archibald Alexander Hodge.

12.1 Timeline of Benjamin B. Warfield's Life.

12.2 Selected Works of Benjamin B. Warfield.

12.3 Timeline of J. Gresham Machen's Life.

12.4 Selected Works of J. Gresham Machen.

12.5 Pictured here are the graves of Archibald Alexander (left), James W. Alexander (middle), and Joseph Addison Alexander (right) in Princeton Cemetery. The Hodges, Samuel Miller, and B. B. Warfield are buried close by, as are Aaron Burr Sr., Aaron Burr Jr., Jonathan and Sarah Edwards, Samuel Davies, Samuel Finley, John Witherspoon, Samuel Stanhope Smith, Ashbel Green, and Grover Cleveland. Taken by the author.

12.6 Drawing of Princeton Theological Seminary from Mercer Street (c. 1843). In the middle is the main seminary building, in which Machen lived on the fourth floor throughout his entire Princeton career. On the far left is Archibald Alexander's home (built in 1819), and on the far right is Charles Hodge's home (built in1825). A. A. Hodge and B. B. Warfield later lived in Hodge's house as well. Miller Chapel, just to the left of Alexander Hall (built in 1834), was moved in 1933 toward the middle of campus. The proposed library (just to the right of Alexander Hall) was never built in the location shown here, but was built on the other side of Mercer Street. Perhaps the library was drawn in here to represent the balance and dual emphasis given to both piety and scholarship. From *The Journal of Presbyterian History* 6, no. 7 (Sept. 1912): 246.

INDEX OF PERSONS

INDEX OF SCRIPTURE

Gary Steward (B.A., South Dakota State University; M.Div., The Southern Baptist Theological Seminary; Th.M., Westminster Theological Seminary) is an adjunct professor at California Baptist University in Riverside, California, and at Liberty University in Lynchburg, Virginia. He served as pastor of Calvary Baptist Church in St. John's, Newfoundland, Canada, from 2004 to 2011, and is currently pursuing a Ph.D. in church history and historical theology at The Southern Baptist Theological Seminary in Louisville, Kentucky. He has coauthored, with Sally Michael, *Rejoicing in God's Good Design*, a youth-oriented curriculum on biblical manhood and womanhood for Children Desiring God. He is ordained with the Southern Baptist Convention, and lives with his family in Louisville, Kentucky.

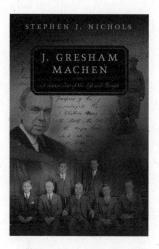

Also from P&R PUBLISHING

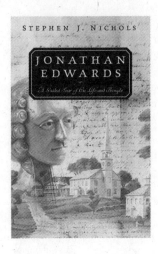

BY STEPHEN J. NICHOLS | PRICE: $14.99
TO ORDER, VISIT WWW.PRPBOOKS.COM OR CALL 1(800) 631-0094

"A lively and vivid introduction to America's greatest theologian—
the best one yet for use in most churches and Christian colleges."
—DOUGLAS A. SWEENEY

"Nichols is an enthusiastic, experienced, and reliable tour guide to the
theology of Jonathan Edwards. If your experience is like mine, these
pages will make you want to visit Edwards on your own for frequent
and extended periods. An excellent introduction."
—SINCLAIR FERGUSON

"Edwards is still America's greatest theologian, and his works remain
of lasting value to the church. This book is a useful introduction
to the great man's message and ministry. Nichols has chosen his
material carefully to help readers begin to understand Edwards's
most important writings."
—PHILIP GRAHAM RYKEN

Also from P&R PUBLISHING

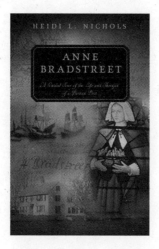

BY HEIDI L. NICHOLS | PRICE: $13.99
TO ORDER, VISIT WWW.PRPBOOKS.COM OR CALL 1(800) 631-0094

"This book does a masterful job of performing the task identified in the subtitle—it is a guided tour of the life and work of Anne Bradstreet, conducted by a wonderfully talented tour guide. For anyone wishing to acquire or renew an acquaintance with Anne Bradstreet, this is the book of choice."
— LELAND RYKEN

"Puritan pioneer Anne Bradstreet, solid believer, ardent wife, faithful mother, wise woman, and gifted poetess, is a lady well worth meeting. Dr. Nichols arranges that meeting beautifully in these pages, and merits our gratitude for doing so."
— J. I. PACKER

"Nichols not only illuminates the poet's life and social context, she makes it possible for a new generation to savor Anne Bradstreet's own words and to share the sorrows, joy, and hope of her inner journey."
— CHARLES HAMBRICK-STOWE

Also from P&R PUBLISHING

BY STEPHEN J. NICHOLS | PRICE: $13.99
TO ORDER, VISIT WWW.PRPBOOKS.COM OR CALL 1(800) 631-0094

"For over half a century Roland Bainton's *Here I Stand* has been the best popular introduction to Luther. Stephen Nichols's engaging volume is in many ways better than Bainton's for this purpose. It deserves to be widely read, and as an unashamed Luther-lover I hope it will be."
　—J. I. PACKER

"How do you do a book on everything from training children to hymns to preaching to political conflict—and have it running over with the glorious gospel? Nichols has done it. Be alert: people forget how life-changing the gospel really is—and then are astonished to remember it again as they read Luther."
　—D. CLAIR DAVIS

"Since Luther published a printed work about every two weeks of his adult life, there is a lot of ground to cover. But Nichols knows the terrain well and opens up its treasures with a deft touch."
　—MARK NOLL

Also from P&R PUBLISHING

BY BRANDON G. WITHROW | PRICE: $13.99
TO ORDER, VISIT WWW.PRPBOOKS.COM OR CALL 1(800) 631-0094

"This well-researched study of authoress Parr, Henry VIII's surviving queen, contains full reprints of her *Prayers or Meditations*, drawn from various sources, and her precious autobiographical account of authentic Reformed piety, *The Lamentation or Complaint of a Sinner*. These are worth more than the price of the book!"
—J. I. PACKER

"This is a very helpful book on a most courageous woman—one of the most important women of the entire Reformation. Parr's story ought to be better known by evangelical Christians, who often forget the roles that women have played in shaping their faith and practice."
—DOUGLAS A. SWEENEY

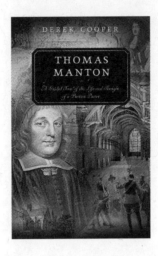